THE LONDON CAGE

THE
LONDON CAGE

The Secret History of Britain's World War II Interrogation Centre

HELEN FRY

YALE UNIVERSITY PRESS
NEW HAVEN AND LONDON

For information about this and other Yale University Press publications, please contact:

U.S. Office: sales.press@yale.edu   yalebooks.com
Europe Office: sales@yaleup.co.uk   yalebooks.co.uk

Set in Adobe Garamond Pro by IDSUK (DataConnection) Ltd
Printed in Great Britain by Gomer Press Ltd, Llandysul, Ceredigion

Library of Congress Control Number: 2017942331

ISBN 978-0-300-22193-0

A catalogue record for this book is available from the British Library.

10 9 8 7 6 5 4 3 2 1

For Frank Gent

'A small body of determined spirits
fired by an unquenchable faith in their mission
can alter the course of history.'
Mahatma Gandhi

CONTENTS

ACKNOWLEDGEMENTS

My sincere thanks to Heather McCallum, managing director at Yale University Press, for commissioning this book and for being so enthusiastic about the project; also to Marika Lysandrou of the editorial team for her excellent insights and sharp observations, which have significantly enhanced the book, and Rachael Lonsdale and staff at Yale for their professional advice, patience and expertise in publishing the book. These sentiments are echoed, too, for my copy editor, Clive Liddiard, who has been meticulous. I am very grateful to my incredibly hard-working and dedicated agent, Andrew Lownie, for his support for my projects, particularly this book, and for understanding what makes me tick (thus enabling me to write the books that I feel drawn to write).

This book could not have been written without the generous support of veterans and their families: to the veteran who wishes to remain unnamed – a real gentleman, who has discussed his memories of the London Cage over coffee and lunch in wonderful restaurants in London – thank you. Also to Second World War veteran and MI19 secret listener Fritz Lustig for translating extracts from the original German; Lucy Sheffel; Mrs Pamela Coate (widow of Randoll Coate); Geoffrey Marx; the late Marika Rotter; Peter Leon; Nigel Morgan; Barbara Lloyd, granddaughter of Colonel Thomas Joseph Kendrick; and Carol Curties, granddaughter of Bertie Acton Burnell.

A huge amount of support has been given to me by Mark Birdsall and Deborah McDonald of *Eye Spy Intelligence Magazine*. They have also kindly provided photographs for the book. From museums and archives, I am indebted to Fred Judge and Joyce Hutton for giving access to unpublished material at the Military Intelligence Museum, Chicksands, and also to staff at the National Archives and Historic England. A number of colleagues, fellow historians and researchers have advised and shared the fruits of their research. Sincere thanks to Derek Nudd for material relating to Naval Intelligence and MI19 from his own research; historian and expert on SOE, Steven Kippax; MI5 expert and historian Phil Tomaselli; Lee Richards, historian of psychological warfare (psywar.org); military historian Dr Roderick Bailey; Julian Putkowski, Mark Scoble, Peter Lawrence, Colonel John Starling and Norman Brown of the Royal Pioneer Corps Association; and Dick Smith for information on Camp 21.

Sincere thanks to a number of friends – too many to list – who support me throughout my work, but especially Alexia Dobinson, James Hamilton, Daphne and Paul Ruhleman, Frank Gent and Brana Thorn, Stanley Gilbert, Alan Perkin, Claudia Rubenstein and Trudy Gold.

Sincere thanks to my family, who are a constant support and who enable me to carry out my research and writing. And finally, to my creative, artistic friend Louisa Albani, without whom this book would not have happened.

INTRODUCTION
Impounding the evidence

In 1940, Kensington Palace Gardens, a gated street known as 'Millionaires' Row' and belonging to the Crown Estate, boasted one of the most exclusive and expensive residences in the capital. The broad tree-lined private road was home to the Russian Embassy and some of the richest men in the world, including the shah of Persia and the premier prince of India. For the neighbours, there was no inkling of what was going on behind the bravura Victorian façades of Nos. 6, 7, 8 and 8a. Here, set up in the unlikeliest of locations, was the London Cage, a clandestine Second World War interrogation centre where German prisoners of war who could not be broken under normal conditions of interrogation at any of the other eight 'cages' in Britain were subjected to 'special intelligence treatment', designed to break their will to resist. As a transit camp, the London Cage should have appeared on the wartime lists of the Red Cross. It did not – because officially it did not exist. Its commanding officer, Colonel Scotland, set the cage rules; and this is where the controversy emerged. At the end of the war, he faced repeated allegations from German prisoners of mistreatment and even torture. And all this just a stone's throw from Kensington Palace.

In June 1954, officers from Special Branch at Scotland Yard drew up outside 19 Clarence Gate Gardens, the residence of Colonel Alexander Paterson Scotland, a retired officer of the British Secret Service and nephew of famed Nobel Prize-winning playwright George Bernard Shaw. As the former head of the London Cage, Colonel Scotland was about to go public with sensitive revelations.

How far was Scotland prepared to go? The intelligence services were taking no chances. Scotland's memoirs had been written in collaboration with Alan W. Mitchell, a published author and client of literary agent John Farquharson, and neither MI5 nor the Foreign Office had any idea how explicit they would be. So, at exactly the same time as officers went to Colonel Scotland's residence, Scotland Yard dispatched two other teams across the capital to raid the offices of John Farquharson Ltd and publisher Evan Brothers. The brief from the intelligence services MI5 and MI6 was the same – to seize all copies of a typed manuscript that ran to over 350 pages and described life inside the secret wartime interrogation centre.

The papers, when they arrived back at headquarters, sent shockwaves through the corridors of MI5, the War Office and the Foreign Office. They landed on the desk of Colonel Lionel Johnson Wood, the man responsible at the War Office for reading any manuscripts that were intended for publication by former members of the armed forces. The opening phrase of the second chapter was dynamite enough: Scotland had written 'Abandon hope all ye who enter here.'

Transit camp or interrogation centre?

Having conducted intelligence work for the British for over four decades, Scotland should have known that his revelations were not only explosive, but also highly sensitive. (His early intelligence career abroad is outlined in more detail in chapter 2.) The problems for both MI5 (the home security service) and MI6 (the foreign security service) were numerous: the memoir revealed precise irregularities in the interrogation of prisoners, disclosed methods used during interrogation and provided details of infringements of the Geneva Convention. It prompted Lieutenant Colonel J. Broughton of the Directorate of Military Intelligence to write to MI5:

> The publication of a work giving considerable insight into British military methods of interrogation and the lines of enquiry that our interrogators pursue in wartime, is highly undesirable from the point of view of security.[1]

Part of the problem stemmed from a blurring of the boundaries between the cage's original function as a transit camp and its role as an interrogation centre. The Geneva Convention made provision for prisoners to be assigned basic chores for the daily running of a transit camp, but the intelligence services did not consider the London Cage to be such; therefore, Scotland's allocation of chores to prisoners could be interpreted as a contravention of international humanitarian law. MI11, part of the War Office and the section of the Directorate of Military Intelligence that dealt with field security, raised objections along similar lines.

But the issue went far deeper than a disagreement over whether the London Cage should be categorised as a prisoner-of-war camp or a transit camp. Section 2(1) of the Official Secrets Act 1911 contained an absolute prohibition on the communication of any information that a Crown servant 'has obtained, to any other person without authority'. And Section 2(2) made it an offence for any person to receive information 'knowing that it had been communicated to him/her in contravention of the Act'. Although the official MI6 response to the 'Colonel Scotland crisis' remains classified, its views are known because of copies of documents in the files of other government departments. MI6 argued that Scotland's knowledge was only gained by virtue of his privileged position:

> If permission was granted [for Scotland to publish his memoirs], it would be paramount to allowing an ex-military officer to recount actions which he took in the performance of his military duties and in compliance with his military orders. We have always maintained that where such duties and orders contain secret information, no publication of them should be allowed.[2]

Methods of interrogation used by British intelligence in any theatre of war could not be disclosed, because the same techniques might be used in a current conflict. Britain and the West were entering a dangerous period in the Cold War – an era fraught with danger from the old Soviet enemy, and a time when neither MI5 nor MI6 wished to expose operational methods and weaken their position. Ongoing intelligence operations were critical in preventing the world from sliding into nuclear war and possible extinction.

As far as MI5 was concerned, the decision on the Scotland case was straightforward: it ordered his damaging memoir to be suppressed, and three copies were successfully consigned to a basement of the War Office. (One of those had been seized from the editor of *Empire News*, who had purchased the serial rights for 100 guineas.) However, Special Branch failed to retrieve a fourth copy, which was being held by the publisher, Evans Brothers. It agreed not to publish the memoir, but wished to hold on to the manuscript for its own legal records. In the end, the problem for the intelligence services was not the publisher, but the 72-year-old maverick colonel himself, who appeared not to care much for boundaries.

On 20 January 1955, seven months after the three manuscripts had been impounded, Scotland appeared in person at the War Office, threatening to go ahead with publication. His motivation for such blatant disregard of the Official Secrets Acts was never clear. Did he believe he had the right to tell his version of events? Was he driven by money or the prospects of fame? Or was it simply that he had always invented the rules and never played by any of them?

The dispute rumbled on, with Scotland issuing a veiled threat that if the book was banned completely, he would simply publish in America. But the intelligence services were taking no chances.

Search warrant

On 7 February 1955, Chief Superintendent George Smith of Special Branch called at Colonel Scotland's home and, armed with a search warrant, formally asked Scotland to hand over all official papers retained by him after he had relinquished his appointment in the army. Scotland's response revealed a man of deep patriotism: 'Certainly, as a Lieutenant Colonel and in regard to the honour and duty which I owe to my country, I will produce and let you have any other matter which I brought with me when I left the London Cage.'

Smith, who could see that Scotland had not given up on the idea of publishing his memoir, also secured the following signed statement from him:

As an officer of H.M. Forces with more than fifty years service in this country's interest as a volunteer intelligence officer, I refuse to give any such undertaking [not to publish his book], but should the War Office agree to collaborate with me in modifications in the wording of material used in the book, I am willing to rewrite, I think to their complete satisfaction those portions of the book to which they take exception, before attempting to have it published.[3]

A list survives in the National Archives of nearly 100 items seized that day. They included a typescript of 'The Scotland Story, Part 1', typed articles categorised as 'Intelligence and Various case Reports', a folder of miscellaneous papers with a 126-page case file index detailing names of cases and places crimes were perpetrated, plus transcripts relating to various major war crimes investigations: 'Wormhoudt: 28.5.1940', 'The Le Paradis Murders', 'Sagan' and 'The German Police'. There was also a scrapbook that ran to 134 items, including a signed letter to Colonel Scotland from Field Marshal Montgomery (1947), an aerial photograph of an unnamed prisoner-of-war camp, numerous memos from members of the intelligence services and Naval Intelligence Division, reports on the interrogation of high-ranking German prisoners such as SS Lieutenant-General (Gruppenführer) Jakob Sporrenberg and SS Lieutenant-General Oswald Pohl, and a report on 'Atrocities Committed by Units of the Waffen SS'. It was believed that Scotland had no right to hold on to these documents after retiring from government service. Papers of a personal nature were eventually returned to him, but all official documents and reports relating to the London Cage were retained. Their whereabouts today are unknown.

Behind the scenes, an emergency meeting was convened for 15 February 1955 between the director of public prosecutions, Sir Theobald Mathew, Mr Bernard Hill of MI5, and Chief Superintendent George Smith and Commander Burt, both of Special Branch. The four parties concerned (Scotland, Mitchell, the publisher and the literary agent) were given a warning yet again that any publication of the book would amount to a breach of the Official Secrets Act.

In his defence, Scotland argued that the only reason he wrote his version of events was for his own personal safety: 'I may become the target of attack by vindictive relatives of men who were hanged or imprisoned as the result of the work done at the London Cage.'[4] However, the intelligence services had the upper hand; on 3 September 1940 Scotland had signed a statement declaring that 'All official and military information acquired by me in or from the War Department is to be regarded as the property of that department.'[5] Despite this, and although Scotland was threatened with arrest if he published a single word, the War Office knew it could not hold out for long. The memoirs could be published in America and the fallout felt across the Atlantic. A deal was brokered. Scotland could publish his book, but heavily redacted by MI5.

The cutting-room floor

How extensively were the memoirs redacted and what ended up on the cutting-room floor? In a four-page report compiled by MI5 officer Bernard Hill, the objections to the memoirs were outlined. The problematic passages were primarily on pages 57–78, where Scotland recalled incidents of undue pressure being applied to extract information from prisoners, and ways in which they were occasionally disciplined at the London Cage.[6] Scotland admitted that a number of U-boat officers sent to him for interrogation had been required to undertake certain chores:

> The next thing that the U-boat officers knew was that their beds had been turned right over and that they were underneath. We took away their uniform and set them to work in denim suits on cage chores for three days . . . We found the ruling of the Geneva Convention that prisoners may be employed on various duties and chores in transit camp to be useful on many occasions . . . it was a salutary exercise in discipline when awkward prisoners found themselves put to work with a bucket and scrubbing brush.[7]

Although this was not technically a breach of the Geneva Convention, it was noted to be against the spirit of it.

Joining these excerpts on the cutting-room floor was Scotland's mention on pages 67–8 of prisoners being forced to stand for twenty-six hours to 'discipline' them if they had been initially uncooperative, so that they would answer questions more readily during interrogation. Also removed from the original manuscript was the case of a German officer who had been forced to kneel before officers and non-commissioned officers (NCOs) of the guard to have his ears boxed – described by MI5 as a clear example of physical violence. Any mention of intimidation techniques was excised from the memoir; for example, the case of a German Merchant Navy captain who was threatened with being shot as a spy if he refused to provide information.[8] In another incident, the failure of Scotland's interrogators to 'break' a resilient group of U-boat officers led to Scotland resorting to the bucket-and-mop tactic for three days.[9]

The section of the memoir that dealt with Nazi war criminals proved equally problematic. It revealed precisely how Scotland had obtained their statements to be used as evidence at the war crimes trials. If a prisoner refused to answer questions, he was subjected to certain degrading duties that eventually broke his morale. He would become quite docile and would compliantly write down an account responding to the charges against him.[10]

MI5 objected to Scotland making public the methods by which Nazi war criminals were cross-examined at the cage, with examples of how unwilling witnesses were frightened into giving the desired answers.[11] A number of cases were cited in Scotland's memoir, including how General von Falkenhorst, the German commander in Nazi-occupied Norway, was instructed to write down each charge against him precisely and sign the document.[12] Another war criminal, Erich Zacharias, was psychologically worked on to make him sign a confession to war crimes of which he had originally claimed to be innocent; he was subsequently hanged.[13] Such methods did not mean the prisoners subjected to them were necessarily innocent; but the cases did highlight the unacceptable methods employed to extract statements. All this was potentially embarrassing for both the War Office and MI5, which feared that German defence lawyers might seek to reopen the cases of certain war criminals and challenge the verdicts.

The final version of Scotland's text excluded all examples of interrogation, anecdotal stories about named and unnamed prisoners, general life inside the cage and precise methods of questioning. In reality, it meant that there was very little of the original manuscript left which was of any real interest. Apart from its early chapters, which provided a safe but scant overview of the wartime role of the London Cage, the memoir focused mainly on war crimes investigations after 1945. In so doing, it revealed nothing publicly that could not have been gleaned by attending the war crimes trials. This sanitised version of Scotland's memoirs was finally published in 1957 – the year in which Scotland was asked to be a technical adviser on a Hollywood film of his life called *The Two-Headed Spy*, in which he was played by Jack Hawkins.

In subsequent decades, rumours continued to surface about irregularities at the London Cage. From the British Secret Service there was only silence. But when the official files of the London Cage were released into the National Archives in the 1990s, some were clearly missing. Enquiries addressed to the Ministry of Defence produced a response that they had been contaminated by asbestos and destroyed by floodwater, fuelling speculation that the files had been destroyed to hide damaging evidence.

Now, drawing on the unredacted, declassified manuscript, it is possible to reveal that even Scotland did not tell the whole story. There were aspects of the treatment of German prisoners that even he was not prepared to disclose. What emerges in the following pages is an often grim picture of life inside the London Cage, with fresh insights into the terrible treatment of enemy prisoners of war – dark secrets involving the intelligence services that have lain dormant for decades.

1

GENESIS OF THE CAGE

In the autumn of 1940, the Battle of Britain raged in the skies of southern England. The future of Britain hung in the balance with the wide expectation of an invasion by Adolf Hitler. Only four months earlier, German troops had overrun the Low Countries and France, forcing the retreat of the British Expeditionary Force and the mass evacuation of 300,000 Allied troops from the beaches of Dunkirk in small boats and fishing vessels. Militarily, that retreat may have been a disaster, but British intelligence viewed it merely as a temporary setback. At SIS/MI6 headquarters at Broadway in London, the service's head, Stewart Menzies ('C'), believed that Britain could win the war, despite the odds stacked against her. Encouraged by the unofficial motto 'Whoever wins the intelligence game wins the war' (a 1715 quip by the Duke of Marlborough), Menzies knew that his intelligence officers needed to be prepared for military gains – and to be ready to receive thousands of captured Germans. Their interrogations would now have to take place in England rather than in France. A clandestine interrogation centre was to open just yards from the royal palace in Kensington.

On 15 October 1940, with the fear of invasion still looming, Mr Nulty, the gatekeeper of Kensington Palace Gardens, received an unexpected visitor. Three of the millionaires' mansion houses in Europe's most select residential street were to be requisitioned under Defence Regulations 1939 by Major Dale Glossop of the Military Police, on the orders of Requisition Officer Colonel L.M. Gibbs. The freehold of Kensington Palace Gardens still belonged to the Crown Estate; indeed, the land occupied by the road had once formed part of the grounds of Kensington Palace, and the current road's eastern boundary bordered the formal gardens of the palace.

Just the previous day, Kensington Palace had received a direct hit from an incendiary device that fell on Apartment 9 (home of Lady Bertha Dawkins, Queen Mary's former lady-in-waiting), inflicting the worst damage that would be suffered by the palace during the war:

> The fire had spread to the Athlone's [*sic*] apartment (No. 4), the Keppel's [*sic*] (No. 5), Lady Milford Haven's (No. 7) and Lady Patricia Ramsay's (No. 8) as well as the Queen's State Apartments. Despite the efforts of thirty fire engines, the blaze was not extinguished until 3am.[1]

So the smell of scorched timbers still lingered in the air as Glossop arrived at Kensington Palace Gardens the following morning. It remains a puzzle why the intelligence services should have requisitioned properties in a street near to which several bombs and incendiary devices had already fallen. Locating an interrogation centre here risked the lives of intelligence officers and valuable German prisoners. Indeed, only eight months earlier, another secret MI9 interrogation and bugging site had been moved out of the Tower of London to the country estate of Trent Park in north London precisely because of the risks posed by the Blitz.[2]

As Major Glossop passed through the ornamental black iron gates, so reminiscent of Victorian London, and exchanged a few words with Mr Nulty, little appeared to have changed in this wealthy enclave in a hundred years. As he made his way down the street, it was clear that the three-storey mansions, with their impressive cream-stuccoed fronts, had seen better days. Hidden from public view, the street could be described as very secluded. It was because it afforded complete privacy that the intelligence services had been eyeing it up ever since November 1938, when an unnamed man from the 'German Section of the Foreign Office' (a section of MI6 based at Hayes in Middlesex) discreetly photographed the gatehouse and exterior of Nos. 6–8 and No. 8a. His eerie black-and-white photograph of the gatehouse could have been straight out of Dickensian London.

Baron Joseph Duveen of Millbank

The first property on Glossop's list was No. 8 and the adjoining No. 8a. Built by John Marriott Blashfield in 1843 to the designs of Owen Jones, its Byzantine style – so reminiscent of a Black Sea resort – was nothing if not exotic; it was, according to the *Illustrated London News*, 'novel to this country'. Inside, few traces remained of the grandeur of its pre-war occupant, Baron Joseph Duveen of Millbank, who had died of cancer at the age of sixty-nine on 25 May 1939. One of the wealthiest and most prominent art dealers of the twentieth century, Duveen had been born in Hull on 14 October 1869. He was the eldest son of Sir Joseph Joel Duveen, a highly successful Dutch businessman of Sephardic Jewish origin, who had made his money in the import business and who, in the 1880s, became the first Jewish resident of Golders Green.[3] After Sir Joseph's death in 1908, his ambitious son turned his attention to the highly lucrative, if risky, business of selling art. He realised that Europe had a great deal of art and America a great deal of money; this was a synergy that he would harness. His foresight soon saw him shipping masterpieces across the Atlantic, many of which survive to this day in America's greatest museums. His clients were often self-made industrialists, whose wealth had left the traditional, increasingly impoverished British aristocracy behind. Among his American clients were the banker John P. Morgan, the oil magnate John Rockefeller (founder of the Rockefeller Foundation), gas businessman and philanthropist Frederick Taylor Gates and industrialist Henry Clay Frick.

Raised to the peerage as Baron Duveen of Millbank in 1933, Duveen's connections took him into the heady world of espionage, art dealers and collectors, royalty and aristocracy. His royal friends included Edward VII, whom he provided with art for the walls of Windsor Castle. Duveen moved in the same circles as Sir Philip Sassoon, who was from a wealthy Baghdadi-Jewish family that had made its fortune trading in opium and who was a close friend of Edward VIII. Sassoon was to pass away within a week of Duveen, and his stately home at Trent Park was also requisitioned by the same branch of the intelligence services, MI9.

Duveen and Sassoon were immersed in the art world: both were involved with the Tate Gallery and the National Gallery; both were friends of Evan Charteris, trustee of the National Gallery and the Wallace Collection, and of Sir Kenneth Clark, director of the National Gallery. In his lifetime, Duveen funded the construction of the Duveen Gallery at the British Museum to house the Elgin Marbles and financed the Modern Foreign and Sargent Galleries at the Tate, opened by King George V in June 1926 (an event captured in a painting by the Irish artist Sir John Lavery). By then, Duveen was also director of the Duveen Galleries in New York. But his life was not without controversy, as he became enmeshed in disagreements over the extent to which the grand masterpieces should be cleaned up for his new clients, and embroiled in a scandal and court case about fake art (never proved in his lifetime).

Duveen was also a friend of the Anglo-Austrian art collector and art historian Count Antoine Seilern (who, on his death in 1978, bequeathed his famous art collection covering the Renaissance period up to the twentieth century to the Courtauld Institute in London). In 1938, Seilern was living in Vienna at a critical time in European history when Hitler annexed Austria. He became caught up in the crisis facing Austria's Jewish intellectuals and began to smuggle prominent Jewish art dealers and their art out of Europe, helping figures like Ludwig Münz and Johannes Wilde and his Jewish wife to escape. Some of the priceless masterpieces were stored temporarily at Seilern's new home at Hog Lane Farm, in the village of Ashley Green in Buckinghamshire, which he had purchased in 1939. Transferring into the Intelligence Corps in the war, Seilern was sent on secret missions abroad, information about which is still deemed too sensitive to declassify. He was also a close friend of MI6 spymaster Thomas Joseph Kendrick, one-time British passport officer in Vienna, who in the Second World War became head of a unit that bugged the conversations of German prisoners of war. It was a small world, because Kendrick was also a close colleague of Colonel Scotland, who had provided Kendrick's original reference to enter the intelligence world in the First World War.[4] Scotland and Kendrick both worked for MI9 (later MI19) during the Second World War, and would liaise over German prisoners of war in an effort to extract maximum intelligence.

When the War Office took over Nos. 8 and 8a on the east side of Kensington Palace Gardens, it signed an agreement with the late Lord Duveen's executors, to whom the lease had transferred upon his death. The lease still had forty-nine years to run: it had been signed by Duveen on 5 July 1929 for a period of sixty years, at a rent to the Crown of £1,060 per annum. There were no concessions made to the War Office when it took on the high rent due to the Crown, equivalent to approximately £40,000 a year in today's money. Under the terms of the requisition order, nothing in the street could be visibly changed. The War Office was under a strict obligation to keep it a private road and to ensure the privacy of the other inhabitants. Safeguards in the requisition order guaranteed a fair value to Duveen's estate for the lease, as well as compensation and repair work for any damage caused during the war by the new occupant. No one could have foreseen that the compensation bill would eventually run to a staggering £1 million when the London Cage closed in 1948.

Prisoner of War Interrogation Section

Just days after the requisition, Scotland, then a lieutenant colonel, arrived at Kensington Palace Gardens to open the interrogation centre. Under the auspices of MI9 (from 1941, MI19), it became the headquarters of the Prisoner of War Interrogation Section (PWIS(H)), a unit that had more than eight other 'cages' – slang for interrogation quarters – around Britain.[5] In the closed circles of the intelligence world, it became known as the 'London Cage'. On 23 October 1940, the first German prisoners arrived and were initially housed in Nos. 8 and 8a under heavy guard. No. 8, with its grassy lawn at the rear, had been vacant since Duveen's death the previous year. It was soon reserved as the quarters for the guards and the camp commandant. During the course of the war, it would have its own dark secret.

The adjoining No. 8a had been in a state of total disrepair for some time. Its music room, drawing room, library and large dining room were but shadows of their former glory. Duveen had planned to demolish and rebuild the house, but his death had intervened. At the rear was a disused hard tennis court and surrounding paths, borders and shrubs. The War Office agreed that the garden space in front of the house would not be tampered with.

Shortly after the London Cage opened, it was agreed that the basement of No. 8a could be used by a balloon squadron of the RAF as a rest room, recreation area and shelter for airmen. The squadron was under the command of Flying Officer W.W. Spooner of RAF Kensington, based at 11 Kensington Palace Gardens. The squadron used it until the house reverted to the Crown in October 1942.[6] The property then remained empty until new leaseholders demolished it after the war and constructed luxury flats.

The number of staff rose to ten officers and ten NCOs, in addition to the guards. With the requisition of Nos. 6 and 7 Kensington Palace Gardens, Scotland and his team had at their disposal a further twenty-eight rooms that provided facilities for up to sixty prisoners at a time. This included quarters suitable for solitary confinement and five interrogation rooms. Occasionally, the third floor was full to capacity with prisoners. The front entrance at No. 6 was sealed off so that the premises were only accessible via

No. 7. A connecting door was knocked through between the mansion houses to allow intelligence officers and interrogators to pass between Nos. 6 and 7 without having to use the street, largely to avoid attracting suspicion from the outside world.

As Colonel Scotland passed into No. 8 through the portico, he would first enter a large vestibule-hall which led into the rotunda. This rose up through the upper floors to a glass dome. Double doors on the left of the rotunda led directly into the main hall, with its grand staircase. Here, too, doors led off the main hall into the dining room foyer and then the dining room. Double doors to the right of the rotunda opened into the south hall (a room in itself that stretched half the length of the front of the house), leading into a traditional library that overlooked the ornamental garden. To the rear of the house, a 20-foot-by-20-foot drawing room and adjacent 27-foot conservatory led out to a terrace. The house benefited from two lifts. On the first floor were six double bedrooms, each with its own separate bathroom, quarters for a lady's maid and a valet, and the rotunda continuing upwards. Large, airy and spacious, these rooms became the cells: carpets and rugs were removed, leaving draughty bare floors, the only furnishings a single bed, a chair and a chamber pot. Larger rooms could hold between eight and ten prisoners. The smaller rooms were used to segregate men who were undergoing special interrogation and who needed to be kept in solitary confinement. In winter, the unheated rooms were bitterly cold and grim. Laundry facilities were poor, and harassment of inmates was a frequent occurrence. There were no home comforts for these prisoners, in complete contrast to MI19's site at Trent Park, where German generals roamed the stately house in comfort and luxury. Treatment at the London Cage was deliberately harsh, to cow the prisoners into submission.

The basement at No. 8 was extensive, stretching some way under the back terrace. In Lord Duveen's day, it had accommodated a long billiards room, with its own separate staircase and exclusive access to the ground floor. There was a servants' hall, kitchen, scullery, storeroom, butler's pantry and butler's office, a silver vault, and cellars for beer, wine and coal. Now it housed the interrogation quarters.

In its heyday, the adjoining property at No. 8a was just as grand, although smaller overall. The ground floor boasted a library, music room, hexagonal-shaped drawing room and grand dining room. Its basement had a kitchen, larder, two coal vaults, a billiard room, a scullery, butler's pantry, toilet and servants' hall. The first floor had a generously proportioned boudoir, two large bedrooms, each with its own dressing room and one with its own bathroom. This floor also had a separate room with a toilet and washbasin. On the second floor, there were several smaller bedrooms, bringing the total number of bedrooms in the house to nine. No. 8a had a distinctive tower-turret, with a single room at the top described as the 'third floor', reached via internal stairs. Its use at this time was never specified, but it had excellent views over London. In October 1942, No. 8a reverted to the Crown and remained vacant.

The London Cage was always intended as a temporary camp for the interrogation of enemy prisoners of war and the War Office sought to impose a five-day limit on their stay. Colonel Scotland, who did not want the length of stay of POWs to be restricted (as interrogations might take longer), wrote to the War Office:

> it [is] difficult, if not impossible, for us to observe strictly the 5 day limit of stay which you have allowed at the London District Cage. We do not mean to imply that we require an indefinite stay for enemy prisoners-of-war but it appears to us necessary that we should be given latitude in this respect, we on our part undertaking to release prisoners-of-war at the earliest possible date.[7]

Forward cages

The role of the London Cage was clearly defined by the War Office as providing for the interrogation of German prisoners of war captured within the London District, as well as prisoners transferred from other cages for interrogation to glean 'hot' information.[8] Its primary purpose was to assist MI5 and MI6 in gaining intelligence from German prisoners whose examination under military conditions had a stronger chance of yielding results.[9]

The London Cage became the headquarters of the other cages around Britain. Known as 'forward cages', these were responsible for the interrogation of POWs in each of the military command areas in the country. Cages were established at Kempton Park, Lingfield, Ascot Park, Dunstable, Swindon, Catterick, Doncaster, Newmarket, Edinburgh, Preston and Colchester (the latter, Camp 186, provided one interrogation room and quarters with the capacity to hold up to thirty men). All prisoners captured in Britain or transferred from the European theatre of war were sent to a regional cage for interrogation – usually to the one nearest the port of entry. The cages were serviced by intelligence officers from the army, navy and air force in a joint services venture to maximise the extraction of information. Colonel Scotland had twenty interrogators attached to his particular unit. Wounded prisoners were taken first to the Royal Herbert Hospital in Woolwich (London) and held under military guard until they were well enough to be interrogated at one of the cages. The hospital reserved 200 beds for Colonel Scotland for wounded German servicemen.

Two primary forward cages were established for army staff to undertake the registration and search of prisoners: one at Kempton Park racecourse, the other at Lingfield racecourse. It was not uncommon for U-boat crews to discover later that some of the best items in their kitbags had been confiscated and never returned: the spoils of war. One of the first priorities was the delousing of prisoners using DDT – especially important if they had served on the Russian front after June 1941. Between registration and the search of a prisoner, a rapid preliminary interrogation was conducted by an interrogator from Section ADI(K), the section of Air Intelligence that dealt with the interrogation of prisoners of war.[10] It was important to interrogate a prisoner while he was still disorientated from his capture and at his most vulnerable in terms of divulging information. Important prisoners were swiftly identified and transferred to the London Cage for more detailed questioning.

Lingfield was the preferred immediate processing cage up until D-Day, after which the flow of German prisoners from the Continent reached such a level that Kempton Park took most of them, via Southampton. On arrival at the camp, the prisoners were escorted through a barbed-wire tunnel under the railway and onto the racecourse. The on-site stables became primitive makeshift sleeping quarters, enabling the processing of 120 prisoners at a time. The suites where rich punters once watched the races were converted into interrogation areas. Kempton Park had three interrogation rooms, plus a large workroom. Operating out of this camp was Captain Lawrence Green, whose role was to sift out any German prisoner who might be induced to work for the British, specifically on a radio propaganda station run by former journalist Denis Sefton Delmer of the Political Warfare Executive. The station masqueraded as a German radio station broadcasting from within Germany, but in reality its headquarters were at Milton Bryan, a few miles from Bletchley Park.

Prisoners processed at Kempton Park included Russian POWs who had been captured by the Germans and drafted to fight in the German forces.

Their subsequent capture by the British or Americans did not exempt them from interrogation for useful intelligence, and they found themselves at Kempton Park before members of the Soviet Military Mission, headed by General Ratov. Soviet interrogators were overheard using undue physical force or torture on their prisoners; one poor man was found in a hut with his hands and feet bound. Ratov was dispatched back to the Soviet Union in disgrace by General Firebrace, head of what was then called the British–Russian Liaison Group.

The British cages worked in close cooperation with United States forces. The Americans had a POW camp under their own command at Devizes in Wiltshire, for prisoners captured by their forces. Their prisoners arrived exclusively via the port of Weymouth and were interrogated by US personnel. Around half of the prisoners captured after D-Day were sent to POW camps in America.

Among the duties of the cages were: providing expert interrogators for the War Office; examining all classes of POWs who came to Britain and interrogating them on any subject; selecting suitable POWs for long-term interrogation by a sister unit (the Combined Services Detailed Interrogation Centre: see page 19); and providing advice on the handling of large numbers of POWs passing through Britain.

Across the various cages in Britain, Colonel Scotland's officers carried out the detailed interrogation of German and Italian POWs captured in North Africa from 1942, and helped in the sorting and handling of thousands of POWs evacuated to America via British ports. German prisoners, especially after D-Day, generated so much work that Scotland's men drafted several thousand reports. Some were of such importance that up to 100 copies were requested for distribution by various wartime departments. By June 1944, Scotland's team consisted of twenty-nine officers and thirty-five sergeants who undertook the arduous but necessary task of processing and classifying the prisoners – tens of thousands of them in the course of the war. Reports specifically emanating from the London Cage were identified by the preface PWIS(H)/LDC. An average of twenty-five German prisoners of war passed through the doors of Kensington Palace Gardens every day. That alone generated reports in their thousands.

As the war progressed, the London Cage was used for the interrogation of prisoners who had escaped from other British POW camps and been recaptured, and of prisoners who had committed serious disciplinary offences in other camps, such as illegally passing documents from one

POW camp to another in an effort to facilitate an escape. Scotland assisted the security services, MI5 and Special Branch during periods of tension, such as the planned mass outbreak from Devizes camp at Christmas 1944.

Handling so many prisoners across the war required the right training at all levels. Among Colonel Scotland's duties was the training of staff across PWIS – not just those officers working at the London Cage. He personally hand-picked and trained his own interrogators, as well as assisting in the training of British and Allied interrogators of other military units, making Kensington Palace Gardens an important training centre. He visited cages around Britain to give lectures to field officers who worked alongside the intelligence officers at the special cages. He allocated an interrogator to lecture at the interrogation courses held at Cambridge, where an estimated 1,200 officers passed through the school; and there was special tuition for 700 German-speaking personnel in the Home Guard.[11]

Over 250 security troops received training from Scotland himself on the proper handling and transfer of prisoners between sites. He delivered lectures on how to march prisoners en masse from one destination to another, how to prevent their escape (especially near bridges) and how to bark orders at German troops to ensure their compliance. Scotland exhibited his own style and authority, characteristics which would mark him out as different from other intelligence officers during the war – with the possible exception of Colonel Robin 'Tin Eye' Stephens. Stephens was the commanding officer of MI5's clandestine camp for captured German spies, known as Camp 020, and based at Latchmere House, Ham Common, near Richmond. It was there that MI5 successfully 'turned' a number of German spies to work as double agents as part of the Double Cross System, overseen by the Twenty Committee (or XX Committee). Its work included the successful turning of such famous double agents as Zigzag (Eddie Chapman), Tate (Wulf Schmidt) and Summer (Gösta Caroli). Colonel Scotland went to Camp 020 occasionally to interrogate prisoners. An unpublished source notes that on 10 April 1941 'Scotland arrived with JHM to Ham to interrogate Norwegians.'[12] JHM refers to John Marriott, secretary to the Twenty Committee.

After the war, Colonel Stephens faced court martial for alleged brutal mistreatment of prisoners while running a special camp at Bad Nenndorf in Germany. Some of the techniques employed by Stephens were strangely reminiscent of those alleged to have occurred at the London Cage.[13]

Combined Services Detailed Interrogation Centre

The Combined Services Detailed Interrogation Centre (CSDIC) was a branch of MI9/MI19 that worked alongside the London Cage and its forward cages. It, too, was a clandestine interrogation unit in Britain dealing with German prisoners of war. The cumbersome title masked a fascinating long-term deception plan. A prisoner would be subjected to a 'phony' interrogation, then returned to his cell, where he would chat away with his cellmate discussing what they thought the interrogation officer should have asked. What the prisoner would not have realised was that the cell's light fitting contained a tiny hidden bugging device that was wired back to an 'M Room', where teams of secret listeners recorded anything of relevance that was said.

The CSDIC's commanding officer was Colonel Thomas Joseph Kendrick, Scotland's intelligence colleague and friend from the days immediately after the Boer War and during the First World War. Seconded to MI5 from MI6, Kendrick headed three covert prisoner-of-war sites in requisitioned stately homes where the prisoners' conversations were secretly bugged. Prisoners who required long-term interrogation and who could yield more information from secretly bugged conversations with their cellmates were selected from cages like Lingfield and Kempton Park and transferred to one of Kendrick's three sites.

This elaborate deception began in the Tower of London in September 1939. With an insufficient allocation of space there, and the risk of bombing in London, three other sites were opened: at Trent Park in Cockfosters, north London, in January 1940, and Latimer House and Wilton Park in Buckinghamshire in 1942.[14] CSDIC operated in a joint services capacity, having a strong team of interrogators from Naval Intelligence Division (NID), Air Intelligence (ADI(K)) and the army's Intelligence Corps, as well as teams of American intelligence officers. Although an entity of the War Office, CSDIC consisted of intelligence officers from MI6 and Intelligence Corps personnel.

Prisoners transferred to the CSDIC sites were those who had special information or who had been earmarked for long-term interrogation. From May 1942, Trent Park was reserved for captured German generals, the first of whom, General Ludwig Crüwell, arrived that month. It was run like a 'gentlemen's club' by British intelligence, where the life of relative luxury and stately surroundings fooled the German generals into thinking that they were being treated according to their military rank. They had already had a phony interrogation elsewhere – some at the London Cage, which was devoid of any comforts. Life at Trent Park was extraordinarily good for the generals, so they relaxed, their conversations were unguarded and they chatted among themselves about a host of top-secret military subjects. These conversations yielded revelations about Hitler's secret weapon programme: the V-1, V-2, V-3 and atomic bomb projects.[15]

Located only 10 miles from Trent Park, the London Cage also acted as a transit camp for high-ranking German officers and generals who were being moved between different locations. When the London Cage or CSDIC had finished with the lower-ranking prisoners, they were transferred to a regular POW camp, where they received no further interrogation and where their conversations were not bugged.

CSDIC processed over 10,000 German prisoners of war between September 1939 and May 1945, as well as a few thousand Italians. The bugging operation generated in the region of 100,000 transcripts of conversations, intelligence reports and miscellaneous documents. No report of prisoner mistreatment was ever filed against any of the three CSDIC sites or their commanding officer, Colonel Kendrick. He and his team realised that vital intelligence could be gathered through a mixture of cunning and a soft approach. Prisoners could be rewarded for their cooperation with day trips into central London or extra rations of cigarettes. A late-night glass of whisky with a British officer was a particular favourite for softening up a prisoner, and this often induced them to talk or inadvertently give away information.[16] It raises the important issue of whether Scotland's actions and his particular style at the London Cage came with the sanction of MI5 and the War Office, or whether he was acting alone. The clever methods of deception employed at CSDIC suggest that there were more effective ways of gaining intelligence from prisoners than resorting to physical or psychological abuse.

Kensington Palace

Over the boundary wall, Kensington Palace remained vacant, except for a handful of staff. It had no royal occupants in 1940 when the War Office requisitioned the houses in Kensington Palace Gardens for the London Cage. In spite of its proximity to the cage, no officials at the palace had any idea of the conditions inside the POW quarters. Nearby was Kensington Barracks, which housed soldiers from the Royal Army Service Corps

(RASC) whose duties included acting as the palace garrison. They also knew nothing of life inside the London Cage.

In 1941, the War Office sought to extend the facilities at the London Cage and set its sights on the paddock behind the palace. A large grassed area that ran almost the entire length of the boundary wall of Kensington Palace Gardens, from the royal palace to the Bayswater Road, it had been given to HRH Princess Louise during her lifetime by her mother, Queen Victoria. On the death of Princess Louise in 1939, the land was considered for incorporation back into the gardens of the palace.

During her lifetime, Princess Louise had issued keys for the gates at the northern end of the paddock to various individuals (unnamed in official records) as a favour, so that they could take their leisure in the area. She had also allowed soldiers from the barracks to use the land for games of football. In addition to the northern gates, some wealthy inhabitants of Kensington Palace Gardens had access through the dividing fence between their properties and the west boundary wall of the palace, and were allowed to enjoy this part of the gardens. Security was tightened during the war, and the Crown Commissioners brought in measures to issue keys only under special licence so that there could be no unauthorised access. Privileged access was granted to the Duke of Marlborough (then living at No. 11 Kensington Palace Gardens), the Marquess of Cholmondeley (No. 12) and Sir Alfred Beit (No. 15). The area of the paddock immediately behind the palace was given over to Kensington Council as allotments for growing vegetables due to the wartime food shortages.

In December 1941, King George VI received a formal request from the War Office via his equerry, Sir Ulick Alexander, asking for the paddock running north and west of Kensington Palace to be 'given over for secretive purposes' as a centre for 'examining enemy prisoners'. It was accompanied by a request to gain access via a pathway between Nos. 3 and 4 Kensington Palace Gardens on the Bayswater Road that ran directly into the royal gardens, 'To increase accommodation available by erecting accommodation huts and an exercise area for the prisoners in the northern half of the paddock.'[17] The area remained fenced in with a triple layer of barbed wire until 1946.

The king granted permission and the paddock became an extension of the London Cage until 1946, with two segregated areas: accommodation and support. An aerial photograph taken by the RAF in 1946 shows that it was a triple-fence-secured compound with a dividing fence between the two areas and a guard tower in each. In the accommodation area, there were dozens of tents: five marquees and forty-nine bell tents (seven rows of seven); two bell tents and two marquees; and in a support area, three bell tents and two marquees, along with eleven single-storey, mainly flat-roofed support buildings. The marquees were probably British army hospital marquees.[18]

The king and the palace officials were unaware of what was unfolding. For the duration of the war, the London Cage did not appear on any official list of POW camps under British jurisdiction. The International Red Cross would not find out about its existence until 1946. What went on behind closed doors remained a closely guarded secret until complaints of ill-treatment emerged at the end of the war from Nazi war criminals held there. Foliage and bushes obscured the barbed wire along the boundary fence. No unsuspecting member of the public would notice the bars on the windows, painted white to blend in with the frame. To an outsider, the London Cage would pass as a grand residence for a wealthy businessman or a foreign prince. Its millionaire neighbours never suspected that the real occupants of Nos. 6–8 were the British intelligence services.

2

A VERY 'GERMAN' ENGLISHMAN

At the outbreak of war in September 1939, British intelligence lacked any formal guidelines or training in the interrogation of enemy prisoners of war. The scope and possibilities of interrogation were little known and entirely unpredictable. A full policy was urgently required and interrogators needed to be swiftly trained. British intelligence turned its attention to its most experienced interrogator from the First World War, the 57-year-old Alexander Scotland. With years of experience in the handling and interrogation of German prisoners from 1915 to 1918, Scotland headed a new interrogation unit within Military Intelligence branch MI9, called the Prisoner of War Interrogation Section (PWIS), which included personnel from the Intelligence Corps. Known for his tough approach, Scotland was tasked with setting up its headquarters in one of the most exclusive streets in the capital.

A man of strong personality and with a formidable reputation as an interrogator, Scotland was disliked by most people who crossed his path, including many of his own staff at the London Cage. In stark contrast to his humorous, conversationalist playwright uncle, George Bernard Shaw, Scotland was not a popular choice of guest at the dinner table. But he had an unusual past, and that made him both controversial and interesting. Scotland spoke German, Spanish, Dutch and Afrikaans. Moreover, he thought and acted like a German. One of only two British officers ever to have served in the German army (1904–07),[1] he had a comprehensive understanding of the German mindset and psyche, garnered from having lived among the Germans in South-West Africa immediately after the Boer

War. His experience made him invaluable to British intelligence in the First World War, the inter-war years and into the Second World War, during which he was able to develop urgently needed and successful methods for the interrogation of German prisoners based on his understanding of their psychological profile and, therefore, on how best to make them talk. As commanding officer of the London Cage for five years, then the War Crimes Investigation Unit for three years, Scotland set the rules. How different the story might have been if a different commanding officer had been appointed. In army circles, the London Cage was rumoured to have 'a bit of a reputation' – not a place a prisoner would wish to be sent.

South-West Africa: A melting pot

Alexander Scotland sailed for German South-West Africa in 1903, a young man with idealistic dreams in search of a promising new future. Born on 15 July 1882 in Middlesbrough in the north of England, he came from humble beginnings, the son of a railway engineer and one of nine children. He left school at the age of fourteen, worked for a time in London in an office, and spent a year in Australia.

He had entertained hopes of joining the British forces in South Africa, but with the end of the Boer War those hopes were dashed. He took up work with a trader in German South-West Africa, now Namibia.[2] The biggest customer was the German army, but only a member of the German armed forces could trade with it. That is apparently why Scotland decided to enlist in the kaiser's army in German South-West Africa at this time. The Khoikhoi Wars, which had kicked off in 1903, were then raging, and Scotland served in the German army for four years until 1907. At the end of his service, 'Herr Schottland', as he was known, was awarded the Order of the Prussian Red Eagle.

On demobilisation, the 25-year-old Scotland fortuitously crossed paths with Major Wade, British attaché to the German forces in South-West Africa. Scotland was immediately recruited into intelligence activities and tasked with spying on the German army. Major Wade told him: 'Learn all you can about the German army and one day you will be a valuable man for your country.'[3] How true that turned out to be, for it marked the beginning of a distinguished four-decade-long career in British intelligence, during which Scotland became one of its most prized German experts. It is my belief that Scotland's unusual career over several decades, often abroad in interesting places at key moments in history, meant that he might have provided information to SIS on a casual basis.

In 1908, Scotland was posted to Keetmanshoop to carry out intelligence duties under the guise of being a trader.[4] He was to observe the German military forces in the region and assess their strength and the new weapons being deployed. It was here that Scotland discovered that the Germans were using a secret new gun. From 1910, he surreptitiously photographed the weapons and reported back to General Jan Smuts at British intelligence headquarters in Cape Town.

Although the Boer War had formally concluded in 1901, it had not ended the conflict in the region. South Africa witnessed numerous uprisings between native Khoikhoi and German forces in a four-year battle. From Keetmanshoop, Scotland was transferred to Cape Colony as a civilian clerk representing a successful enterprise company, South African Territories Ltd, again as a cover for his intelligence work.[5] It is perhaps one of the oldest ruses in the book: to place an agent in a business to mask his real duties as a spy. Stationed at the remote backwater of Ramonsdrift, between Cape Colony and German South-West Africa, Scotland travelled widely and spied for the British. Here he rapidly learned to speak fluent German and Cape Dutch. German forces in the region unexpectedly became his biggest customer, purchasing cans of food, biscuits and soft drinks from his company. He began to follow Major Wade's advice and became an expert on German troop movements and rearmament, travelling regularly from Ramonsdrift to Cape Town with his precious information.

Much of Scotland's work was carried out on horseback and took him close to the protected diamond region of Lüderitzbucht. On one occasion, he was assigned to investigate two rogue diamond traders who had moved into the Lüderitzbucht area in search of a new stream. This was the stomping ground of two other British intelligence officers: Thomas Joseph Kendrick and Kendrick's brother-in-law, Rex Pearson, both of whom would serve the British Secret Intelligence Service for over forty years.[6]

Another figure in British espionage in South Africa at this time was Claude Dansey, who had also been drafted into intelligence duties in the region immediately after the Boer War. Having served with the British South African Police during the Matabele Rebellion (1896–97), he had gone on to fight bandits in Borneo. From 1899 to 1901, he was a lieutenant involved in reconnaissance missions, and from 1904 to 1909 he served as colonial political officer in Somaliland. It is believed that the paths of Dansey and Scotland crossed in South Africa, at a time when both were carrying out intelligence duties; Dansey and Kendrick were among the early members of the Secret Service Bureau, founded in 1909, before it split into MI5 and MI6. Decades later, Dansey would rise to become deputy head of MI6.

A prisoner of the Germans

At the time of the fatal shooting of Archduke Franz Ferdinand and his wife Sophia in Sarajevo on 28 June 1914, Alexander Scotland was living in Keetmanshoop. There were immediate signs of war in South-West Africa as the German forces embarked upon their expansion. In response, neighbouring Dominion forces mobilised against them. A priority for British forces was the capture of the key ports of Lüderitzbucht and Swakopmund, where German troops had radio equipment that could transmit messages as far as Nauen in Germany in good weather conditions. Knocking out the coastal wireless transmitters was one of the first priorities to protect the British Empire in the region.

Although Scotland had served for four years in the German army, the Germans were unsure which side he was really on, and he immediately fell under suspicion as a British spy. His lodgings in Keetmanshoop were searched by German military police, but no incriminating evidence was found. This did not prevent Scotland's arrest, but nevertheless he fortunately managed to get a message to General Smuts in Cape Town about German troop movements.

Scotland was taken to Windhoek prison to begin what turned out to be eleven months behind bars. His ability to withstand his German captors' isolation treatment – holding him in solitary confinement in a narrow cell measuring 5 feet by 12 feet, with no newspapers or books – tells us much about his character. He had already been warned that if he tried to escape, he would be shot. Not knowing whether he would ever be released, Scotland made the conscious decision to use the situation to observe and understand how the Germans treated their prisoners. It gave him a unique and unprecedented insight into the German psyche and military method. During the long hours of many interrogations at the hands of German officer Lieutenant Hepka, Scotland observed the techniques being used and resisted being broken. Whenever he protested about his incarceration, he was told: 'Don't worry, you will never leave this place alive. We are going to shoot you.'[7]

It can be argued that Scotland's own later success as an interrogator and expert 'psychologist' of the German mind was honed during his long hours of solitary confinement in Windhoek prison, during which he processed what was happening to him and stored it in his mind for future use. Living with the possibility that he could be shot any day was an invaluable, if disconcerting, experience. He later wrote:

> I gained a first-hand knowledge of the hopes and fears of a prisoner-of-war so that in later years, I could guess pretty well what a German prisoner might be hoping to hide when he was interrogated, how he might conceal useful information by verbal false scents and how ultimately his 'front' might be broken down.[8]

Within a year, the tide had turned for German forces in South-West Africa. On 9 July 1915, they surrendered to the Union Defence Forces under Afrikaner General Louis Botha. Just days before his thirty-third birthday, Scotland was released from prison.

The Intelligence Corps

Scotland sailed for England, hungry for action and determined to be drafted into Military Intelligence. He soon realised that enlisting in the Intelligence Corps would be harder than expected. No Whitehall department seemed willing to recruit him into its intelligence section. But Scotland was not the kind of man to let bureaucracy or officialdom stand in the way of his ambition or belief that he had an expert knowledge of the German forces that would be of value to the War Office. He attended an interview with the Inns of Court infantry battalion, but initially received no encouragement unless he could provide a strong reference. Scotland offered the name of General Smuts and waited for the reaction. It worked. General Smuts cabled a reference a few days later from South Africa.

From December 1915 to May 1916, Scotland underwent officer training with the Inns of Court, followed by a course of instruction on intelligence duties in London up to July 1916. He was then dispatched to General Headquarters in France at Le Havre with the rank of second lieutenant for 'special intelligence duties', and was briefed by Captain James (later General Sir James) Marshall-Cornwall of the Intelligence Corps.[9]

The next three years marked an exciting time for Scotland, as he was sent on several covert reconnaissance missions behind enemy lines in Belgium. He often went on undisclosed intelligence forays into neutral Holland and passed easily as a Dutchman because he spoke fluent Cape Dutch. The sandy-haired Scotland had no striking physical features (something of an asset in the world of espionage), which enabled him to blend into the background. He linked up with a network of civilian Belgians called La Dame Blanche, which was being run from Paris by British intelligence, and which sent coded messages in newspapers and knitwear across the lines from Belgium to France.[10] They observed and collected valuable data for British intelligence on German troop movements, numbers and equipment being moved by train across Belgium towards the front line. It enabled the British to begin to work out the Germans' ensuing battle plans.

During a period of leave in England, Scotland met his future wife Roma at a party at the Savoy Hotel and they married a short time later. But that did not stop Scotland's intelligence work. As the war entered its final year, and with the capture of thousands of German prisoners of war in France, Scotland was tasked with classifying the prisoners in 'the cage' – the transit camp and interrogation quarters – at Le Havre. He collated vital information for the British military authorities and was subsequently appointed their 'German expert' in France. There was much speculation among the prisoners about Scotland, given he could speak fluent German with no accent, and behaved like a native German. At Le Havre he interrogated over 3,000 German prisoners of war; the success he achieved seemed to be down to his understanding of their mindset.

In a reference at the end of the war, countersigned by Lieutenant Colonel A. Fenn, Major Wynne of the General Staff wrote of Scotland that he had 'compiled most valuable information regarding German manpower. His experience while working with the Germans in their South West African Campaign has given this officer an insight into the German character, which he has used successfully in the present war.'[11] There was a glowing reference, too, from Lieutenant Colonel Marshall-Cornwall, who wrote that Scotland was a man of ability and high energy whose 'knowledge of the German language and of the German character enabled him to render the greatest assistance to the British General Staff in conducting the interrogation and classification of thousands of German prisoners which fell into our hands during the battles of 1916, 1917, and 1918.' Because of his competence, discretion and energy, Scotland was placed in charge of this entire duty.[12]

After the Armistice on 11 November 1918, Scotland returned to South-West Africa where he worked on a farm estate. In 1929, he sailed with his wife to Argentina to work for an unnamed enterprise company. He spent the next six years travelling around the Argentine, Brazil, Paraguay and Uruguay, discreetly gathering information on the immigrant German community for British intelligence.[13] Oral tradition suggests that Scotland worked for MI5, but it has not been possible to provide credible evidence to support this.

While he was in these parts of South America it is possible that Scotland acted as an 'along-sider' for SIS (the latter of course cannot be acknowledged or denied by MI6). South America in the late 1920s was a hotbed of espionage, business and diplomatic parties, with secret agents working out of embassies and consulates. In Argentina, Scotland lived and worked as a company manager in the north-eastern regions of Corrientes and neighbouring Entre Ríos between the Paraná and Uruguay rivers. He discovered that it was general practice for a German national to make contact with the local German consulate and offer his services in a loose espionage role. He was in the region during the crucial Chaco War – the bloody struggle between Bolivia and Paraguay that lasted nearly three years and led to the death of over 100,000 native troops. According to Scotland's official military record,[14] he himself served in the Chaco War between July and September 1932. Although his record makes no reference to his regiment for those three months, it is likely that he was there on intelligence duties.

Scotland had accumulated a substantial picture of German espionage activities in South America by the time Adolf Hitler rose to power in Germany the following January. 'By 1933,' Scotland commented, 'I watched the spectacle of a country gone mad.'[15] It was perhaps no coincidence that he made three tours of Nazi Germany between 1935 and 1937. On his itinerary during one visit was a meeting at the Colonial Institute in Stuttgart with its head, Captain Schmidt. According to Scotland, during the meeting Schmidt raised the issue of a scheme to enable 200 German-Jewish families to emigrate to South America. There is no apparent reason to doubt Scotland's testimony. He kept in touch with Schmidt and discovered several years later that the Colonial Institute had become the main centre for controlling German agents based in Africa and South America. Scotland also made a point of visiting old friends in Germany from his days in South-West Africa. His 'HUMINT' – human intelligence – was all about building up contacts and friends in Germany and casually enquiring about life under Nazism.

Coffee with Hitler

In 1937, Scotland took another trip to Germany. In Munich, he sought out a wealthy old friend from his days in South-West Africa, identified only as Herr K. A life of luxury could not hide the fact that Herr K was in very poor health. But his mind remained sharp. He kept asking Scotland about his experiences during the Khoikhoi Wars and in the Orange River valley, and his relationship with the German colonial administrators. The conversation rolled on from afternoon tea to evening and supper. Scotland had no inkling that it was all was being recorded.

The following day, he received a phone call at the hotel to say that Herr K's colleagues were interested in talking further with him. A car would be ready to collect him. Scotland arrived back at Herr K's house to find a silver coffee service laid out in the dining room surrounded by half a dozen chairs. As coffee was poured, the entourage of expected guests entered. Scotland found himself being introduced to the Führer himself. What did the Nazi leader want with him? If Scotland's memoirs are to be believed, Hitler commanded him to be seated and asked him about his years in South-West Africa, whether he was still an army officer, and what the situation in South America was. Coffee was passed to Scotland and the two aides who had accompanied Hitler, but the Führer 'was given a separate jug on a small silver tray and a plate of plain biscuits which he proceeded to nibble throughout the interview'.[16]

It was an informal chat rather than an interrogation. The Führer commented that 'South-Africa is a rich country. It should come back to German control.'

Scotland disagreed: 'Your German residents there simply do not want the return of the old stiff-necked officials telling them how to run their farms and businesses.'

'What stiff-necked officials?' retorted Hitler. Did the German dictator have a sense of humour? Scotland replied: 'Did you ever meet Herr Governor Seitz?'

Hitler is said to have pulled a face and replied: 'Yes, I know what you mean.' His parting words to Scotland were: 'You are an ingenious man, Schottland. Now I understand the reports we have on our files about you.'[17]

What exactly was known? Had the Führer been shown a German intelligence file on 'Herr Schottland'? It is perhaps surprising that Scotland was not arrested on suspicion of espionage – after all, he was in Germany gathering vital information on the ground and meeting interesting political figures in local government. Unfazed by this meeting with the Nazi leader, Scotland continued his tour and searched out comrades from his days in the kaiser's army; some turned out to be pro-Nazi, others anti-Nazi. Eager to share their views, they sat down with him, deliberated on the country's current circumstances and analysed the latest events. From them Scotland gained an important insight into the political situation and true state of affairs in Germany. He wrote:

> The enemies of Nazism, Jewish or non-Jewish, were being disposed of with ruthless speed. In addition, vast sums of money were being made available to engineering firms engaged on the production of armaments. Throughout Europe and South America and many other parts of the world, Nazi intelligence men were at work, and from sources on both sides of the fence I was learning, with some alarm, about the fantastic scale of the plans for setting up penal camps by the hundred.[18]

Scotland had no hesitation in crediting himself with much of the useful intelligence being gathered for London. The emerging picture crystallised as he travelled the country further, noting how the SS conducted themselves and how they watched the German populace closely. The nature of Nazi Germany was well known from information supplied by people like Frank Foley and Thomas Kendrick, and attachés across Europe.

On his return to London, Scotland wrote a paper for the War Office on the fast-changing political situation in Germany, the formation of a new army of SS and the rearmament programme that threatened the stability of Europe. His paper underscored the value of studying manpower in the German armed forces as a prerequisite for any intelligence service to understand the capability of the Nazi regime in the event of another war. When Scotland submitted his report, war was less than twelve months away.

The Second World War

After Hitler's annexation of Austria on 12 March 1938, Scotland offered his services again to the War Office. But it was two years before he was back in uniform. On his re-enlistment papers he declared the countries of which he had knowledge to be Germany, South-West Africa, Paraguay, north-western Argentina and Uruguay. In March 1940, Scotland was summoned to the War Office and given instructions to fly to Amiens in France, and from there to Arras for an interview with General Noel Mason-MacFarlane, the then director of Military Intelligence. Two decades after the last world war, Scotland found himself back on intelligence duties in France and promoted to the rank of major. At Arras, he was greeted by Lieutenant Colonel Jock Whiteford, a former colleague from the First World War, who was working for Mason-MacFarlane.[19] Whiteford had briefed his superior on Scotland's extraordinary background and knowledge of all things German.

The interview with Mason-MacFarlane was brief. He wanted Scotland to organise prisoners of war in France, far away from his own headquarters. He was to establish a suitable site as a 'cage' to process and interrogate captured German POWs for special military information. After looking around for a suitable location, Scotland chose the Normandy port of Dieppe for the interrogation quarters. The War Office approved his choice. Scotland was promoted to lieutenant colonel and (from July 1940) re-enlisted in the Intelligence Corps. From an office in the former Metropole Hotel in London he began the task of selecting suitable interrogators. From there, his team was dispatched to France and he arrived as commanding officer.

The swift and unexpected invasion of the Low Countries and France by German forces in May 1940 meant that the cage in Dieppe never opened. Scotland was forced to evacuate his personnel. He commandeered two fishing vessels at Dunkirk and arrived back in England with his team and seventeen German prisoners of war, most of them Luftwaffe pilots. He handed the prisoners over at Newhaven and headed to London to organise the setting-up of cages around Britain, believing that he would soon have prisoners to fill them. He was tasked with increasing the number of interrogators who could move between the various cages, depending on the workload. Not only did he select his interrogators, but he also trained them. The training included lectures by Scotland himself, based around what he had learned about Germans in South-West Africa after the Boer War, in France in the First World War and in Germany during the rise of the Third Reich in the 1930s. On 13 July 1940, he formally established the Prisoner of War Interrogation Section (Home Section), with twenty officers as interrogators.

In those early days, Scotland posed a direct challenge to his own boss, Major Rawlinson, the head of MI9a. Scotland refused to sign the Official

Secrets Act when presented with it by Rawlinson, arguing that, as an interrogator, he would be discussing secret matters with German prisoners that would necessitate him breaking it. Rawlinson insisted that Scotland and his intelligence officers sign it. To break the impasse, or perhaps because he was a man who traversed conventional boundaries, Scotland devised a special statement for his interrogators to sign:

> British secrets must not be discussed with German prisoners-of-war except in the presence of the British officer who wants the information the German may have. German secrets, if known to the enemy, are not secrets under the Act. What is secret is that we know them.[20]

Until the cages were fully functioning, Scotland travelled from the War Office in London where he was mainly stationed to interrogate newly captured German prisoners of war at various locations around Britain. He also placed single interrogators at strategic points around the country to conduct interrogations should lone German pilots be shot down there.

In June 1940, a batch of over 400 German prisoners who had been captured by the British during the retreat from Dunkirk entered England via the port of Southampton. They comprised mainly young soldiers with only a superficial understanding of weapons and fighting. But among them was a small number of older soldiers who had served in the German armed forces for a number of years as part of the limited 100,000-strong army permitted by the Treaty of Versailles. They had received first-class military training and were found to be highly efficient soldiers. From them, Scotland and his interrogators were able to evaluate the German army's capabilities, and could report to British intelligence that the Germans' fighting ability and efficiency in the early stages of the war was mixed. The fall of France and the retreat from Dunkirk yielded no more German army prisoners for two years until the influx of prisoners captured in North Africa. Instead, Scotland and his staff received naval and air force prisoners.

Scotland himself admitted that his years of experience living among German nationals after the Boer War, serving in the German army and later interrogating thousands of German prisoners of war in the First World War enabled him to form an opinion as an intelligence officer rather than as a politician. He believed that this provided a unique tool for understanding how to glean information from his prisoners.

Scotland analysed Nazi philosophy and observed an unqualified respect for all things military. As he noted, 'the common desire for a leader and a national identity with which all sections of the German nation can be content, or reasonably content, is engrained deeply'.[21] He detected that professional rivalry in the German army had always been fierce, because its base was tribal and not national. There was also a belief that the army had never really been defeated in 1918:

> The force of 100,000 men allowed to Germany by the Versailles Treaty ensured the unbroken continuation of the German Military Spirit; and since the Wehrlister [sic] (which contained the names and particulars of all men due for military service) had been left intact by the Allies in 1918, it was a comparatively simple matter to select an elite force and for Hitler to build on it.[22]

During the 1930s, Germany had expanded its armaments and spy networks and had re-established contacts in South America, South Africa, Australia and elsewhere. Scotland also argued that the German respect for strict authority made it easier for Hitler to gain blind obedience from his people. Hitler brought new traditions to German culture – the oath of secrecy and 'loyalty in the SS'. This 'broke family ties and encouraged men to inform on family and friends who criticised the Third Reich. The army was loyal to its old traditions, but the Waffen SS and Gestapo were not. Their loyalty was to Hitler.'[23]

Introducing equality of rank and no hierarchy in the SS created a virtually impenetrable brotherhood of blind obedience. It led Scotland to conclude of the SS that the removal of any hierarchy was 'the wrong way for Germans to be controlled':

> They are content to take orders from above – it fits in with the old family tradition of parental authority and also of the state being led by a single leader, but give the Germans equality with one another and they rapidly became arrogant, domineering and fools.[24]

It was this premise that led Scotland to ensure that, wherever possible, a German prisoner was interrogated by a higher-ranking British officer, because the prisoner would respect his authority and rank and be more likely to cooperate.

It was largely due to Colonel Scotland's expertise that by the end of the Second World War British intelligence had an impressive and adaptable interrogation policy that produced intelligence of the highest quality, unequalled in any other country. It was because of this that in February 1946 he was decorated with the American Bronze Star by Major-General William Biddle,

> for outstanding cooperation in enabling field interrogation detachments of G-2, ETOUSA [European Theatre of Operations, United States Army], to be quickly established, for generous sharing with United States Field Interrogation Detachments of the British experience for the speedy and complete reporting of the results of PWIS interrogation; and for exceptional contribution to Anglo-American cooperation and outstanding devotion to duty.[25]

However, allegations of a sinister nature began to emerge publicly. Colonel Scotland's conservative, gentlemanly, military appearance belied a man with a penetrating gaze, Afrikaans twang and tight-clenched manners that made him feared by most German prisoners. To those on his side, Scotland was a charmer, but he was brutal and ruthless to anyone who stood in his way, especially the German prisoners who refused to cooperate in his cage.

3

CAGE CHARACTERS
The interrogators

The majority of enemy prisoners captured in the early stages of the war were not willing to give away information voluntarily. They believed that Germany would win the war. And who could challenge that belief, given that England faced the very real threat of invasion in 1940–41? Obtaining vital intelligence from prisoners as quickly as possible became the immediate task for the London Cage interrogators and for those at other cages around the country.

'Interrogation is an art,' wrote Scotland. 'A good interrogator is partly born, partly made.'[1] The role of interrogators was critical in the immediate period after a prisoner's capture. Timing was all. In a fast-moving war, a piece of intelligence one day was history the next. But the interrogators' role in the London Cage has been obscured, even by Colonel Scotland himself, who makes no reference to them in his memoirs (apart from a fleeting mention of senior interrogator Major Terry). Nevertheless, they were essential to the 'success' of the London Cage: without their skills, a vast number of pieces of the intelligence jigsaw would have been unavailable to the British military authorities. Having signed the Official Secrets Act, they knew the consequences of talking about their work – consequences that Scotland himself faced when he crossed the intelligence services by trying to publish his own memoirs.[2]

The interrogators were all male; the London Cage was no place for women. Only two Auxiliary Territorial Service (ATS) women were known to have worked there for a few months after the war, when it became a centre for war crimes investigations: the British-born Lucy Haley and the German émigré Miss Metzler, neither of whom ever saw any prisoners in the cage. They were billeted in a building of the Music College next to the Royal Albert Hall, and every day travelled the short distance to the London Cage, where they were engaged in taking down letters in English for the sergeants. Before the end of the Second World War, it was rare for the military to use female interrogators. The exception was Naval Intelligence and MI19's Combined Services Detailed Interrogation Centre in Cairo.[3]

Scotland's experience had taught him that German prisoners in uniform were very different in attitude and behaviour from the civilians in peace-time Germany. His interrogators faced soldiers who were indoctrinated in Nazi ideology – especially the SS officers, who belonged to highly efficient units that had sworn blind allegiance to Adolf Hitler.

The art of interrogation

The interrogator had to produce immediate results while a prisoner was still disoriented by the shock of capture. His duty was to obtain from the prisoner all information required by the army and security services as swiftly as possible. This included building a picture of the prisoner's war service since enlistment; where he had served before capture; his regiment and training; the Germans' fighting capability; and the state of morale among the general population in Germany. Prisoners could be talkative and egotistic, which boded well for their interrogation because it often took little for such men to cooperate. Prisoners could also be timid and fearful of punishment, or just plain foolish and unable to see the verbal trap that was being laid for them. The hardest prisoner to interrogate was the polite, cheerful one who suspected various ruses and was firm in his refusals. He could only be overcome with perseverance.

The London Cage was a tight-knit unit, and Colonel Scotland insisted on hand-picking his interrogators. Although fluency in German was a requirement of the job, Scotland insisted that any good interrogator or intelligence officer had to have an intuitive understanding of the German mindset: understanding the psyche of the prisoner meant that information could be extracted from him. He honed his interrogators' intuitions, so that they could conduct interrogations methodically and extract information in the shortest possible time, before the prisoner became uncooperative.

Scotland looked for five qualities in an interrogator: 1) a first-class memory; 2) keen observation; 3) infinite patience; 4) knowledge of psychology; and 5) the ability to act.

A good memory enabled an interrogator to check a prisoner's story for consistency. Sharp powers of observation meant he could detect subtle changes in the prisoner's mannerisms and behaviour during interrogation. Infinite patience was required to see the job through to its conclusion, however long it took: there could be no shortcuts and an interrogation could not be rushed. At the London Cage there was sufficient time to study prisoners, unlike at some of the cages near the front line, where prisoners needed to be moved on quickly.

An interrogator had to be a practical psychologist with an ability to appraise character rapidly and swiftly understand the type of man about to be interrogated. He needed to understand when to change his mood; a swift judgement had to be made as to whether to adopt a friendly or tough attitude. The interrogator had to judge whether a prisoner could be won over by a soft approach of discussion, argument and befriending; by a hard approach of anger and even veiled threats; or by small favours, such as extra chocolate, cigarettes or alcohol.

Some German prisoners could be bluffed into obedience by a reminder of military authority. Interrogation was found to be more effective when the interrogator was of a higher rank than the prisoner. Successful interrogation was based on an interrogator's personal art, playing a confidence trick, getting the prisoner to talk, often without knowing that he was revealing new information. The interrogator was the master – or was to give the impression of being the master.

Another successful technique was for two interrogators to play off against each other. The one who failed to induce a prisoner to talk could indicate to the prisoner that he was about to be interrogated by a sterner officer. The other officer was called in and the two interrogators pretended to disagree over how the prisoner was to be treated – with harshness or mercy. It was often enough for a prisoner to begin to cooperate.

The best interrogators came from particular professions: lawyers and academics, who were used to sorting through volumes of unfamiliar evidence, and journalists and businessmen, trained to worm their way into a new situation. In essence, an interrogator had to be a good actor. Displays of impatience or anger could be effective, but loss of temper was always fatal. Scotland believed that 'an interrogator must be subtle and disarming in his approach to a prisoner'.[4] This could be achieved by talking to him about his background, family life, grievances and political beliefs. This enabled an interrogator to build a comprehensive picture of the prisoner. The main disarming technique employed on a prisoner was to reveal so much information about him that he felt the interrogator knew everything and so he might as well cooperate.

Identifying a prisoner's rank and the markings on his uniform could tell an interrogator his situation and enable him to work out the German order of battle. This would be presented to the prisoner during interrogation, before he had time to adjust to his new status, and he might be deceived into inadvertently giving away more information. One of the key areas to ascertain was what a prisoner knew about new technology. This helped paint a picture of the broader military capability of the German armed forces. Also crucial was any information on developments in the manufacture of tanks, U-boats, planes, weapons, mines and industrial chemicals. Interrogators often worked with technical experts and scientists who were drafted in to help on matters relating to technology. These technical officers received a short training course at the London Cage before being deployed to other cages to aid interrogations. They also had to sign the Official Secrets Act and not disclose the nature of their work or location.

Prisoners were interrogated about their service history, battle campaigns and geographical aspects of their country, including the locations of industrial plants, so that the interrogator could identify potential bombing targets: railways, bridges, industries, factories and ships. In the end, few refused to cooperate, though it could take up to nine days for them finally to talk.

A combination of aerial photography from the Royal Air Force and the United States Army Air Forces, captured documents, enemy propaganda and prisoner-of-war interrogation all fed into the intelligence picture and provided the Allies with a far-reaching appreciation of the enemy's situation during the war.

The 'actors'

The chief 'actors' among the interrogators at the London Cage were Major Randoll Coate, Major Antony Terry, Kenneth Morgan, Captain Ryder, Theodore 'Bunny' Pantcheff, Lieutenant Hepton, Captain George Sinclair,

Captain W. Kieser, Captain Hay, Captain Egger and Captain Cornish. They were aided by Warrant Officer Michael Ullman, who took statements from the prisoners. Biographical information on many of the interrogators is very sketchy.[5] Few personal details are known about Captain George Sinclair, except that he was drafted into the Intelligence Corps and served at the London Cage from 2 October 1941 until 11 August 1944. Similarly, little is known about Captain W. Kieser, who had been a schoolmaster in civilian life. Kieser was commissioned into the Intelligence Corps on 14 May 1942 and transferred to the London Cage. He was described as a 'careful and reliable interrogator especially on technical subjects, his all-round knowledge of German [making] his services particularly sought after as an interpreter'.[6]

Interrogator Randoll Coate, who had a quiet flair and sense of adventure, suggested to Colonel Scotland that at least one interrogator should accompany the clandestine commando night raids into coastal areas of France and Norway, so that any prisoners could be interrogated for swift 'hot' information while they were still disoriented and in shock from capture. He was successful in persuading his superior, and so all the now-legendary major raids and their diversionary actions had at least one of Scotland's interrogators attached to them. These interrogators were an integral part of the perilous night raids on the Lofoten islands (1941), Vågsøy (1941), Bruneval (1942) and Saint-Nazaire (1942), and the German prisoners captured during them were taken back to Britain to undergo detailed interrogation at the London Cage or the CSDIC sites run by Colonel Kendrick. These were high-risk ventures: Antony Terry was captured and remained a prisoner of the Germans for most of the war; later released from a German POW camp, he returned to work as Scotland's deputy at the London Cage.

Randoll Coate

Randoll Coate served as an interrogator from the beginning of the London Cage in 1940 until 1944. Born in Switzerland in October 1909 to British parents, he was educated at the Classical College in Lausanne and Oriel College, Oxford, where he read French and German. He was fluent in German, French, Dutch and Italian and travelled widely in France, Italy, Switzerland and Germany. By profession he was a journalist and commercial artist. After the outbreak of war, the Coate family sold the house in Lausanne and returned to Britain. Coate noticed an advertisement in *The Times* for people fluent in languages and replied. He subsequently turned down a job in Romania and trained at the officer training unit at Weedon. Although he was offered a commission in the Tank Corps, he declined and was commissioned on the General List instead, 'specially employed'. He joined No. 8 War Intelligence Course at Swanage and then transferred to the Prisoner of War Interrogation Section at No. 2 Eastern Command cage at Hounslow.

On 15 July 1940, he joined the Intelligence Corps and was posted for interrogation duties at the London Cage. Coate accompanied the commandos on a number of raids and was able to question prisoners shortly after their capture. In December 1941, he took part in Operation Archery against the German garrison on the island of Vågsøy as a Combined Operations raid by the Marine Commandos, Royal Navy and elements from the Norwegian forces. Their aims were to capture enemy troops and equipment, destroy industrial plants (including fish oil factories), seize documents and codes, and arrest collaborators. Several ships were successfully sunk and a number of shore facilities destroyed. At least 98 prisoners were taken, 64 collaborators captured and 154 enemy killed. The commandos suffered 17 dead and 54 wounded. On return to the home port, the main priority for Coate was to make sure he disembarked with the prisoners quickly, to avoid any delay in interrogation that could reduce the intelligence value of any material or prisoners captured.

The following year, in April 1942, Coate was selected to take part in Operation Myrmidon, an abortive raid on the Adour estuary in south-western France.[7] He sailed with his group of commandos to the mouth of the Bordeaux estuary. Their objective was to sail up to the town in landing barges, inflict as much damage as possible on the German garrison, take prisoners for interrogation and return to ship. A major Naval Intelligence mistake meant they did not realise that the sandbar at the mouth of the river was so high at that time of year that the naval destroyer could not cross it, and even the troop landing craft could go no farther. The operation had to be abandoned.[8]

By 1943, Coate was busy interrogating prisoners at the London Cage, lecturing to various army groups on interrogation and the morale of the German forces, and attending intelligence meetings at the War Office. His advice and analysis were based on the results of interrogations of over 10,000 German prisoners of war by MI19 at various cages around Britain. In 1944, he was posted from the London Cage to the Middle East Forces, where he was tasked with acquiring intelligence on the German presence in Greece; it is now thought that he was working for SIS. While Coate was in Cairo, it was decided that he should be sent to Bari on a parachute course. He obtained his parachute wings, but his first operation into Greece was by boat. After landing, and unsure of who he was, the partisans nearly shot him as a German spy; with the aid of a small Greek medallion, he was able to convince them otherwise.[9] Later, Coate was posted to Rome and was eventually discharged with the rank of honorary major in April 1946.

Maurice Cornish

Captain Maurice Frank Cornish was described as 'a sound interrogator and successful with the difficult sort of prisoner of war'.[10] According to records at the Military Intelligence Museum, he served with the Political Warfare Executive (PWE), MI19 (Prisoner of War Interrogation Section) and possibly the Special Operations Executive. He was commissioned on 7 June 1941 and 'specially employed' with MI19 from 1942 as an interrogator with a mobile unit of the CSDIC in the Western Desert. On 29 June 1942, he was captured by the Germans in North Africa. It is possible that he managed to escape, because he was mentioned in records in 1943, again as 'specially employed'. Nothing else is recorded about his wartime activities, except in an account by Colonel Scotland in his book *The London Cage* about how Cornish was sent to Moscow to interview Nazi war criminal Scharpwinkel about fifty Allied prisoners of war who had escaped from Stalag Luft III and who had been summarily executed by the SS and Gestapo after their recapture. On the recommendation of the director of the Political Warfare Executive, Cornish was decorated with an MBE in 1946 for 'gallant and distinguished service whilst a prisoner of war'.[11]

Hans Kettler

Born in Germany, Hans Kettler arrived in England in 1925 and studied at Magdalene College, Cambridge. On 2 March 1942, he was commissioned into the Pioneer Corps. Six months later, on 20 September 1942, he transferred to the Intelligence Corps and was posted to the London Cage as an interrogator. In the summer of 1944, he was listed as a captain on a regular emergency commission, still at the London Cage.

Matthew Sullivan, MI19 interrogator at Latimer House and Wilton Park, wrote:

> No one was physically touched [at the London Cage], but it could be a traumatic experience for a burly submarine petty officer or an SS corporal to be confronted hour after hour by the diminutive Major Kettler, with his slightly deformed body, boring into him with his quick mind and dynamic energy.[12]

The prisoners nicknamed him *der Giftzwerg* – 'the poison-dwarf'. The toughness of certain prisoners was matched with equal toughness on the part of Kettler. Facing a prisoner who had clicked his heels and proudly saluted 'Heil Hitler!', Kettler responded: '*Jetzt sind Sie der Amboss, und ich der Hammer*' ('Now you are the anvil, and I am the hammer'). Strong, die-hard Nazis were said to quail before him. Kettler had great professional pride and 'would rather break his heart and his larynx than fail to break a man'.[13] When Kettler finished an interrogation, he apparently threw off the seriousness with a flippant laugh, leaving a subdued – if not bewildered – prisoner staring after him.

After the war, he was promoted to the rank of major, on a short service commission to the sister interrogation site at Bad Nenndorf in Germany. He was granted the rank of honorary lieutenant colonel in 1954, when he relinquished his commission. Kettler was regarded as 'outstanding in his rough treatment of prisoners'.[14] As a historian and writer, he published a book in 1943 called *Baroque Tradition in the Literature of the German Enlightenment, 1700–1750*.

Theodore 'Bunny' Pantcheff

Theodore Xenophon Henry Pantcheff, known to his contemporaries as 'Bunny', was commissioned into the Intelligence Corps on 7 March 1942 and was 'specially employed' from the following month. His wartime career thereafter was relatively unknown and shrouded in secrecy until the London Cage files were declassified. He was described as a naturally gifted investigator.[15] He probed the planned mass escape of prisoners from Devizes, the murders at Camp Comrie, the Channel Islands atrocities and the Wormhoudt massacre. Following the liberation of the Channel Islands in Operation Nestegg (1945), Pantcheff was involved in investigations into civilian collaboration with the Germans. From 1948, he was employed by SIS.

Antony Terry

Antony Frederic Aime Imbert Terry, nicknamed 'Afie', was born in north London in 1913. A journalist, he had spent most of his life outside Britain, growing up in pre-war Berlin where his father was attached to the British Embassy. This gave him an invaluable knowledge of pre-war Germany, as well as of the inner workings of the Nazi military and civilian regime.

Terry was commissioned on the General List in July 1940. British intelligence files described him as 'bi-lingual German with good French, a highly efficient interrogator, a first-class office organiser and gets on well with all contacts'.[16] A rather enigmatic man, Terry was of slight build and was known for his nondescript dark suits; these features enabled him to blend into a crowd. It is unclear when he transferred from the General Service Corps to the Intelligence Corps, but from the London Cage he was temporarily attached to Combined Operations for the raid on the dry docks at Saint-Nazaire on 28 March 1942.[17] Terry was reported missing afterwards. His bravery in action meant that he was immediately awarded the Military Cross in absentia.[18] The citation was signed by Lieutenant Colonel A.C. Newman, VC, military commander of forces at Saint-Nazaire. Part of it read:

> Capt. TERRY started with the very definite disadvantage of taking part in an operation in which all ranks had been very highly and strenuously trained, whereas he had had no training whatsoever. To say that he stood up to the very gruelling operation without flagging would be an understatement; for his actions from the moment of setting foot on French soil until taken prisoner, some ten hours later, were outstanding. Captain TERRY displayed courage, great initiative and was, at all times, of great assistance to me. On one occasion during the street fighting in the town of SAINT NAZAIRE, Capt. TERRY went off alone to find out what was the position with regard to the enemy in the adjacent streets. At great personal risk, armed only with a revolver and showing total disregard for his own personal safety, he carried out this reconnaissance, bringing back the most valuable information of the actions and

whereabouts of the enemy. It was only when all ammunition had been expended and with a great many seriously wounded, the Headquarters Party, with Captain TERRY, were taken Prisoners-of-War.[19]

As a prisoner of the Germans, Terry was sent to a POW camp for three years where he put his journalistic skills to use running a clandestine newspaper and keeping the whole camp informed of developments in the war. On his release from captivity at war's end, he was posted back to the London Cage with the rank of major. There he became Colonel Scotland's deputy and interrogated high-ranking Nazi war criminals, compiling evidence for the war crimes trials.

Kenneth Morgan

Born in Gloucester on 30 March 1912, Kenneth Morgan was fluent in French and German, having obtained an MA in Modern Languages from Cambridge. On 1 September 1940, he transferred to the Intelligence Corps and attended the nineteenth security course at the School of Military Intelligence at Matlock, Derbyshire. From October 1940 until February 1942, Morgan served in 21 Field Security, attending four months of officer training at Sandhurst. He then attended a one-month German interrogation course in Cambridge. From 15 December 1942, he was 'specially employed' and transferred to the Prisoner of War Interrogation Section with the rank of lieutenant, later captain. Morgan looked steelier than he was, being 'the gentlest of the London District Cage interrogators'.[20] An insight into what Morgan felt about his job at the London Cage is offered in former MI19 interrogator Matthew Sullivan's book *Thresholds of Peace*:

> I found it harder to get my blood up than 'Scottie' [Colonel Scotland] who was motivated by past experiences or Kettler who had his own reasons for enjoying these battles. A whole submarine crew would suddenly arrive, just fished up out of the sea. Living comfortably in London, it was a real emotional strain to make oneself hard, to work oneself up into the required state of anger or annoyance. Fortunately for me, other methods were also necessary: jigsaw work on the small details picked up in an interrogation or scrutinised out of the prisoner's papers; or playing on some factor like a man's family situation or his Christian background, appealing to something sentimental in his nature.[21]

Campbell Macintosh

Captain Campbell Dundas Macintosh was commissioned into the Intelligence Corps in October 1940 and began work with MI5 at Camp 020, the camp for captured German spies.[22] His work involved interrogation and eavesdropping on prisoners' conversations,[23] and he was particularly engaged in the case of Dutchman Charles Albert van den Kieboom, a German spy who landed with three other agents near Dungeness in September 1940. Van den Kieboom was taken to Camp 020, where he refused to be 'turned' as a double agent and was hanged at Pentonville prison on 17 December 1940.[24]

In October 1940, while with B8L,[25] Macintosh interrogated another German agent, Karl Theo Druecke, one of three agents who had landed on the coast of Banffshire the previous month. He also refused at Camp 020 to become a double agent, and he and another member of the party were hanged on 6 August 1941 at Wandsworth prison.[26] From Camp 020, Macintosh transferred to the London Cage as an interrogator.

Arthur Ryder

Major Arthur Ryder was attached to the London Cage as an interrogator from 12 January 1945. He already had a distinguished record as a military security officer in the period leading up to and during the campaign in north-western Europe, including work in Belgium. He played a considerable part in assisting the Belgians to establish their security services by providing training and advice, which led to him being honoured as Chevalier of the Belgian Order of Leopold II with Croix de Guerre and Palm. He was also mentioned in dispatches in November 1945.[27] He was 'a painstaking interrogator who is successful with the more ready and willing prisoner'.[28]

Working with the Americans

After the surprise attack on Pearl Harbor by the Japanese on 7 December 1941, America entered the war on the side of Britain. It was just a matter of weeks before US personnel began to arrive in England, and with them officers of the newly established intelligence service, the Office of Strategic Services (OSS, forerunner of the CIA). They were posted to a number of clandestine sites run by British intelligence and assisted in the interrogation of enemy prisoners of war.

By 1942, the Joint Intelligence Committee and MI19 had agreed to share intelligence with the Americans, including interrogation reports. They liaised directly with Mr Whitney Shepardson and Mr Maddox of the OSS.[29] Colonel Scotland was responsible for training US interrogators, and he used a pool of his interrogators as instructors across various sites. But his treatment of Allied personnel was just as brisk and efficient as his treatment of prisoners. A team of American intelligence officers arrived with their commander at Wilton Park, Beaconsfield, another MI19 site. The loyalty of the American commander, who was of Italian-American origin, came into question when he was overheard informing Italian prisoners that they were not to give any information to British officers. Word got back to Colonel Scotland, who immediately left for Wilton Park and called the American commander to a meeting. Scotland did not mince his words as the commander stood before him, refusing to give any explanation for his action. 'I shall dispense with your help,' Scotland told him. 'You can take back your troops to wherever they came from.'[30] The American intelligence officers were paraded before Scotland, instructed as to why they were being sent away, and ordered to 'Quick march!' That was not the end of the matter, though. Scotland's unauthorised dismissal of the American unit led to his being hauled before Colonel Conrad, commanding officer, for a dressing-down. But age and experience as a soldier carried little weight with Colonel Scotland, who ignored the reprimand.

The special Anglo-American cooperation in interrogation and intelligence gathering continued successfully throughout the war. The various branches of MI19 conducted immensely important work, interrogating prisoners and eavesdropping on their conversations. But it has rarely received its due recognition in books on the Second World War or espionage.

Later in 1944, trained British and American interrogators accompanied the invasion forces into Europe and worked in forward-field interrogation units. Underpinning all their work was the conviction that psychology was at the heart of successful intelligence operations. It was believed that Nazi youths would yield nothing during interrogation, and by 'a careful study of the psychology of this new type of prisoner of war, methods were evolved to overcome his resistance and useful information was obtained from even the most resistant of these highly trained members of the enemy forces'.[31]

In July 1945, Colonel D. Macmillan, the senior British intelligence officer at the office of the assistant chief of staff, Allied Forces Headquarters, concluded: 'There is very little glamour attached to the work of interrogation.' That would certainly be the experience of the London Cage interrogators as they entered the most difficult phase of their work and prepared to receive many ardent Nazis, who would sorely test their patience. They were about to face the perpetrators of horrendous crimes in the concentration camps and those responsible for murdering Allied soldiers in cold blood. It would be full-time work to bring them to justice.

All too often the focus is on the interrogations' impact on the prisoners, but the work also affected the interrogators. Living in a virtually closed world, their task could lead to mild psychosis.[32] How difficult was life in the London Cage? What were the realities that the interrogators faced on a daily basis? And did they cross the line and break the Geneva Convention?

In his uncensored memoirs, Colonel Scotland wrote: 'No physical force was used during our interrogations to obtain information, no cold water treatment, no third degrees, nor any other infringements; for not only is it the firm rule of the British Services that no physical force may be used to induce a prisoner to talk, but I have always considered it to be useless as well as unnecessary.'[33] What emerges is a very different story.

4

CAGE CHARACTERS
The 'guests'

In the course of the war, over 3,000 German prisoners of war – from the air force, navy and army – crossed the threshold of the London Cage. It became the most valuable centre for those prisoners of war who required special attention. It dealt with German prisoners who had special military information, but who were proving uncooperative during interrogation at the other cages. Interrogation was permitted under the Geneva Convention, but a prisoner was only required to give his name, rank and number. The official files and interrogation reports for the London Cage between 1940 and 1943 have never been released. Nor is there a surviving list of prisoners who were held there. Piecing together the details of exactly who the early prisoners were and what information they gave during interrogation has only been possible thanks to Colonel Scotland's published memoirs and uncensored manuscript, and a few short summary reports in the files of the War Office and Air Intelligence.[1]

Prisoners captured during the first year of the war were ideal material for the new interrogators to practise their skills on – as in the case of 200 German paratroopers captured in May 1940 near Rotterdam. They had parachuted into the Low Countries ahead of invading German forces and had attempted to capture strategic airfields in the Netherlands, aided by an assault on the Dutch port of Rotterdam by General von Sponeck's forces. The unsuccessful enemy action on Rotterdam left thousands of German troops scattered across the sand dunes and in hiding. Over 1,200 were captured and shipped to England via Dover, with 200 being taken to the London Cage for interrogation. The remaining German troops in the

Netherlands escaped capture only because of Hermann Göring's order for the Luftwaffe to pound Rotterdam. Back in London, Colonel Scotland's interrogators soon established that their new prisoners had no previous military career, but had been trained up quickly by the Nazi regime. Attempting to establish the fighting ability of the German forces was to be a recurring theme in the early days of the London Cage.

U-boat crews provided Colonel Scotland and his interrogators with details of their training and naval background. German naval personnel let slip technical details about specific battleships, their armour, armaments, construction and engines: the *Bismarck*, *Tirpitz*, *Gneisenau* and *Admiral Graf Spee*. The crews discussed the movements, tactics and exploits of their own vessels, as well as of the heavy German battleship *Scharnhorst*. They revealed vital information in the early days of the Battle of the Atlantic.

Among the earliest prisoners at the London Cage were survivors of the *Bismarck*, the German battleship sunk by the British 350 miles west of Brest, France, on 26/27 May 1941. Their interrogation reports from the London Cage have not been released, but their bugged conversations from their time at Trent Park survive in the National Archives, in series WO 208 of War Office files. In his memoirs, Scotland spoke of the survivors of the *Bismarck*, who described her last voyage in considerable detail, including the damage inflicted on her during her fight with the British warships *Hood* and *Prince of Wales*. They told how they had been spotted in the water, and how the British destroyer *Maori* had moved in to pick them up. In total, 110 survivors were pulled from the waves – from an original crew of 2,200. They were taken first to the London Cage for initial interrogation and were then transferred to Trent Park, where their conversations were secretly bugged. One of the youngest *Bismarck* survivors arrived at the London Cage suffering from severe shock. He was given only light work by the intelligence staff and was befriended by the interrogators, who took a soft approach. He gradually recovered and the interrogators learned that he was one of 500 young men drafted aboard the *Bismarck* to give them experience at sea. When the battleship had come under fire from the Royal Navy, they were all locked in the hold. It was a terrifying experience, from which most were unable to escape.

If a question or ambiguity arose over a prisoner's nationality or status that required more detailed investigation, he was transferred to the London Cage to establish whether he was a member of the German armed forces, a merchant seaman or a civilian. It was important for a man's identity to be established because he could be a German spy or a traitor – in which case the London Cage liaised with MI5 or Special Branch. In the early days, the London Cage held anti-Nazis who might be at risk from fellow Nazi prisoners in an ordinary POW camp. This cautionary approach proved sensible: in 1944 at Comrie Camp, die-hard Nazis murdered a fellow prisoner. There were serious consequences (as detailed in chapter 8). The London Cage was also a beneficial location for holding prisoners who had special information and who needed to be interrogated by technical experts. In such cases, expert specialists aided Scotland's interrogators in securing the right information during interrogation.

The one that got away

During the Battle of Britain, rooms at the London Cage were filled with Luftwaffe pilots, nicknamed 'the weekenders' by the interrogators. These particular German pilots had realised that their reconnaissance missions over England were becoming increasingly dangerous. Flying at the weekends, they expected to have to bail out, and so they packed an overnight bag with pyjamas, a toothbrush and razor. Their interrogations were easy, because they were ready to talk. One German pilot anticipated that he might be shot down and simply landed his plane in a field near Dover, declaring to the interrogators that his aim was to reach America and Hollywood. From men like him, Scotland's team gained extensive information about the low morale among the German air force and where various Luftwaffe squadrons were based.

The most renowned Luftwaffe pilot captured in 1940 was the German flying ace Franz von Werra, whose daring escapades were immortalised in the 1957 British film *The One That Got Away*. The movie claimed that Werra spent a short time at the London Cage, and was possibly even interrogated there. It is a claim repeated online. But there is no evidence that Werra was ever at the London Cage – indeed, it had not yet opened when Werra was interrogated.

On 5 September 1940, his plane was shot down over Kent during the Battle of Britain. After being held in barracks in Maidstone for a few days, Werra made his first escape attempt. He was transferred to Trent Park, at Cockfosters, and was interrogated by Captain Denys Felkin, the head of Air Intelligence there. Werra was then allegedly transferred to the London Cage, and from there to Grizedale Hall, a prisoner-of-war camp in Cumbria, known as No. 1 camp. Run by Lieutenant Colonel Morton, it had been used for senior German prisoners of war during the First World War. On 7 October 1940, Werra escaped from Grizedale Hall and was recaptured on 12 October 1940. The London Cage was not requisitioned until 15 October 1940, and its first prisoners arrived on 23 October. This makes it highly unlikely that Werra was ever held at the London Cage.

After his recapture, Werra was sentenced to three weeks in solitary confinement at Camp No. 13 in Swanwick, Derbyshire. In January 1941, he was transferred, together with other German POWs, to a camp in Canada, from where he escaped and eventually made his way back to Germany. Later that year he saw active service on the Russian front and continued his dangerous missions. He died young, at the age of twenty-seven, on 25 October 1941, after crashing into the sea north of Vlissingen, off the Netherlands.

Rudolf Hess

The highest-ranking German prisoner ever held by British intelligence was Hitler's deputy, Rudolf Hess. He flew solo to England on a peace mission, seeking to offer terms to the Duke of Hamilton, who he thought would offer a sympathetic ear. Late at night on 10 May 1941, Hess parachuted out of his plane when it ran out of fuel, landing south of Glasgow. He initially concealed who he was, and was carrying papers identifying him as Alfred Horn, so it took three days to establish his true identity. Whether Hess was ever taken to the London Cage is a subject of speculation. In his memoirs, Colonel Scotland claimed 'We interrogated Hess.' What is unclear is whether Scotland meant 'we' as in British intelligence or 'we' as in his unit in Kensington Palace Gardens. It is known that Hess was interrogated by a number of officials, and analysed by psychiatrists and psychologists. And he was certainly interrogated by the head of Air Intelligence from Trent Park, Captain Felkin. But it is not known where Felkin saw Hess; it was possibly at the Tower of London, where Hess was held for four days after being transferred by train from Scotland.[2] He remained a prisoner of MI6 for the duration of the war and stood trial at Nuremberg in 1945–46.

***

The London Cage also debriefed British prisoners, mainly pilots, who had escaped from German POW camps on the Continent. Of particular interest to Military Intelligence were their successful methods of escape and evasion, and details of any military installations that they might have observed while being escorted as prisoners through enemy territory. These men were relatively small in number, however, compared to the main focus of the work of the London Cage. From 1942, British pilots who escaped from POW camps were debriefed at another MI9 site, Wilton Park, Beaconsfield.

Fighting capacity

British interrogators had to learn all German ranks, recognise badges and understand military formations and the structure and division of the German armed forces. Such information could reveal a fair amount about a prisoner, even before he was interrogated. In the early days of the war, knowledge of the training methods of the German army was patchy. Interrogating prisoners of war about their training became a priority, to enable British intelligence to understand the German military morale, ability to fight under certain conditions, fighting qualities and the prisoners' will to resist.

From those early prisoners at the London Cage it was discovered that the Luftwaffe pilots had not been trained in Germany in matters of security: some carried papers and documents that were found and confiscated during the search of the prisoner and his registration, and these proved a good starting point for interrogation. The identity cards provided a clue as to the prisoner's unit, and, in contravention of orders given to them in Germany, one in ten German pilots carried their savings bank book, which showed where they had last deposited their pay; this allowed British interrogators to trace where a pilot's unit was stationed. German officers were often found to be carrying notebooks containing lists of their men and codes for all kinds of aircraft, as well as notes on difficulties within the unit. This information could be leaked during an interrogation without the prisoner realising where such precise information had come from. It gave the impression that the interrogator was omniscient and British espionage highly efficient, so that the prisoner decided it was not worth withholding answers to questions. It was an effective tool to break down resistance with little effort.

Colonel Scotland claimed in his unpublished memoirs to have left the London Cage for a short time to accompany the commando raid on the German-occupied Norwegian islands of Vågsøy and Måløy on 27 December 1941. Apparently much to his disappointment, the commandos would not allow him to go ashore, and he had to wait on the boat. He subsequently spoke about the bravery of these special forces:

[They were] by far the bravest of all invaders of Europe during the war, particularly those with the special role of obtaining information about the Germans' beach defences. These men were based in the most remote spots of the south coast of England, from which they slipped across in small crafts to France and returned with valuable knowledge. Necessarily, they were unpublicised but they did their lonely, dangerous work with cheerfulness and resolution, bearing their occasional losses with fortitude.[3]

Codenamed Operation Archery, the aim of the raid was to destroy key German installations and defences, oil tanks and ammunition stores, and take prisoners for interrogation. The dawn raid took the German commander completely by surprise and succeeded in its objectives, with 154 Germans killed and 98 captured. It came at a heavy cost to the Allied Combined Forces, with the loss of fifty-three officers and other ranks, including thirty-one from the RAF.[4] For the British, it yielded some particularly useful German prisoners of war, who were passed over to Scotland for interrogation. The first priority was to question the German commander, an affable man who, Scotland found, could easily be befriended. Scotland described how he nicknamed him 'Buddie' because of the commander's willingness to sit down with him with a cigarette and a beer. Apparently, Buddie had been so surprised by the attack that he had surrendered in his pyjamas. He jovially complained to Scotland that it was quite unfair of the British not to have given him the chance to use his guns against their ships.

Whether Scotland actually accompanied this raid is open to doubt, as is the interrogation of Buddie on the island of Vågsøy. His intelligence officer Randoll Coate did accompany the commandos during Operation Archery, and it is therefore probable that Scotland used some artistic licence by claiming to have been on the raid himself. The interrogation of Buddie that he described probably took place at the London Cage and not on Vågsøy; it is unlikely that Scotland would have shared a beer with a prisoner on the beach. Clearly, some caution should be exercised when reading Scotland's memoirs: one should not assume that all he recounts is accurate.

Buddie may have proved an easy prisoner, but some of his men were tough, sullen Nazis who were unimpressed by their capture. Their interrogations took longer and required a bluff tactic by Scotland, who leaked information provided by their commander. This soon convinced them that their interrogator knew everything there was to know. The interrogations revealed that the unit had indeed been completely unprepared for an attack. Importantly, it provided British intelligence with a comprehensive understanding of the German occupying forces in Norway, in particular their strength and locations. Louis Mountbatten, then adviser of Combined Operations, had recommended that a concentrated effort on Norway would divert German troops away from other parts of Europe. He was proved right: after Operation Archery, Hitler diverted over 30,000 troops away from other European fronts to secure the Norwegian coastline.

North Africa

The defeat of General Rommel and his forces in the Second Battle of El Alamein, North Africa, in November 1942 produced the first large-scale influx of Wehrmacht prisoners of war. The Anglo-American capture of Tunisia several months later brought the number of Axis soldiers who needed to be processed, identified and interrogated to over 230,000. It was a logistical challenge for Allied interrogators. Some prisoners were transferred to camps in Britain, others to Canada or America. Among them were a number of high-ranking German officers, including General Wilhelm von Thoma and General Hans-Jürgen von Arnim. Both would soon be held by MI19 at Trent Park, north London. They came with an important cache of documents: 5 tons of material, which a special unit at the War Office sifted for intelligence. In cooperation with the Americans, who had joined the war after the attack on Pearl Harbor in December 1941, a special document section was established.[5] Later, after the invasion of Germany, it would prove invaluable when hundreds of thousands of documents were impounded by the Allies.

By the time German prisoners arrived at the London Cage from North Africa, they were invariably ready to talk. Communications personnel held grievances against Hitler for being posted away from the comparative safety of their German homeland to the conflict in Africa. It seemed to make little sense to them to send them to an area where they risked capture and interrogation. They had vital knowledge of German communication lines and signals, as that was what they had been working on. Once captured, predictably they provided British interrogators with a wealth of intelligence on the railway network in Germany and underground cable communications. The interrogators played on the prisoners' discontent to soften them up. They needed little encouragement and spoke freely to British technical experts, readily drawing detailed sketches and plans of sites and technology. Again, later this was to prove of immense value to the Allies during the invasion of Germany.

Italian soldiers were also taken prisoner in North Africa. They were found to harbour a deep mistrust of Germans, an attitude which British interrogators could use to their advantage. Of these prisoners, only one refused to talk in interrogation. This unnamed Italian was transferred to the London Cage, where Colonel Scotland decided to see him personally. He found the prisoner feeding breadcrumbs to the sparrows from the window of his room. A period of solitary confinement had been prescribed to break his silence, but the tactic had failed. Now Scotland needed to know this man's particular war service. However, the prisoner told him there was nothing he could do to make him talk. Scotland left him for a while, then asked the guards to bring him to his office. Scotland explained to him that he knew everything there was to know: his staff had the testimony of the other prisoners, as well as the captured documents. It was one of the oldest tricks in the trade: convince a prisoner that everything was already known about him. Persuaded now that there was no point in holding back, the Italian finally opened up.

The most valuable German prisoners were those whom Hitler had transferred to the front line in North Africa from the secret weapons development site at Peenemünde. They resented being moved away from their interesting work on the V-1 and V-2 programme on the north German coast. After capture, they readily provided British interrogators at the London Cage with information, sketches and drawings of the secret programme.

The London Cage was still assisting the security forces with the interrogation of special prisoners from North Africa in 1943 – a task that took three months to complete because there were so many of them. These particular prisoners were deemed more likely to open up under stricter military conditions, and so they were interrogated at either the London Cage or at another cage at Bourton, Gloucestershire. Much of the early work was routine, but the progression of the war saw the arrival of die-hard Nazis and SS officers who changed the tone of life inside Kensington Palace Gardens.

999 Division

The most difficult prisoners of the war began to arrive at the London Cage after the defeat of Rommel in 1942. Described by Colonel Scotland as 'rabid Nazis', they included SS officers and indoctrinated members of the Nazi armed forces.[6] The staff became efficient at quietening them. Among them was an unusual set of prisoners – men from 999 Division, made up of men who had been incarcerated for a time in a concentration camp and had volunteered to serve in the German forces in order to avoid a slow and painful demise in Dachau or Bergen-Belsen; the risks of fighting on the front line were preferable. These men came under the command of SS divisions and were formed into 999 Division. One of these prisoners harboured a deep hatred of Hitler and the Nazis, in spite of having served in the German forces. He spoke freely to interrogators and fellow prisoners about the terrible things he had suffered in the concentration camps. Scotland believed it important that other prisoners should hear about these atrocities, and encouraged the guards to put certain men together in the same cell. There is no doubt that Scotland and his staff knew of the atrocities in Nazi Germany and of the brutality of the regime. Sometimes that played out in incidents inside the cage, as in the case of two men from 999 Division who arrived for questioning. They were taken to Room 22 for initial interrogation. They stood in front of a table at which sat two interrogators. On hearing the door open, the prisoners turned to see the guards march in with a rabid Nazi. Again, he is not named in Scotland's memoirs, but his Hitler salutes in another POW camp, as well as his refusal to obey orders, were causing problems. He had been transferred to the London Cage for disciplining. The guards left him to face the inter-rogators.

What transpired next calls into question why this prisoner was brought before the two men of 999 Division during an interrogation session. The interrogators watched as the two prisoners began to shout at the Nazi, lunging at him and beating him. The two interrogators leapt up from behind the table and tried to separate the fighting men as punches were thrown. The assault was serious enough to call back the guard, who sepa-rated the prisoners and hauled the Nazi out of the room.

The interrogators wanted to know what had provoked the outburst of violence. Composing themselves, the two men explained that the Nazi had been one of the guards at a concentration camp and had assaulted them on numerous occasions. They had promised each other that if they were ever captured by the British and their paths crossed with the Nazi guard's, they would kill him. What happened next to the Nazi is not recorded, but Scotland does comment that he was 'made to submit' and returned to his original prisoner-of-war camp a subdued man.

Men of 999 Division continued to be used in Scotland's attempt to confront ardent Nazis and SS prisoners with their past. They poured out their stories of the terrible suffering that had been inflicted on them, their loss of homes and possessions. The Nazis had no response, but neither were they cured of their ideology. However, it gave the staff satisfaction that the Nazis were being confronted with their brutal and sickening actions.

Intelligence asset

Intelligence gathered from POWs at the London Cage could be used to identify key targets in Germany that could be bombed or sabotaged. In July 1943, 122 Polish prisoners of war arrived at the cage. Short summary reports of their interrogations survive in the National Archives and provide an insight into the kind of intelligence being gathered by the interrogators.[7] High on the interrogators' list of priorities was to obtain economic information about the Nazi regime and the relocation of key German industries to the east. However, most of these prisoners were young men from subsidiary occupations (waiters, barbers) who had been conscripted into the German armed forces. They had been told to report to German police headquarters, where they had unexpectedly been handed their call-up papers. From 1940, this had been happening to many Poles who were working in Germany. Sometimes financial incentives were offered to join up.

These particular prisoners are not named in the intelligence files. The first is simply called 'Informant A' and was born in Graudenz (Polish Grudziądz) in 1921. He told interrogators about a firm where he had worked as a draughtsman and construction engineer. After the invasion and occupation of Poland by the German forces on 1 September 1939, the firm received contracts for the construction of new aerodromes and factories that would manufacture new German planes. The first to be built was the Flugzeugwerke (aircraft factory) in Graudenz, which became a subsidiary of the famous German industrial company, IG Farben. Informant A said that from the end of 1942, the factory was producing fifty Ju 88s (fast bombers) a month; it manufactured various parts, like wings and rudders, but it imported the engines. He told the interrogators that the aeroplanes were tested at an adjacent airfield and collected by operational crews. The airfield accommodated a technical school that could train eighty men. The next airfield to be constructed was at Rippin in Prussia, and came directly under the Luftwaffe.

From 10 October 1942 until 3 December 1942, Informant A had been stationed at Delmenhorst, Lower Saxony. He told interrogators how the workers were marched past the local airfield and saw operational two-seater planes along the road and how they were camouflaged: 'In the woods, ammunition dumps and bomb dumps were disguised as barns with camouflage nets in place of roofs. In a couple of cases, these were built to look like hills or mounds.'[8]

Informant A was not the only prisoner to provide intelligence on IG Farben. Informant M said that the company was building chemical works at Auschwitz in 1941, 'covering an area of about 13 sq. km, in the triangle formed by the villages Oswiecim–Dwory–Monowice'.[9] He had worked there until March 1942 building shops and had witnessed the construction for himself.

Informants B and C had worked in a factory concealed in the woods between Vistula and Birkenthal. They provided interrogators with a sketch of the layout of the factory. It showed that wooden barracks adjacent to the factory's pumping station were living quarters for foreign workmen. The factory itself consisted of numerous bunkers dispersed throughout the woods and protected by flak guns. Informant B was able to provide precise details of the concrete mix used in the construction of the 6-metre-by-6-metre bunkers. The walls were reinforced with rods, but the foundations were not. The roof was dome-shaped and reinforced, extending over half the bunker, and was concealed by earth and trees. The bunkers were so well camouflaged that they were invisible from the air, and were so spread out that any individual bomb would only cause localised damage. Only the destruction of the pumping plant could put the factory out of action. Construction of the factory had begun in November 1939, first using a German workforce, then thousands of French, Russian and British prisoners of war. Production output began in February 1942. Informants B and C were able to describe the cylinders and other parts being manufactured. Informant C provided information that the machinery used in the factory was brand new and came from Essen, Düsseldorf and places in Belgium. The electrical machinery was sent from Siemens in Berlin.

Informant D's interrogation was particularly disturbing. He had been sentenced to two and a half years in a detention centre in 1935 for distributing socialist newspapers, then two and a half years under preventive arrest in Buchenwald concentration camp, where he had worked long hours on camp construction. The intelligence files record:

The stories he has to tell of this camp are of such a nature that they could not be committed to paper, but it may be recorded that of 12,000 men in the camp, the average death toll was 200 men monthly and in June 1939, apart from other deaths, 400 Jews were killed.[10]

He told interrogators that he had witnessed the ceremonial hanging of a Jewish man in Buchenwald. The man had killed an SS guard, escaped and had eventually been found in Czechoslovakia. From there he was abducted by Gestapo agents and brought back to Germany. Informant D also witnessed the shooting of the Hamburg socialist leader Hans Brehm. He confirmed that the camp leader was SS General (Obergruppenführer) Koch and his second-in-command was Roedel. Those men would eventually be hunted down at the end of the war and stand trial for war crimes. Informant D provided important information that the Hermann Göring works on the Gleiwitz–Laband–Heidebruch road was making liquid air bombs and shells.

The continued build-up of the industrial Nazi war machine was clearly evident from the testimony of the Polish prisoners. Another prisoner spoke about a new factory that was producing synthetic petrol from coal and outputting one trainload a day. By-products of the factory were lubricating oils, tar and turpentine. The factory had been steadily enlarged and employed a few thousand men, working in twelve-hour shifts.

Informant H had been employed as a joiner for the firm of Wilhelm Ritterhauser at Neuenhagen near Berlin. It produced large plates for U-boats and small aircraft parts. All its products were dispatched by rail. He told interrogators: 'Hidden in the woods at Neuenhagen is a vulcanisation factory re-treating old tyres for the army. About 400–500 men are employed but no foreigners because the process is highly secret.'[11]

Informant I worked at a factory that employed 2,000 people in the production of gas masks, lifebelts and rubber equipment for the German army. He also knew about a small shell-filling factory and bunkers scattered in the hills near Graudenz, employing around 200 people. Informant J spoke about a former machine factory in Upper Silesia that was milling parts of large guns, aeroplanes and tanks. Informant K worked from January 1941 until September 1942 in a factory at Graudenz producing ammunition and bombs, thought to be the same ammunition factory that Informant A referred to. Informant K also spoke of an airfield near Graudenz that employed 1,000 men and was producing Messerschmitt planes. Other prisoners told of the military build-up, much of the information not available from RAF reconnaissance missions, thus underlining the importance of the interrogations at the London Cage.

Various prisoners talked about factories outside Berlin that were building component parts for aeroplanes; of work at Schildau-Ebbing on the production of Tiger tanks; chemical works near Riesenberg, East Prussia; and an underground munitions factory at Münsterlager that employed 1,000 Polish workers. Mention was made of a Krupp factory in Poland that was well camouflaged in the forest and that in 1940 had had an output of 30,000 hand grenades a month; by April 1942, it was outputting 150,000 a month. Another prisoner spoke about a U-boat factory in the forest north of Lübeck that employed 6,000 Polish men and women.

The value of this kind of information gathered from prisoners of war cannot be underestimated. From them, British intelligence could map a comprehensive understanding of the Nazi military capability and see that the pace of rearmament showed no sign of slowing down. These prisoners were interrogated a year before the invasion of Europe by the Allies on 6 June 1944. But in 1943, the Allies were already preparing for D-Day, and intelligence such as this was used in military planning and strategic bombing raids on the German industrial heartlands, whether in the cities or the countryside. Copies of these interrogation reports were distributed among the key intelligence agencies: MI5, MI6, the Foreign Office, MI3, MI10, MI14, CSDIC, Naval Intelligence Division, Air Intelligence, the Joint Intelligence Committee, the Political Intelligence Department of the Foreign Office, and American intelligence in Washington.

British intelligence issued guidelines on interrogation that stated: 'the interrogator must be careful to avoid any suggestion of having threatened the prisoner with physical violence. His art must consist of suggestions and innuendo rather than the use of threats.'[12] Naval Intelligence Division, which undertook many interrogations for MI9 and MI19, also concluded: 'Instruments of torture, drugs, etc., are pointless.'[13] Group Captain Denys Felkin, head of Air Intelligence Section ADI(K) attached to another MI19 site, wrote: 'It is always easy enough to persuade any prisoner to say what the interrogator thinks he ought to say, but the essence of interrogation is the honest reporting of unprompted statements made by the prisoner.'[14] Intelligence gathered under duress was always suspect and was of no use to the intelligence services, because they could not act on unreliable testimony.

There is no doubt that the interrogation work at the London Cage was absolutely vital to the war. What is particularly sensitive and controversial today is not what was gleaned in interrogation, but how that intelligence was obtained. Colonel Scotland commented: 'There was no need to use force here; disgruntled and disillusioned men will invariably speak freely with others, even though they be enemies, when they talk the same technical language.'[15] But what about the uncooperative prisoners? And how did that affect life inside the cage?

5

DOWNSTAIRS
Interrogation methods

How do you make a difficult German talk? That was one of the main challenges that faced interrogators throughout the war. Colonel Scotland stated in his unpublished memoirs that, from time to time, 'it was necessary to discipline tough, arrogant and impudent prisoners. We had our methods for these types.'[1] During training, Scotland taught the interrogators techniques that were underpinned by his belief that 'One of the most important aspects of a war is to know as much as possible about the enemy, not only about his military forces, his weapons and the distribution of both, but above all about his mind – how he thinks along certain lines and why.'[2] The ideal scenario was to break a prisoner in interrogation through a combination of cunning and psychological deception; but what if that failed? It can be argued that at various points in its history, the London Cage slipped into unorthodox interrogation methods that went against official policy. The authorised military manual on interrogation in war stated: 'The interrogator must strictly adhere at all times to the terms of the Geneva Convention . . . Interrogation by torture or ill-treatment in any way is not, in any circumstances, permitted.'[3] That manual was not declassified until decades later. The general public knew nothing of interrogation techniques, and during the war did not give them a thought.

When MI5 censored Scotland's original manuscript in 1957, it catalogued a list of offending pages where clear contraventions of the Geneva Convention were deemed to have taken place at the London Cage.[4] Mistreatment of uncooperative prisoners appeared to have been commonplace there, and extended to a variety of methods usually associated with

Soviet Russia. Prisoners were allegedly locked in narrow sentry boxes for hours and doused with cold water; forced to clean their rooms with a toothbrush; subjected to sleep deprivation for up to five or six days; and endured periods without food. Field Marshal von Rundstedt was allegedly asked to scrape a toilet with a razor.

The interrogators also seem to have used various intimidation techniques and innuendoes that they knew played on the German psyche and ingrained fears. Relying on the prisoners' unqualified respect for military discipline, whether German or British, the prisoner was reminded that he fell under British military rules in the cage. This was known as 'soft' brainwashing. If that failed, 'hard' brainwashing was used, extending to verbal threats of being deported to Russia. It was believed that German prisoners feared the Russians most because of possible imagined reprisals and brutal revenge for the atrocities committed by the German army on the Russian front from 1941. An interrogator at the London Cage could play on that and stamp a prisoner's file *NR*, which the prisoner assumed meant *Nach Russland* ('To Russia'). In fact, it meant 'Not Required' – i.e. the interrogators had finished with him.[5] If a prisoner saw *NR* swiftly stamped on his file in front of him, he generally backtracked and became cooperative.

In his published memoirs, Gary Leon, a German-Jewish refugee who was transferred from the Pioneer Corps into the Intelligence Corps in 1944, barely mentions the nature of his work at the London Cage, but he does cite one incident of psychological blackmail of an unnamed German sergeant who had taken part in the shooting of British soldiers captured in battle. Leon tried to gain a confession from him about his role in the atrocity:

> He would not talk. I asked him if he was married and he told me that he had a wife and daughter. I asked where they were and he told me. I then put it to him that the Russians were about to take that town, if indeed they were not already in it, and a word from me to the Soviet Embassy next door would make sure that he would never see his wife and child again. He broke down and told me enough for the case to be brought to trial after the war in Hamburg.[6]

The postscript to the story is that, during his trial, the prisoner claimed that undue influence had been brought to bear during his incarceration at the London Cage, and that his confession had been extracted by threats. It was enough for the prosecution to drop the case, and he never faced justice for his war crimes.

Another example of psychologically unnerving a prisoner was the case of an SS colonel whose cell was searched at night by a guard who taunted him with the words, 'I'm searching for nails in the wall. Don't hang yourself here; that's for later.'

In the case of three German prisoners who claimed to be doctors, Scotland suspected from their interrogations that only two of them had received full training. It was important to work out the profile and history of each prisoner who was sent to the cage. To test the case, the men were brought to Scotland's office. He instructed the suspect 'doctor' to remove the appendix of one of his comrades. The other two prisoners, a senior doctor and surgeon, protested that there was no need for an operation – no one had appendicitis. At this point, Scotland exhibited his sinister side and called their bluff. 'If I say that you are to have an operation, you will have an operation!' he barked at them in German. The third prisoner then stammered that he was only a second-year medical student. Perhaps he was the lucky one; having secured the truth, Scotland ordered him to be posted off to another prisoner-of-war camp as a medical orderly. It is not known what happened to the other two doctors.

When Scotland's instincts told him that a prisoner was hiding something, he appears to have been determined to extract the secret by whatever means necessary. That included forcing a prisoner to run for up to six hours around the paths in the paddock area of the cage (see chapter 1). There were numerous cases of prisoners collapsing on the parade ground and of temporary hospitalisation during exercises. Prisoners could find themselves bound and locked in thin-walled lockers and rolled around the parade ground for forty minutes. Many returned from their outdoor exercise in a state of exhaustion. It was all apparently designed to break their will to resist, and it usually succeeded. But four prisoners whom the interrogators failed to break ended up as 'suicide cases' (discussed in chapter 15).

Discipline

The prisoners who arrived at the cage were often deeply imbued with Nazi ideology and committed to the belief that Germany could still win the war. These were some of the toughest men that the interrogators encountered throughout the war. The challenges were numerous, and success relied on their careful handling; and that was usually down to Colonel Scotland, who, as the commanding officer, ran the cage according to his own tough rules. The guards sometimes came up against resistance from German officers who refused to get out of bed. They dealt with the Germans the same way as they would any British soldier who refused to get up: 'Their beds were turned over and they found themselves underneath. Their uniforms were taken away and they were set to work on cleaning the London Cage and other manual chores for three days.'[7]

Barking orders at prisoners was apparently commonplace. Fritz Wenzel, a U-boat commander who first spent time as a prisoner at MI19's Trent Park site, knew about the harsh conditions in the London Cage. In an interview, he recalled: 'Their tone was very harsh and even brutal. I shouldn't have liked an extended cure at their hands. I get naturally obstinate and resentful if anyone bawls at me, and I shouldn't have had much to laugh at with them, for they were bawling all the time.'[8]

Disruptive prisoners were sent to the London Cage from other camps or cages for disciplining. One particular ardent young Nazi who had been causing trouble in his POW camp felt that he was waging a private war on the British army – a war which, in Scotland's view, he adamantly believed he could win.[9] He was summoned to appear before Scotland, who decided to challenge him to a test of toughness. Knowing the German would obey orders from someone of higher military rank, even if British, Scotland ordered him to remain standing bolt upright and not speak unless spoken to. Scotland carried on with work at his desk, ignoring the sullen, defiant Nazi, who was given food and taken to the toilet whenever necessary. Then Scotland left for the evening.

The incident was censored out of his original manuscript by MI5, but in it Scotland recalled:

> Hour after hour the Nazi stood in my room. The light was kept on during the night and he was not allowed to sleep. He stood there for twenty-six hours. Then the young Nazi declared, 'I give in.' He asked to speak with me. I mellowed towards the submissive German, offered him a chair and a cigarette.[10]

No longer resistant to questioning, the German gave Scotland the information he asked for. Why did Scotland believe he had succeeded? In his words: 'I was able to discipline this man in such a manner because he was foolish enough to let me challenge his toughness and his pride, and ignorant enough to think he could not be handled or out-witted.' Scotland achieved results with 'minor discomfort on the part of the prisoner'.

Little patience was reserved for another unnamed prisoner, who had caused trouble in his camp by reading anti-Jewish literature and being so abusive to the guards as to provoke an incident. The uncomfortable surroundings of the London Cage did not necessarily dampen the Nazi's ego and objectionable attitude towards the guards. Sergeant Prion is said to have cautioned Scotland that his guards were close to physically assaulting the prisoner. Scotland called all officers and NCOs of the guards into Room 22. The prisoner was brought in. Scotland reports that he confronted the prisoner with the facts and laid before him his belief that he was trying to provoke a violent reaction or physical assault in order to make a formal complaint about the London Cage. Scotland ordered the prisoner to kneel down and, in his own words, 'proceeded to box his ears' with his bare hands.[11] According to Scotland, the prisoner sprang to his feet, ready to strike back, but Scotland was already rounding his desk. He explained in fluent German how the punishment was no different from that meted out by a commanding officer in the German army for such riotous behaviour and lack of discipline. Although this was the last of any trouble from this particular officer, he was called as a witness during the Sagan trials in 1946 to testify to the ill-treatment of prisoners at the London Cage. The 'regimental box on the ears' became sixty punches with a clenched fist. Even allowing for a degree of embellishment of the truth, the military court decided to dismiss this evidence against Scotland.

Scotland may have believed that it was acceptable to apply moderate physical force to discipline a prisoner, but not to obtain military information. He wrote: 'Nazi prisoners expected to be beaten up; after all, they were past masters in the practice . . . but this occurred only in one instance at the cage and that was after the war.'[12] Predictably, this was edited out of the final version of his manuscript by MI5 and the War Office.

Occasionally, Colonel Scotland was called upon to deal with particularly disruptive and volatile incidents at other POW camps. This took him to Oldham, Lancashire, where trouble had flared up and some 500 paratroopers and SS men had taken over the third floor of an old cotton mill. Scotland arrived at a tense moment, with the staff having withheld food from the insurgents for two days in an attempt to discipline them. Scotland explains how he refused to be intimidated by the sheer number involved or by their uncooperativeness.[13] His first move was to call for the 500 men to be brought before him for an inspection. The camp staff looked on in disbelief as he entered the room alone, with no guards, to find the prisoners standing bolt upright. Scotland knew he could rely on the German sense of military discipline when asked to stand to attention by a senior ranking officer. Walking down the line, he paused occasionally to look them up and down. There was total silence.

According to Scotland, he stood behind the prisoners and barked 'About turn!' The men obeyed. Scotland turned to the senior German NCO and remarked that he was disappointed with the discipline of the men, because they did not know how to parade. And why, he asked, did their eyes follow him when he moved around the room? Scotland proceeded to address the men with a speech they were not expecting; it is reproduced in full in his unpublished memoirs, but censored out of the book by MI5. Scotland told them that they were prisoners of war who would be punished with bare rations and no privileges if they refused to cooperate. He reminded them that their rations were generous, and if they continued to rebel, they would be kept in the room until their repatriation to Germany and given very little food. 'By then,' he told them, 'you may not be strong enough to march.' He acknowledged that they had grievances and gave them the option of sending a deputation of six men to him at any time to discuss the matter. He then left the room. Four hours later, a deputation came to see him. Their grievance was quite basic: some prisoners of war were allowed outside the camp for work duties, but they had to stay within the camp's confines. Scotland told them frankly that prisoners who behaved in camp would have privileges. He agreed that 15 per cent of the SS and paratroopers could work outside the camp immediately, and that if their behaviour improved, that number would increase. 'Make no mistake,' he told them. 'Those men who won't work and won't obey orders and don't behave will remain in that room.'

Scotland left the camp and life there settled down. He himself said that he always worked on the golden rule that German prisoners of war should be treated as they expected to be treated. When they broke the rules, all were to be punished, and the whole group would find a solution to the ill-disciplined comrades.

Colonel Scotland was at pains to protect some prisoners from rough treatment if they were proving to be a valuable asset. One such person was 24-year-old Kurt Koenig, aka Karl Kubelka, who arrived in Britain in the autumn of 1942. A deserter from the German army and an anti-Nazi, he was interrogated by Colonel Scotland and Captain Cyril MacLeod at the London Cage on 12 October 1942. He was questioned about his time in Madrid in order to establish whether he was, in fact, a German spy. Koenig was allegedly in trouble with the Gestapo for subversive activities.

Scotland was particularly concerned 'lest MI5 should handle Koenig in a manner which would disturb his present cooperative state of mind'.[14] Koenig was considered by Scotland to be 'of somewhat higher education than the average German and exceptionally reliable'.[15] The interrogation report survives and demonstrates the valuable material that Koenig was able to provide to MI19, ranging from key military installations in Germany to field posts, German units, ground personnel, railway engine sheds, bridges, camouflaged water works, and a plan of the port and town of Bremen. Koenig revealed during interrogation that the crack battalions of SS units were given the best-quality equipment and the newest wireless transmitter sets. Scotland told MI5 interrogator Helenus 'Buster' Milmo that Koenig was, in his view, 'one of the most valuable prisoners of war who had been handled by his department since the beginning of the war'.[16] He was in no doubt that Koenig could have supplied him with a considerable amount of further military information, but did not do so.

Scotland concluded that Koenig was 'an exceptionally fit and strong man for an ordinary soldier. The worse impression he makes on me is his obvious unsuitability for normal infiltration operations. In conclusion, to me it does not all add up.'[17] He wrote to Victor Caroe at MI5 a letter marked 'MOST SECRET', dated 28 October 1942:

> The amount of general knowledge he [Koenig] has is far above what could be considered normal in even a high class workman . . . his spoken German is that of the local lower class in Bremen. He gave us a great deal of general information which he knew would be helpful and full details of his own small military unit. But on a point of precise information on the use of diesel motors in transport vehicles of a certain kind, he became vague and unhelpful.[18]

Koenig was transferred from the jurisdiction of the Prisoner of War Department to Brixton prison as a civilian internee. He was interrogated by Victor Caroe on 30 October 1942 and expressed his keenness to work for the British. Like Colonel Scotland, Caroe could not make him out. On

1 November 1942, Caroe offered him to Major R.H. Thornley of the
Special Operations Executive (SOE). Koenig was released from prison and
trained with SOE to undertake sabotage missions behind enemy lines. A
memo from 'C' (head of MI6) to SOE, dated 1 March 1943, read: 'He is
now hidden in San Sebastian.'

Koenig was exceptionally brave in serving Britain. He was parachuted
into Germany on a number of occasions, including as part of Operation
Squad and Operation Calvados. He paid the ultimate price – being captured
by the Germans in January 1944 and executed the following February.[19]

The case of Otto Witt

The files and interrogation reports for anti-Nazi prisoner of war Otto Witt
survive in the National Archives and provide clarification on the controversy surrounding his treatment at both the London Cage and Latchmere
House. This kind of material is rare for other prisoners of the London
Cage, either because not much information was recorded in their files or
because they have not yet been declassified.

Witt claimed to have been struck during interrogation in the week that
he was at the London Cage.[20] It was serious enough for Maxwell Knight of
MI5 to formally raise the case with the secretary of state for war in 1943.[21]
Witt arrived in Britain from Stockholm on 5 May 1942 at the suggestion
of SOE, which had been tracking his political activities in Sweden. As a
political refugee from Germany, Witt had worked as a journalist in
Denmark until the Germans invaded in April 1940, whereupon he had
fled to Sweden, initially as a turncoat, to carry out anti-Czech propaganda.
Described as 5ft 7in with grey hair, blue eyes and a fresh complexion,
Witt was known to be working simultaneously for Czech intelligence
and the Polish Secret Service. MI5 always seemed to doubt his testimony
and suspected that he may even have been a German spy, though his
intercepted letters to friends in England before he arrived showed him to
be opposed to the Nazis.[22] From Sweden, he made contact with the British
and Allied governments, claiming to be in touch with German anti-Nazis
and seeking to advise the British on the right kind of propaganda to
feed them.

SOE installed Witt in a flat in London that had been prepared before his
arrival, and gave him £5 a week and a wireless set. Sefton Delmer, a former
British journalist and spy in Berlin in the 1930s, who worked for the Political

Warfare Executive in the Second World War, was suspicious of Witt and, after interviewing him, summed him up as 'a typical Nazi of the minor official class'.[23] As a result, Witt was transferred to Camp 020 at Latchmere House for suspected enemy spies. Here he spent eight months in solitary confinement, during which time he was interrogated for a total of five hours. He was informed that his testimony was believed and would lead to his early release. Instead he was transferred in February 1943 to the Brompton Oratory School in London, where he was questioned by the chief interrogator, Major Sampson. Witt was subjected to very harsh treatment; he was locked in a narrow cell, approximately 9 square metres, and the windows were smashed.[24] As a result, Witt developed life-threatening bronchial pneumonia, but despite having a high temperature, he was offered no medical help. After being transferred to a different cell, a 'stool pigeon' by the name of Hans Kretschmer was placed with him. Stool pigeons – cooperative prisoners who agreed to guide conversations with their cellmates in a particular direction – were useful to the intelligence services, as they were never usually suspected of being anything other than a genuine prisoner of war. Witt confided in Kretschmer about his connections with the Abwehr in Hamburg and about his fears of being handed over to the Czechs, who would torture him. MI5 could play on this fear during interrogation.

Witt became the subject of several entries in the personal war diary of Guy Liddell, MI5's director of counter-espionage. The first was made on 8 March 1943 and referred to a meeting convened by Liddell to discuss the Witt case with Czech officer and interrogator Lieutenant Wiesner, and MI5's officers Buster Milmo, Francis Aitken-Sneath and Dick White (later director general of MI5). Liddell recorded:

> Wiesner was very confident that if he could employ his own methods he could break Witt down within three days and suggested that Witt should be interrogated at frequent intervals during both the night and day.[25]

It was agreed that Witt would be given to Wiesner for three days, after which Wiesner agreed to 'hand him back without a bruise on his body'. MI5 appeared to view Witt as arrogant, but a coward who would probably cooperate readily.

Liddell's next diary entry concerning Witt was 11 March, the day he was transferred to Brixton prison. Liddell recorded a visit by MI5 officer Victor Caroe, who gave Witt a final opportunity to speak the truth before being handed over to the Czechs. Witt broke down and said that he had been lying and would now tell the whole truth. Caroe told Witt that he did not believe he was a German spy. Liddell then commented in his diary:

> We feel that it is now desirable to bring in some new military person to do interrogation and have obtained the services of Major Scotland. We want if possible to carry out the interrogation at the London District prisoner-of-war camp, but this will have to be subject to Home Office approval.[26]

Since Witt was being detained under the royal prerogative, he could be held wherever MI5 decided. The following day, a diplomatic incident arose with the Czechs. Liddell wrote in his diary that they were

> a little crestfallen about the Otto Witt case being taken over by Major Scotland but everything has been smoothed over to their satisfaction. Scotland will commence on Monday. When we have got a statement, the Czechs will be brought in to cross-examine.[27]

Two days later, on his birthday, Witt was transferred at midday to the London Cage, where he found himself before Colonel Scotland. Despite all his interrogation skills, Scotland could not induce Witt to talk.[28] Witt was treated as a normal prisoner undergoing intensive interrogation; the frequency and length of his interrogations were recorded in his personal file as follows:

Saturday 13 March:	one hour, three hours and 35 minutes, and one hour
Sunday 14 March:	1 hour 50 minutes, 2 hours 35 minutes, 10 minutes, 3 hours and 10 minutes, 1 hour and 40 minutes, 1 hour and 20 minutes, 2 hours and 30 minutes and 1 hour
Monday 15 March:	one period of 30 minutes
Tuesday 16 March:	one period of 1 hour and 30 minutes
Wednesday 17 March:	1 hour 30 minutes, 1 hour 5 minutes, and 3 hours 5 minutes
Thursday 18 March:	40 minutes, and 2 hours 55 minutes
Friday 19 March:	one period of 35 minutes

A separate MI5 file reveals more detail about these encounters. On 15 and 16 March, Colonel Scotland began his interrogation by announcing that Witt was an agent of some kind. He could not get Witt to confess. Guy Liddell noted in his diary: 'The trouble is this case has been so messed about that Witt is now convinced that we have nothing on him and cannot bring him to justice. Scotland thinks that Wiesner should now return to the charge [interrogate].'[29]

One of Witt's extensive personal MI5 files summarised his treatment at the cage as 'several days of almost uninterrupted interrogations by means of the most severe pressure, both physical and psychological'.[30] Witt described his time there, when he was subjected to the kind of treatment 'which I thought indeed to be the privilege of the Gestapo and I was told "You are here in the English Gestapo." '[31] The interrogators played him various sound recordings that had allegedly been confiscated from his room and were composed of Morse signals. During interrogation, he was forced to strip naked and stand. The interrogations took place under bright light and lasted for up to three hours without a break. For four days, the only sustenance he received was bread and water, and one midday meal. He was not allowed to wash or shave; and at night he was woken every half an hour. He was told that his secret execution was set for Wednesday at 10 o'clock, and his body would disappear without trace.

Witt made several attempts at suicide in the cage. Because of these, he was placed on hourly watch throughout the day and night. On 17 March, he was questioned by Captain Kettler and Lieutenant Wiesner, in the presence of wireless expert Warrant Officer Maly. He was promised immunity and was 'very hard pressed at this interrogation'.[32] He was also asked to reveal his contacts in Britain, Sweden and Germany. At this point, Aitken-Sneath interrogated him strenuously from 11 p.m. until midnight. Witt denied using Morse code, having any contacts in Germany, or working as a spy for the Gestapo.

The next interrogation was carried out at 2.30 a.m. by Wiesner and Aitken-Sneath, who offered Witt gin. Two drinks later, he became talkative and told his tormentors: 'I didn't come over here for the love of the English, but for the love of the German people whom I wanted to help.' He was at pains to convince them that he was an anti-Nazi, not a spy. He had heard from Count Finckenstein, a fellow prisoner at Latchmere House, that the French used electric torture treatment on prisoners in Britain. He begged Aitken-Sneath: 'I know torture is forbidden in England, but I'll make you this proposal, that you can drug me or torture me with that French electric machine, and then you will see that I'm innocent.' Witt was returned to his cell and an hourly watch kept.

During this period, Witt was also seen in the cage by MI5 interrogator Buster Milmo, who told him it was the British government's belief that it was better for nine innocent men to be executed than for one guilty man to escape. The statement was clearly aimed at frightening him, but it did not bring Milmo any closer to the truth. Witt's MI5 file finally noted that 'the interrogation [at the London Cage] was vigorous and that the methods used at times tended to exceed the bounds of legitimate interrogation'.[33]

Witt wrote letters to his wife from captivity which were checked by the Scientific Section of MI5 for secret writing. He was issued with special paper to prevent him from using invisible ink, and his letters were tested for pyramidon, aspirin and alum.[34]

Witt held out at the London Cage for a week. During this time, he was seen by army psychiatrist Lieutenant Colonel Henry Dicks, a consultant psychiatrist to MI19, based at its headquarters at Latimer House, near Chesham in Buckinghamshire. Throughout the war, Dicks provided psychological analyses of prisoners for MI19, and on several occasions was asked to visit Rudolf Hess and make a psychiatric assessment.[35] Reports written by Dicks about Witt are not in Witt's personal MI5 files, and so it is not possible to ascertain his views on him.

Frustrated by Witt's failure to cooperate, MI5 decided to liquidate the case, and on 30 March 1943 transferred him to Dartmoor prison, where he was held in a special wing. Liddell concluded:

> There is no doubt that he is a confirmed liar, but it seems quite impossible to extract from him the real reason for his visit to this country. I am inclined to think that he is a man who has at one time or another worked for the Gestapo, that they have not got a very high regard for his ability, but that he in his conceit succeeded in persuading them to let him go and try his hand in England by investigating in political refugee circles.[36]

That was not the end of the matter. In May 1943, Witt issued a formal petition from Dartmoor prison about his treatment at the London Cage. The list was serious: starvation, sleep deprivation, drugs, threats against his wife and family, and hints of torture and secret murder. He gave details of how he had been threatened with execution. He maintained that no one knew where he was, that agents disappeared, and that he was told 'we hang people who aren't any use to us'.[37] Scotland described these accusations as 'a parcel of lies and pure invention'.[38] In a diary entry for 26 June 1943, Guy Liddell noted:

> Sir Alexander Maxwell has written a letter intended for the Secretary of State for War in which the Home Secretary expresses his grave displeasure and concern at the treatment of Witt at the London District Cage. Witt has made a number of allegations about ill-treatment which have been denied. The only admission is that Wiesner slapped his face. If the denials are accepted it seems an incredible thing that two Secretaries of State should be drawn into a matter which involves a lying little Nazi having had his face slapped by a Czech. It seems to me that the whole case has got totally out of perspective . . . If the Home Office think they can handle spies with kid-gloves on, it is about time someone disillusioned them.

MI5 offered a formal response to the Home Office, referring to Witt's complaints as 'a gross distortion and exaggeration of the facts',[39] and added that he had been consistently arrogant and insolent. Then came the admission that on two occasions, and only two occasions, Witt had been slapped across the side of the face with the back of the hand. This was 'not intended to hurt him, but humiliate him and induce a proper sense of respect'.[40]

In June 1944, Witt was transferred to an internment camp on the Isle of Man, and finally, in June 1945, moved to the civilian internment camp at Staumühle, near Paderborn in Germany, after which he was repatriated. MI5 officer Buster Milmo never believed that Witt was a spy. He wrote to Colonel Scotland on 20 March 1945, in a letter that provides a glimpse of Scotland's reputation in interrogation, 'For my part, I feel convinced that had this man been a German agent of any sort he would never have survived your interrogation.'[41]

There is no doubt that there were times when Colonel Scotland resorted to rough treatment of prisoners in the cage that extended to physical assault, punching a prisoner, psychological innuendoes during interrogation, and giving prisoners humiliating chores. At the end of the war, as the London Cage began to receive Nazi war criminals, it exhibited an even darker side to its interrogations.

6

PRISON QUARTERS

By the time Scotland took over the premises, any trace of the former glory of Lord Duveen's stately home had vanished from Nos. 8 and 8a Kensington Palace Gardens. Duveen's salons and drawing rooms gave way little by little to the intelligence services as they dismantled the last remnants of luxury. Eventually even the beautiful wood panelling on the ground floor would vanish, used as firewood during the bitterly cold winter of 1946.[1]

Colonel Scotland ran a tight ship, with a team of resilient guards who ensured that the prisoners obeyed cage rules. His intelligence officers worked in sparsely furnished rooms; Scotland's own office, in No. 7 Kensington Palace Gardens, was a degree more comfortable – but not by much, its pastel blue walls being all that remained of its pre-war décor and glory. Furnished with a desk, several chairs and with maps on the wall, it was here that German prisoners had their first encounter with Scotland, and where he made his first assessment of them. Uncooperative prisoners were summoned here, too, for a dressing-down. On arrival at the London Cage, a prisoner faced Scotland himself, who psychologically disarmed him by handing him a pad of paper and a pencil and asking him to write down his story. The prisoner often displayed complete bafflement at Scotland's approach – this half-mad British officer in his sixties. But Scotland was smart. He knew that by giving the prisoner a chance to write down his version of events and signing it, he would be in possession of a legal testimony that could be used in court, if needed.

Life upstairs was run on strict discipline, enforced by soldiers from the Grenadier Guards, Coldstream Guards, Welsh Guards and Irish Guard

Division. Many were from headquarters at Pirbright and had seen service in royal palaces. A Grenadier Guard, Captain Edward 'Ted' Albert Lessing, acted as liaison officer at the cage. Fluent in Russian, he had been military attaché in Saint Petersburg in 1917 and had served as Liberal MP for Abingdon in the 1920s.

The only clue that this cage might not have been like the others came on those occasions when a prisoner was handed over to a guard to be escorted back to his cell and the interrogator would say: 'I don't like this man. Make sure I like him tomorrow.' This was coded language for the guards to rough the prisoner up to ensure that he cooperated in interrogation the following day.[2] The first sergeant of the guard was Sergeant Lewis of the Welsh Guards. Over 6 feet tall, he was firm, commanding, but with a calm disposition. Later, when the site became the War Crimes Investigation Unit and handled die-hard SS and Gestapo prisoners, his successor, Sergeant Prion, appeared equally determined to instil discipline among the prisoners. Both men were tough and effective. Of Sergeant Prion, Colonel Scotland wrote: 'Prion could cow these brutes [the SS] into complete obedience to cage rules.' Prion served in the Grenadier Guards, a regular guard unit.

A cooperative prisoner had nothing to fear. He could expect a reward from the special fund provided by the intelligence services for cigarettes and toiletries. The London Cage drew £8 a month from the fund, equivalent to around £320 today. The official files show the personal ration quotas: 2oz of meat per prisoner every two to three days, or no more than 2oz of offal or 2oz of preserved meat. Staff received the same daily rations. The prisoners were given 2d as a cash allowance, according to the provision made by the Geneva Convention.

The Geneva Convention allowed for chores to be undertaken by prisoners in a transit camp. However, as was mentioned earlier, it was a moot point whether the London Cage should be considered a transit camp or a prisoner-of-war camp. At the London Cage, chores were primarily used as a method of discipline, which was against the Geneva Convention. And yet a mixed picture emerges of life inside the cage. When Nazi war criminal Colonel von der Heydte was held there after the war, he refused to carry out fatigue duties. He was escorted to the guardroom and offered a drink. Later that same week, Sergeant Major White entered his cell and offered him whisky. The two of them sat down together and shared the entire bottle.

Doug Richards of the Welsh Guards arrived at the London Cage in 1945. He was called before Colonel Scotland for a briefing and asked to sign the Official Secrets Act. His duties consisted of internal security, conveying prisoners between locations, and sitting in on interrogations, ready to escort a prisoner back to his cell.[3] Often he was required to carry secret papers to MI9 or the Americans:

> The papers were strapped under my shirt. I personally made the journey from the cage to a building in Bond Street, a distance of some 4 to 5 miles, as well as SHAEF Headquarters in Grosvenor Square, again about 4 miles. I was not allowed to use public transport under any circumstances and had to walk each time.[4]

The guards referred to Colonel Scotland as 'the Boss'. Richards recalled:

> He was always quiet-mannered but when a prisoner tried to make a fool of him, he really exploded. We had some very nasty people amongst the prisoners and they were treated accordingly. No one was above reproach and the prisoners knew that once they were sent for, the end was near.[5]

Room 22

When a new batch of prisoners arrived, there was nothing more effective in the first few hours of arrival than to place them in a room with other prisoners, where their conversations could be secretly bugged for information. Most of the early interrogations took place in Room 22, a large and airy room on the ground floor, formerly the library at No. 8a, but now with bare wooden floors and just two tables. On the wall was a board that listed all the prisoners being held in the cage, together with their room number and whether they were to be interrogated.

On one occasion, two teams of newly trained interrogators were tasked with the interrogation of seven U-boat men who were determined to remain silent. After forty-eight hours, the interrogators had made no progress. Colonel Scotland decided to intervene. He asked the guards to bring in the toughest of the U-boat men, and a big, sullen man was brought before him. In a surprising move, Scotland asked him about his work in civilian life. The man replied that he had been a wagonsmith. Scotland then asked technical questions about how to make a wheel, and soon established that the prisoner knew nothing about wheels. He was escorted back to his cell.

After fifteen or twenty minutes, the next tough U-boat man was brought before Scotland. That interval had allowed the previous prisoner to discuss matters with his cellmates. Scotland asked the second U-boat officer about his civilian work. This prisoner knew more about wheels than the previous one, leading Scotland to conclude that he was partly trained in making them. In a clever move, Scotland sent the officer back to his cell and gave him time to discuss the interrogation with his cellmates before the next prisoner was hauled out for the same questioning. Eventually, all seven crew members were talking among themselves about their civilian skills and work. In this sense, Scotland understood the psychological importance of getting the prisoners to talk freely about their civilian life – something they believed had no relevance to the war. It broke down their refusal to speak during interrogation. Scotland was smart enough not to ask direct questions about their naval training, and soon they were relaxed enough to talk to each other. Little did they suspect that their conversations were being bugged and the information recorded by Scotland's staff in another room.

Scotland's reputation for anger was earned early in the war, during the training of his interrogators. He admitted: 'I always approach a German with a smile, and continue to smile and be friendly – unless he bites. If he bites, I bite back. If he refuses to be anything but rude, then I drop the smile and I am thoroughly rude to him.'[6] Rudeness or extreme anger usually signalled the end of an interrogation, because nothing of use could then be gained from the prisoner and another interrogator had to continue. Far more effective was the use of stool pigeons: fluent German speakers, ex-German refugees from Nazism or 'turned' prisoners, who masqueraded as fellow prisoners and led conversations in a particular direction in a cell.

As early as 1940, Scotland accompanied a group of trainee interrogators to Edinburgh to practise interrogation on 300 captured merchant seamen. The problem was not the ordinary seamen, but their captain, who was resisting interrogation by giving nothing more than his name and rank. Scotland stood back and observed as his officers interrogated the captain without success. Then he intervened and accused the captain of being a spy: as such, he told him, he could be 'tried and shot like a dog'.[7] A screaming match in German is said to have ensued between Scotland and the prisoner as the interrogators looked on, stunned. They little understood what was going on in Scotland's mind; his knowledge of the German regime told him that the captain was no ordinary captain, but SS or SA. The captain denied this. Scotland shouted at him: 'You are a liar!' Nothing could break the captain's will to resist. He and his crew were transferred to an intern-ment camp on the Isle of Man.

Solitary confinement

A stubborn prisoner could find himself in solitary confinement. Psycho-logically, a period of isolation from other prisoners was considered a useful tool in breaking down a man's will to resist as well as isolating him from fellow Nazi ideologists. German prisoners were found to be so dependent on their comrades for moral support that, once deprived of it, they could easily be persuaded of another viewpoint. Contact only with an interrogator could prove effective if the interrogator constantly reminded the prisoner that his ideology was based on untruthful propaganda crafted by the Nazi regime. Sometimes a prisoner who had 'seen the light' could be taken to his cell and used to persuade his cellmate. This ruse was known in interrogation circles as 'political deconditioning', and attached to it were various rewards for the pris-oner, such as being taken to a restaurant, theatre or cinema in central London.

Trips into central London reinforced the political deconditioning because the prisoner was taken to parts of the capital that had not been affected by the Blitz. Back in Germany, the prisoners had been led to believe that London was in ruins and on the verge of collapse. Now they saw for themselves private cars on the streets and a wide selection of goods in shop windows. All this added to the process of transforming opinion. They compared what they had heard from their own propaganda machine with what they were seeing at first hand. It was a hugely effective way of turning a prisoner around. With very little persuasion from an interrogator, the Germans realised that they had been duped by their own commanders and by Nazi propaganda. In some cases, these prisoners were successfully 'turned' to work as double agents against Germany. In many cases, staff at the London Cage found that this political deconditioning by propaganda lasted long enough for an interrogator to extract the necessary intelligence.

The average German soldier could normally be induced to talk by means of a number of clever ruses and frequent long interrogations; and if that failed, then by a period of solitary confinement. But the die-hard Nazis were tough and disruptive. They cared little for cage discipline and appeared unaffected by periods of solitary confinement. A decision had to be made whether to hold them for longer in the cage or transfer them to the special prisoner-of-war camp at Comrie, Perthshire, which was reserved almost exclusively for the toughest Nazi prisoners in British custody. One example was a bullet-headed young Nazi who refused even to give his name, rank and number. He glared at Scotland with a measure of arrogant defiance and contempt, protesting that nothing would make him talk to the elderly gentleman sitting across the desk. It was clear to Scotland, as he thought back to his own period of solitary confinement in Windhoek prison during the First World War, that nothing was going to induce this prisoner to talk. In this particular case, Scotland ordered him to remain in the cage until his will to resist was broken, but it did not work. The prisoner was eventually transferred to Comrie.

Soviet-style prison

The basement at No. 8 was reserved for the interrogation of prisoners who failed to cooperate in Room 22. They were escorted into the basement with a black canvas hood over their head – to disorient them and instil some fear ahead of the next interrogation. It was hoped that the uncertainty over what was to happen next would be enough to prompt the prisoner to open up. Life was straightforward, unless they still proved uncooperative. Out of bounds to most cage personnel except the interrogators, the basement mirrored a sinister Soviet-style dungeon, designed to intimidate. With its dark, damp, isolated position, a prisoner knew that any screams for help would go unheard. If the inferences of the surroundings failed to have any effect on him, then physical abuse and torture seem to have been the next step. Forcing a prisoner to stand naked for up to eight hours, sometimes chained or handcuffed to objects (a chair or pole); making him perch for long periods of time on a one-legged stool or chair; forcing him to pick up and put down oil drums; or keeping him in a cold bath for four hours with cold spray on his head – all these were methods used at the London Cage.

The basement became the domain of physical torture and threats of torture. MI19 files for the London Cage make three independent references to 'secret control gear' – i.e. electric shock equipment and other torture apparatus.[8] Captain Egger and Captain Hay, both German speakers who aided the interrogators, were described as 'assistant interrogators and operators of special gear'.[9] A separate report records that 'Both these officers are experts on the control gear operations.'[10] Those two officers had already served with CSDIC at Latimer House near Chesham. Even after the war, and in fact to this day, there are bleak cells in the basement of the house. When a relative of intelligence officer Leslie Parkin asked about his wartime work at Latimer House, Parkin replied, 'You really don't want to know what we did.'[11]

A prisoner at the London Cage could be threatened with Cell 14, also in the basement at No. 8. Cell 14 was another part of the psychological war waged by the interrogators in their efforts to break the really hardened prisoner. 'From Cell 14 emanated the overpowering stench of dead rats, wet rags and rotting flesh,' recalled one eyewitness, who wishes to retain his anonymity.[12] He shuddered as he remembered, and screwed up his nose. 'But nothing actually went on there. Allegations of torture have always puzzled me, because for the fourteen months that I worked there from 1946, I never saw any mistreatment of prisoners. I attended four or five interrogations which were always in the rooms upstairs. Torture could have taken place at 1 a.m. in the night when I was asleep and I wouldn't know anything about it.' He testifies that he never saw any torture or electric shock equipment at the London Cage.

Such cells existed elsewhere. In May 1945, Lieutenant Colonel Stephens, the MI5 officer who had run Camp 020 at Latchmere House during the war, was posted to Bad Nenndorf in Germany to set up an interrogation centre. Known as No. 74 CSDIC, prisoners were threatened with being taken to what was called 'Cell 12' – and indeed some were taken there.[13] Cell 12 was designed to humiliate, intimidate and weaken their resistance to interrogation. This was the interrogation centre where the conversations of interned civilians, German scientists and political prisoners were secretly bugged. These prisoners were relevant to the Allies' mass hunt for Nazi scientists, technicians and technologists who had to be captured before they fell into the hands of the new enemy – Russia. At Bad Nenndorf, prisoners were forced to scrub the walls and floor for days, with no heating or proper lighting. A prisoner had to sleep on the concrete floor of a cell with only two blankets. Here in this camp, Stephens was accused of resorting to torture and starvation of the internees. Their plight came to the attention of the authorities after many became so ill that they were transferred to a nearby hospital for treatment. They arrived at the hospital in a desperate state, looking like concentration camp survivors. The sight of them was so shocking that staff reported the cases to the Red Cross. Stephens eventually faced court martial for his torture of victims, although he was subsequently acquitted.

There were cases of suicide at Bad Nenndorf, as there were in the London Cage and at five other sites in post-war Germany. At these sites, those who committed 'suicide' died in circumstances of torture, starvation and prolonged periods of solitary confinement. Sir Hartley Shawcross, the chief British prosecutor at Nuremberg, wrote to Prime Minister Clement Attlee:

> If cruelties did occur at Bad Nenndorf they were of the kind systematically adopted as the practice at MI5 Interrogation Centres during the war, and at Camps in Germany subsequently and authorised by ministers through Sir David Petrie [head of MI5].[14]

Camp 020 and No. 74 CSDIC at Bad Nenndorf both sanctioned violence. In the words of historian Ian Cobain: 'The claim that violence was taboo at Camp 020 was a lie. It had been run on the same brutal lines as Bad Nenndorf. It too had been a torture centre.'[15]

Within MI5 and MI6, there were differing opinions over the treatment of prisoners and captured German spies, with some officers endorsing and employing violent methods and even torture at interrogation sites which could not be inspected by external organisations like the Red Cross. Other intelligence officers, like Guy Liddell, placed torture firmly within the realm of foul play and unethical behaviour.[16]

Gestapo methods

Rumours of what happened at the London Cage liken it to the brutality of the Nazi regime. Had British intelligence at this clandestine site behaved no better than Hitler's henchmen? Could there ever be justification for such treatment, even if the man standing before the interrogators had information that could change the course of the war? How far would Colonel Scotland push the boundaries to force information from a completely uncooperative prisoner? Soft methods might quickly turn to harsh treatment in an attempt to get intelligence from him quickly.

Colonel Scotland admitted that on two occasions he had been provoked into using violence against a prisoner. In reality, as we shall see, during the lifetime of the London Cage the figure was much higher. There is an independent source which corroborates the fact that Scotland struck prisoners during interrogation. This evidence comes from the personal war diary of

Guy Liddell, MI5's director of counter-espionage. The diary was extraordinarily helpful in the amount of detail it provided about various double agents before MI5 released their personal files into the National Archives. One incident recorded in the diary concerns double agent Tate. A Danish national born in 1911, Tate's real name was Wulf Dietrich Schmidt. Schmidt parachuted into England in September 1940 on a mission from the Abwehr, the German Military Intelligence. Another agent who had been captured by the British gave advance details of Schmidt's mission in return for an undertaking that Schmidt would not being executed.[17] Schmidt was arrested on landing and taken to Camp 020 at Latchmere House, MI5's secret interrogation centre reserved for captured German spies. It was here that MI5 interrogators tried to 'turn' German spies to make them double agents, as part of the Double Cross System. Initially, they had little success with Schmidt.

On 21 September 1940, Colonel Scotland arrived at Camp 020 to interrogate Schmidt. A full verbatim transcript of Schmidt's interrogation by Scotland has been declassified. The interrogation was recorded via hidden microphones, and provides a rare surviving example of one of Scotland's full interrogations. It was not common practice for an interrogator to take notes during an interrogation, or to have a transcriber present; that is why it was recorded and later transcribed word for word. The transcript reveals Scotland's technique of using threats and intimidation, with persistent accusations that Schmidt was a spy. At one point, Scotland threatened:

> If you don't wish to speak the truth, we have methods to make you speak the truth, which will be very unpleasant for you, because we have complete evidence against you. Do you understand that? Alright. You just make up your mind very quickly what you are going to do, because what will happen to you will be something you will never forget.[18]

The results of Scotland's interrogation reached the ears of Guy Liddell, who wrote a lengthy piece in his diary the following day:

> I have just been told that the officer at MI9 who was present at the interrogation of TATE yesterday took it upon himself to manhandle the prisoner without saying anything to Colonel Stephens, Dick White, or Malcolm Frost. The interrogation broke off at lunchtime when Colonel Scotland left the room. Frost, wondering where he was,

followed him and eventually discovered him in the prisoner's cell. He was hitting TATE in the jaw and I think he got one back himself. Frost stopped this incident without making a scene, and later told me what had happened. It was quite clear to me that we cannot have this sort of thing going on in our establishment. Apart from the moral aspect of the thing, I am quite convinced that these Gestapo methods do not pay in the long run. We are taking the matter up with the DMI [director of Military Intelligence] and propose to say that we do not intend to have that particular MI [military officer] on the premises any more.[19]

Tate, who was issued with false identity papers in the name of Harry Williamson, went on to become one of the longest-running agents of the Double Cross System. He successfully fed his German handlers information that led the Germans to believe that the Allied landings were planned for the coast near Pas de Calais instead of Normandy, and that the Soviets were going to attack through Bulgaria and Norway.

Lieutenant Colonel Stephens banned Colonel Scotland from setting foot in Camp 020, but as we have seen, Stephens himself would face court martial at the end of the war on serious charges of the brutal treatment and torture of German prisoners and civilians.

Back at Kensington Palace Gardens, the surroundings echoed the cage's unsavoury reputation, with the building described as 'tatty and seedy, the brusque bawling of the corporals and sergeants undiminished'.[20] Scotland's establishment was different from the other sites run by MI19, from which he received prisoners who could not be dealt with using ordinary measures: this was where the London Cage slid into unorthodox territory. Rumours began to circulate about the mistreatment of prisoners and terrible happenings in the basement of No. 8, where five interrogation rooms were located. Contraventions of the Geneva Convention were alleged to have taken place throughout the war and into the period when the cage became the War Crimes Investigation Unit.

7

CAGED LIES
The truth drugs

The allegations of brutality at the London Cage are shocking enough, but evidence emerges to reveal for the first time in this book that Colonel Scotland apparently sanctioned the use of 'truth drugs' on his prisoners. Clearly, this needs to be placed in the broader context of the military's experimental use of drugs in this period, but the matter was so classified that even Scotland dared not mention it in his memoirs.

In 1957, when Scotland's autobiography was published, experimentation with truth drugs had become common among the intelligence services of Britain, America, Russia and North Korea. All had their own secret research programmes and experimented with 'truth drugs' on prisoners and enemy spies; in some cases they even used their own civilians. Drugs, hypnosis and mind control – that was the new trend in Cold War espionage. It was believed that these could enable the intelligence services to control a person's mind or induce them to speak truthfully. The idea of mind control and brainwashing was nothing new – it featured in Aldous Huxley's *Brave New World* (1931), Arthur Koestler's *Darkness at Noon* (1940) and George Orwell's *Nineteen Eighty-Four* (1949) – yet, generally, it was seen simply as fiction, pure fantasy; few suspected how close to reality the accounts came, or that the early use of truth drugs dated back to the Second World War, or even earlier in scientific research.

An entry for 22 September 1940 in Guy Liddell's diary reveals that Colonel Scotland threatened to use drugs during an interrogation at Camp 020, Latchmere House. The prisoner was, once more, double agent Tate. The entry read:

I am told that Scotland turned up this morning with a syringe containing some drug or other, which it was thought would induce the prisoner to speak. Stephens told Scotland that he could not see TATE, who was not in a fit state to be interrogated. Actually, there was nothing seriously wrong with TATE.[1]

It was during this same interrogation that Colonel Scotland was supposed to have physically assaulted Tate, which prompted Lieutenant Colonel Stephens banning him from ever setting foot on the premises again – though the ban appears to have been motivated by a dislike of Scotland and personal rivalry, rather than by a policy disagreement over the treatment of prisoners.

Tate finally broke under interrogation and agreed to become a double agent for the British, as part of the Double Cross System that successfully turned a number of German spies. One of the most famous double agents was Garbo (Juan Pujol Garcia), who, like Tate, helped fool the Germans into believing that the main Allied invasion was to take place at Pas de Calais, meaning that Hitler kept an unnecessarily large number of troops and crack Panzer divisions in that region instead of diverting them to Normandy. As a result, they could not get to the beaches quickly enough to fight the Allied troops after the D-Day landings in June 1944.

In the early days of the war, because the fruits of interrogation could be fragmentary, it was necessary to obtain vital information in the shortest possible time. This was when various MI6 intelligence officers began to experiment with drugs. The most common at the time were barbiturates like barbital (Veronal), scopolamine hydrobromide, atropine and later sodium thiopental (Pentothal). These worked by relaxing the subject and depressing higher cortical functions to stupefy them.

In 1932, Dr J. Stephen Horsley at the London Hospital noticed that pregnant women became uninhibited when the barbiturate drug Nembutal was administered to them during labour. The discovery led him to experiment with other barbiturates: amytal sodium and sodium pentothal. After intravenous injection at a slow rate, he discovered that his patients became relaxed enough to recount very personal incidents from their past. Horsley believed he might have discovered 'truth drugs'. The implications could be far-reaching and were of interest to the military and intelligence services for interrogation. Discussions took place about their effectiveness for the police in forensic investigations. Files now reveal that Naval Intelligence was already experimenting with truth drugs in 1939.

Truth drugs and Naval Intelligence

In December 1939, Naval Intelligence Division tried out truth drugs on their own willing intelligence officers. The experiment was, of course, highly classified and not to be leaked into the public domain. It must be borne in mind that a highly effective team of naval interrogators was attached to MI19 at a number of its clandestine sites, in a joint services operation involving the army, Royal Air Force and Naval Intelligence. The first truth-drug experiment was carried out on civilian officer Charles Mitchell of Naval Intelligence Division, but it had no particular effect on him at all. That same month, Vice Admiral John Godfrey, the then director of Naval Intelligence, held two consultations with three unnamed doctors on the effective use of drugs and hypnosis during the interrogation of prisoners of war.[2] One of the unnamed doctors was a consultant psychologist to the army. Godfrey's full report of the meeting confirmed that two of the doctors had already carried out detailed studies for the army on the military use of certain drugs. They advised Godfrey that the use of Evipan, when combined with hypnosis, could put a patient in a condition where he would be unable to resist interrogation. Evipan was used to treat types of epilepsy and certain psychotic disorders, and belonged to a group of drugs that made a person more susceptible to hypnosis. Hypnosis ensured that the patient had no memory of the interrogation.

To get a prisoner to agree to an injection, a ruse was employed: it was said that the POW unit did not know his blood group, and in the event of casualties during the Blitz, the prisoner might need a blood transfusion. The ruse worked; but instead of having a blood sample taken from him, the prisoner was injected with Evipan. First, a number of experiments on prisoners had to take place to assess the value of this in intelligence terms: would a prisoner really tell the truth under the influence of Evipan and hypnosis? After injection, a patient actually fell asleep for a few minutes and was then in a state of drowsiness for three-quarters of an hour. Godfrey was told that during this forty-five-minute period, 'the hypnotic condition can be established and maintained'.[3]

On 12 December 1939, Vice Admiral Godfrey authorised experiments to determine the applicable dose of Evipan. Appropriate prisoners had to be found for the experiment. It was decided to select those who were known to have secret information; the extent to which they divulged those secrets during interrogation under the influence would be a measure of the effectiveness of the 'truth drug'. Under the guise of requiring a blood sample, a small dose of Evipan was administered, enough to make the prisoner slightly drowsy. After two or three days of unexplained drowsiness, the prisoner would probably ask to see a doctor, at which point 'it would be reasonable practice for him [the doctor] to give a dose of Evipan'.[4] The patient would be none the wiser, would still feel sleepy, and Naval Intelligence could observe the effects over a longer period of time. The particular value of using truth drugs and hypnosis lay in the fact that the intelligence services could use anyone to carry out an interrogation if they spoke fluent German. They had to sign the Official Secrets Act, of course, but they may not have known that the patient was under the influence of drugs and hypnosis.

A doctor who was 'prepared to adopt the technique and had no professional scruples about carrying it out' would administer the drugs to prisoners.[5] He would be trained in administering Evipan and in subsequent hypnotic treatment. But the military raised questions about the use of truth drugs, focusing on whether it was morally acceptable, whether it would infringe the Geneva Convention, and on the repercussions if the patient became aware of the process. A key issue was whether any information that could possibly be extracted justified such a drastic method. The disagreement among military advisers was not actually on moral grounds, but was concerned with the potential of scandal. The head of Section XIV of Naval Intelligence Division (whose signature is illegible) said: 'If I were in the Cabinet I would not agree to such a method, as, if by bad luck it leaked out, there would be such widespread popular agitation about it that it would become a first-class political scandal.'[6] The advisory doctors agreed unanimously that 'evil effects might take place in perhaps one in 100,000 cases'.[7] This led Godfrey to conclude:

The method is justified provided the doctors are satisfied that the technique is one that can easily be carried out, and which will have no permanent effect on the patient's health; the information which it is desired to elicit is of vital importance, and the preliminary experiments show that the patient is likely to respond favourably to the interrogation. If these two conditions are fulfilled, the objections on moral and legalistic grounds should not be accepted.[8]

Experimental use of insulin and the hallucinogen LSD on German prisoners of war was known to have been carried out in the Far East.[9] The
Americans also used drugs on German prisoners. One American agent
encouraged an MI5 officer to use Benzedrine sulphate (a truth drug), which
was known to induce sleepiness and was used as an alternative to Evipan.
An official report by a principal medical officer in 1950 concluded: 'Truth
drugs were discontinued in the army after a very short period in the recent
war as found to be unreliable.'[10] With the benefit of hindsight, it is possible
to add that truth drugs nevertheless continued to be the focus of research
and use by the British, American and Russian intelligence services.[11]

Use of drugs by the military

The use of drugs was not confined to Naval Intelligence or the British Secret
Service. Their possible use by the military and by air force pilots remained
high on the agenda of the War Cabinet and other intelligence chiefs in
1940.[12] At the end of July 1940, Winston Churchill asked the Ministry of
Defence for a report on their use by the military. Attention turned to the
drug Benzedrine, which reduced the desire for sleep and any feeling of tired-
ness, a possible asset for troops in combat. Benzedrine sulphate was first
used in 1935 to treat narcolepsy; it was later utilised for conditions such as
post-encephalitic Parkinsonism. A dose of 5 milligrams could ward off
drowsiness or sleep for four or five hours. The Royal Air Force was cautioned
against using the drug on fighter pilots, but it could prove ideal for special
commando and naval operations which put great strain on the body and
necessitated greater short-term endurance than usual.[13]

The Medical Research Council examined the medical findings of
research into Benzedrine, Pervitin and Leonidine, drawing on medical
papers published in Germany in the 1920s, and advised the War Cabinet
and the Joint Intelligence Sub-Committee that different people might
require a higher dose to achieve the desired mental alertness; there were no
after-effects or withdrawal symptoms of abnormal exhaustion or depression, although repeated use of such drugs reduced their effectiveness. The
council recommended their use by the army in emergency circumstances
only, and with certain precautions. Any such drug 'should only be given
under the supervision of a Medical Officer. Where individual judgement
is required in the course of a person's duties, it should only be taken if their
reactions to the drug have been previously tested.'[14] It concluded that more

research was needed to determine whether the effects of these drugs differed in different temperatures (i.e. tropical or temperate climates), and what the optimum dose was. Further controlled trials on personnel were required to observe the effects and after-effects.

In a report dated 27 September 1940, the Joint Intelligence Sub-Committee issued a memo for the meeting of the War Cabinet and Chiefs of Staff Committee that advised:

> There was a net gain from using Benzedrine drugs to stimulate mental alertness and resistance to fatigue. The Flying Personnel Research Committee was already carrying out experiments on this type of drug for stimulating air crews. The Army Medical Service was also carrying out its own research trials.[15]

The report was signed by Victor Cavendish-Bentinck, chairman of the Joint Intelligence Committee and the Services Liaison Department of the Foreign Office; Vice Admiral John Godfrey, head of Naval Intelligence; Major-General Frederick Beaumont-Nesbitt, director of Military Intelligence; and Air Commodore A.R. Boyle of Royal Air Force Intelligence. The consensus was that, provided the drugs were administered under the strictest medical supervision, they 'might have considerable military value'.

At a further meeting on 2 December 1940, General Sir William MacArthur, director general of Army Medical Services, outlined trials and research into the effectiveness of Benzedrine: 'The results of the test so far carried out were inconclusive and further tests are necessary before a definite recommendation on the use of the drug can be made. Any further experimental work should be of a practical kind, using opportunities created by incidents of war.'[16] The report was marked in bold red lettering: 'To be kept under lock and key.' General MacArthur advised the committee that 'I should be totally opposed to wholesale drugging of the troops, and I feel the idea of putting men under the influence of a drug to do their duty repellent.'[17]

Around this time, the adoption of a variety of drugs for military use was becoming commonplace. The SOE gave its agents a cyanide pill to use in the event of capture, the resulting swift death ensuring that they gave nothing away during intense interrogation and torture. From 1942, SOE's special section at the military experimental establishment at Porton Down in Wiltshire worked on Operation Saccharine – research to procure drugs for use by agents.[18] In the declassified files relating to this operation, a number of tablets are listed as being suitable for a variety of purposes:

- A tablets – to aid travel sickness;
- B tablets – Benzedrine, to provide extra energy;
- Mecodrin – an amphetamine, for energy in an emergency;
- E capsules – fast-acting anaesthetic;
- K tablets – could knock out foreign agents, if slipped into their drinks;
- L tablets – suicide pills.

That same year, SOE dispatched truth drugs for use in the field. A memo of 10 April 1942, marked 'SECRET', enclosed 'doctored' aspirin tablets, together with the same number of plain aspirin. The effectiveness of the doctored tablets had been confirmed by experiments on animals. Known as 'A tablets', they looked just like innocent aspirin. A tablet would take effect thirty to forty-five minutes later and would cause death within three to four hours.

SOE also favoured the use of insulin, which, if injected in certain quantities, could cause collapse and unconsciousness within an hour. A single injection rarely had any serious effects, but if followed with a second, 'success would be ensured'.[19]

The military and intelligence services were careful to disguise their use of these particular drugs. In a file marked 'Narcotic Drugs' (i.e. drugs which have a sedative effect), a memo was at pains to emphasise that if they were mentioned in any telegram, the drugs should be described as 'being supplied to our agents for medicinal purposes'; 'telegrams dealing with this subject need to be very carefully worded', it advised.[20] Contained in one dispatch to SOE in the Far East in April 1942 was a small phial marked '7 tablets A, plus six boxes of insulin, totalling 400 units'.

'K tablets' induced sleep that could last for several hours. They took effect thirty to sixty minutes after swallowing. Small test tubes were provided to dissolve the tablets in water, because they could not be introduced in small quantities into drinks or food to produce instant effects – 'Such things can only be done in spy and detective fiction,' wrote one unnamed SOE officer. Guidelines were issued in a booklet entitled *Instructions for the Use of Tablets K*.[21] One tablet was a sufficient dose for a person of slightly less than average bodyweight. Two could be used to produce quicker results, but a dose of three tablets was verging on the dangerous. It was underlined that these tablets were poisonous and any attempt to exceed the recommended dose could have fatal consequences.

Issuing tablets to agents in action behind enemy lines was one thing, but administering experimental mind-transforming truth drugs on unsuspecting prisoners without their consent was quite another, and crossed the boundaries of the Geneva Convention.

The Nazis and truth drugs

The German army and air force were known to be using Benzedrine to increase mental alertness and resistance to fatigue, followed by sedatives like Sedormid to combat the Benzedrine-induced wakefulness. Also in the Second World War, Pervitin was known as the German army's 'wonder drug', as it enhanced performance and gave soldiers incredible stamina and endurance (for example, marching for 90 kilometres without a rest).

The Nazis were known to have been developing clandestine drugs and brainwashing substances as early as the 1930s. During the war, a number of truth drug experiments were carried out in Ukraine and at Dachau and Auschwitz concentration camps. The drugs were being developed because German interrogators had been unable to break Allied prisoners during interrogation. Definitive proof that the regime was testing the truth drug mescaline came from a decoded message deciphered at Bletchley Park on 24 July 1942. The cipher was marked 'Most Secret' and read:

> Experiments to date of injecting parachutists with scopolamine were successful. Therefore, experiments with mescaline are to be undertaken, since these injections produce and enhance effect through intoxication. The above is a request from SS Fuhrer in Ukraine for mind-altering drugs from SS medical headquarters (Berlin).[22]

The mind-altering properties of scopolamine were first discovered in America in 1916 by obstetrician Dr Robert E. House, again in relation to pregnant women. The findings were widely available and were drawn upon by the Nazis. Mescaline, a hallucinogen made from the Peyote cactus, was supposed to induce talkativeness (though ultimately it was found to be unreliable). Experiments continued in Block 5 at Dachau, aimed at 'eliminating the will of the person examined'.[23] The project was supervised by Wolfram Sievers, director of the Institute for Military Scientific Research and a member of Heinrich Himmler's personal staff. Sievers was to stand trial at Nuremberg for his crimes, and would be hanged on 2 June 1948, in Landsberg prison, Bavaria.

Horrific medical experimentation at Auschwitz is well documented. It was carried out there under the authority of the SS doctor Bruno Weber, a German physician and bacteriologist. He experimented with barbiturates and morphine for the purposes of mind control, as well as with psycho-tropic drugs during interrogation. He managed to avoid prosecution as a war criminal and died a free man.

The Nazis were not alone in these types of experiments. In the 1930s, the Soviets had built a covert laboratory in Moscow, where doctors and scientists 'developed new poisons to eliminate enemies of the state'.[24] Its location and function were so secret that even senior KGB officers were not privy to its whereabouts. Soviet botanists began 'cross-breeding hallu-cinogenic and poisonous plant species to create hybrids, producing new drugs with effects on the human body and mind as yet unknown'.[25]

Use of drugs by American intelligence

On 31 October 1942, US intelligence was alerted by the US National Research Council to the Germans and Russians experimenting with truth drugs. A committee was formed to verify the facts and check the effective-ness of truth drugs in interrogation. It came under the auspices of the OSS, and was headed by the main scientist there, Stanley P. Lovell. A chemist from Boston, Lovell invented an entire arsenal for his boss and head of OSS, William 'Bill' Donovan, that could have come straight from the lab of James Bond's 'Q'. Items included detonating household objects, exploding cookie dough and silenced pistols for assassinations. He even produced cocktails of lethal chemicals to use on the Führer, but any imag-ined assassination attempt on Hitler failed.

In May 1943, American intelligence was carrying out research into scopolamine, considered one of the most deadly drugs from the Colombian borrachero tree. The OSS decided to test this 'truth drug' on a group of people who knew the most classified secrets of all – the scientists on the Manhattan Project. The results were limited, because it made most of the scientists violently sick.

Working alongside Lovell were Harry Anslinger (head of the Federal Bureau of Narcotics), Winfred Overholser (director of St Elizabeth's

Hospital, Washington, DC), and CIA operative George Hunter White. Experiments showed that mescaline and scopolamine were not suitable truth drugs. The side effects of hallucinations, blurred vision and head-aches were found to be a distraction during interrogation. They knew this because they first subjected their own team to experimentation, including with different types of marijuana. George Hunter White was one of the first to try out new drugs, on one occasion, when testing the effects of smoking marijuana, knocking himself unconscious. Subsequently, the OSS carried out tests on unwitting members of the public by inserting marijuana into cigarettes and resealing the packets. White once commented: 'the [marijuana] cigarette experiments indicated that we had a mechanism which offered promise in the relaxing of prisoners'.[26] Already in 1946, the OSS had concluded that nothing was more effective on a prisoner than alcohol.

White had attended Camp X, the top-secret spy school in Canada, and had met Ian Fleming, an officer from British Naval Intelligence. He also accompanied Bill Donovan during interrogations of German prisoners of war. White was an interesting character, later becoming the CIA's main federal narcotics agent, involved in the 1950s and 1960s in the highly clas-sified Project MKUltra. Warfare and espionage had entered the shady, dangerous and unpredictable world of mind control.

Experimental psychology and mind control

In addition to truth drugs, MI6 was already testing out new experimental psychological methods on its prisoners. As commanding officer at the London Cage, Colonel Scotland liaised with a number of psychiatrists and psychologists, some of whose work was controversial and unorthodox. Among the list of items impounded by Special Branch during the second raid on Scotland's flat in 1955 was a letter dated 5 December 1944 and addressed to Scotland from William Brown, director of Oxford University's Institute of Experimental Psychology.[27] (All attempts to trace the letter or any archives of William Brown have failed.) Brown founded the institute in 1936 on the academic foundations of experimental psychology, which had begun in a clandestine laboratory in Oxford in the nineteenth century with the controversial psychologist William McDougall. Brown had been McDougall's first student. A parallel department existed at Cambridge University, where Kenneth Craik devised a number of instruments and pioneered research into the sensory system. Much of his work had practical military application and was taken up by the military in the Second World War.

Colonel Scotland's correspondence with Brown raises questions about what Scotland hoped to gain from the connection. It points to his attempt to use experimental, even unorthodox, psychological methods on his prisoners. But further than that, the trail goes cold, and it is not known if the two men ever met. However, it would not be the first or only time that MI6 looked to psychologists and psychiatrists for help with prisoners. The eminent (but controversial) British psychiatrist William Sargant (1907–88), along with psychiatrists Lieutenant Colonel Henry Victor Dicks and Brigadier John Rawlings Rees, carried out work for MI5, MI6 and various other branches of Military Intelligence, including MI9 and Colonel Scotland's unit at the London Cage under the auspices of MI19.[28]

William Sargant was a prominent psychiatrist on the scene during the 1930s and 1940s. He became a household name for his work on brainwashing and for two bestselling books, *The Unquiet Mind* and *Battle for the Mind*. During the Second World War he was primarily based at the Sutton Emergency Medical Service in Surrey. His treatment of patients was controversial – and shocking to many in the medical world. It involved deep-sleep treatment, psychosurgery, insulin shock therapy and electroconvulsive therapy. After the evacuation of Dunkirk in May–June 1940, he was known to have treated traumatised soldiers with barbiturates, sedation and electroconvulsive therapy. The treatment then extended to civilians and other military patients – but what is not known is whether any of the latter were German prisoners of war. A number of psychosurgical procedures were carried out, including deep-sleep and electro-shock treatment on the brain under anaesthetic; leucotomy, which consisted of cutting away connections in the brain to and from the prefrontal cortex; and ablative psychosurgery, which aimed at destroying small areas of tissue in the brain to cure psychological problems. The procedures were highly risky and could lead to seizures, cognitive impairment and even death.

One deeply traumatised evacuee soldier was given a dose of the barbiturate amytal sodium, which produced positive results for Sargant. The soldier went from being nervous and mute to recalling in detail exactly what had happened to him. Sargant started to administer amytal sodium to other traumatised soldiers and they began to talk freely. He discovered that his patients were not merely recalling trauma from the battlefield, but were actually reliving it; and so he extended his research into other barbiturates. He started to mix barbiturates like amytal sodium and Pentothal with amphetamines like Benzedrine or Methedrine. The former removed a person's inhibitions and made him drowsy; the latter increased alertness; and the combination was thought to make the ideal truth drug. The use of ether was found to cause a more violent expulsion of deep-seated emotions and memories, and was therefore avoided. 'With [truth] drugs, Sargant had rediscovered the technique of cathartic abreaction pioneered by Freud and Brevet in the 1890s.'[29]

Sargant's findings were published on 6 July 1940 in the medical journal *The Lancet*, in an article entitled 'Acute War Neurosis'. Six days later, he was contacted by Brigadier John Rawlings Rees (1890–1969), medical director of the Tavistock Clinic in London and chairman of the Army Psychiatry Advisory Committee, who was working for British intelligence.[30] MI5 and MI6 took great interest in Sargant's work: if he could make patients talk, then the drugs could do the same to German prisoners of war during interrogation. Two months after the article was published, Colonel Scotland arrived at Camp 020 with a syringe containing a drug for use on agent Tate, which would 'induce the prisoner to speak', but Colonel Stephens prevented Scotland from seeing the German (see page 87).[31]

From 1948, Sargant worked at St Thomas' Hospital, London, where he continued his controversial treatment in special wards and laboratories away from the public gaze. Many patients were left traumatised: some of the deep-sleep treatment, for example, was carried out without the patients' consent. Sargant worked for the intelligence services and military for over thirty years in this experimental field, which became popular for a variety of clandestine uses.

A CIA document dated 22 June 1948 confirmed the existence of a joint American–British intelligence operation to use truth drugs, with further research into amphetamines and barbiturates. The use of these drugs was never admitted publicly, but an OSS document once in circulation seems to have confirmed the use of 'Truth Serum 5678A' in interrogation.[32] In London, the experiments took place on civilians at the Royal Waterloo Hospital, a branch of St Thomas' Hospital, where William Sargant was operating.

By the 1950s, the British, Russians and Americans were all experimenting heavily with truth drugs. The Soviets gave drugs to people being interrogated while held in jails in the Soviet Union and North Korea via coffee and cigarettes with a strange, unfamiliar odour. British and American intelligence knew that they needed to keep up with the Russians, the new enemy in the Cold War.[33] On 20 April 1950, the CIA authorised a classified project headed by Colonel Sheffield Edwards of the US army: Project Bluebird. A committee was formed to establish how soldiers could resist indoctrination, drug-based interrogation and mind control if captured by the Russians. The following year the project was renamed Artichoke, and two years later, in 1953, was given the cover name MKUltra. What began as a defensive weapon against brainwashing and drug control soon turned into offensive warfare. Apparently, no thought was given to the ethical boundaries.

Truth drugs and Rudolf Hess

The use of drugs at the London Cage must be understood within the wider context of their use by the intelligence services. The most infamous wartime case of truth drugs concerned Hitler's deputy, Rudolf Hess, who in May 1941 was being held by MI6 at Mytchett Place, a Georgian house near Aldershot.[34] There, Colonel Scotland's close MI6 colleagues, Thomas Kendrick, Frank Foley and 'Capt. Barnes' (whose real name has never been released by the intelligence services) were monitoring Hess, having been entrusted with the task of extracting information from their prized prisoner. Hess became convinced that they were trying to poison him, and accused Kendrick and Foley of drugging him with 'Mexican Brain Poison', understood to have been mescaline. It has since emerged that MI5 was also using drugs on Hess, having been encouraged by the War Office to try the barbiturate Evipan. MI5 wrote to the War Office that Hess was 'a poor type, completely devoid of intellectual interests'.[35] The use of drugs on Hess to induce him to tell the truth has never been openly admitted by the intelligence services, but becomes apparent from a careful reading of Hess's Foreign Office files.[36]

Hess had flown to Scotland on 10 May 1941, on a solo flight from Germany. Forced to bail out of his Messerschmitt a few miles from the estate of the Duke of Hamilton, he was captured on landing and taken by the Home Guard before being handed over to the intelligence services. After a few days, Hess was transferred to the Tower of London under heavy guard, and then to the Queen's House, overlooking the White Tower.

Within hours, Charles Fraser-Smith of MI6, working during the war for MI9, received a telephone call from MI5 asking whether he could replicate the uniform of a senior German officer. Fraser-Smith readily agreed: as a member of MI9, the escape and evasion branch, he was used to making gadgets and forging items for the intelligence services. When Fraser-Smith arrived at the Tower, he was informed that Hess had been given 'something to ensure that he doesn't wake up until morning'. A duplicate of Hess's uniform was duly copied before sunrise. 'What it was used for – if it was used,' wrote Fraser-Smith, 'is something I shall be interested to know one day.'[37]

On 20 May 1941, a military ambulance transferred Hess to Mytchett Place, accompanied by medical officer Lieutenant Colonel Gibson Graham. Shortly afterwards, Hess began to notice that his food and medication left him with a distinctly unusual sensation, reoccurring over the next few weeks. He was able to describe it:

> A curious development of warmth rising over the nape of the neck to the head: in the head feelings which are similar to headache pains, but which are not the same: there follows for many hours an extraordinary feeling of well-being, physical and mental energy, joie de vivre, optimism. Little sleep during the night but this did not in the least destroy my sense of euphoria.[38]

Hess observed withdrawal symptoms when the substance was not being given. He felt the difference in his own body, especially after drinking milk. Hess was being given truth drugs by MI6, it can be argued, to loosen his tongue, so that he revealed Germany's most closely guarded secrets.

Lieutenant Colonel Gibson Graham found it increasingly difficult to deal with Hess, who had become unstable and suicidal. Graham was relieved of his duties by psychiatrist Lieutenant Colonel Henry Dicks of the Royal Army Medical Corps, who was already conducting work for British intelligence. This was the same psychiatrist who aided Colonel Scotland with interrogations at the London Cage and who made occasional visits for the interrogation of suspected German spies at Camp 020. The bulk of his clandestine wartime work from 1942 would be carried out at the three CSDIC bugging sites: Trent Park, Latimer House and Wilton Park.

Dicks arrived at Mytchett Place on 29 May 1941 and was joined that same day by Brigadier John Rawlings Rees, consultant in psychological medicine to the army at home, and a fluent German speaker. The psychiatrists made various assessments of Hess which survive in Foreign Office files.[39] On 2 June, it was noted that Hess had periods of restlessness and had requested something to help him sleep. He was prescribed the barbiturate Phanodorm. By the morning, he had become more unstable and suicidal. During this period, Hess was being given sedatives as a sleep aid. During his time at Mytchett Place, he made one suicide attempt – in June 1941. The following year he was transferred to Maindiff Court Hospital, near Abergavenny in Wales, where he remained for the rest of the war.

The Hess case seems to indicate that the intelligence services used truth drugs on prisoners – in his case, with very few positive results. Hess's unstable mental condition and his mood swings between euphoria, deep depression and paranoia may well have been caused by the drug experiments conducted by British intelligence while he was in their custody, rather than by any inherent mental illness. His case does not appear to be unusual; rather, it is in line with the culture within MI5 and MI6, where the use of truth drugs and mind-altering substances on prisoners during the war was apparently considered acceptable (even if their use was not officially sanctioned or recorded in the files). Within that environment, Colonel Scotland had no qualms about using drugs on his prisoners being interrogated at the London Cage.

8

THE GERMAN 'GREAT ESCAPE'

On the night of 14 December 1944, two coaches with a strong detachment of guards left London for Camp 23 POW camp in Wiltshire. When they arrived at Le Marchant Barracks at Devizes, the commandant paraded the whole camp under the lights of the parade ground. Thirty-two unsuspecting prisoners were asked to step forward and were escorted to the waiting coaches. Believed to have been involved in a thwarted daring escape plan that nearly turned into a major breach of security in Britain, they were driven to Kensington Palace Gardens under heavy guard. On arrival, they were taken to rooms on the first floor of No. 8. Over the next five days, the prisoners underwent intensive interrogation to ascertain what had happened, who was responsible, and whether they had had any contact with German agents secretly operating in Britain.[1]

During the war, several escapes were attempted from POW camps, but rarely were they successful; they often failed due to bad planning.[2] Anybody involved in an attempted escape was transferred to the London Cage, which was known in army circles for its extreme toughness. Of the Devizes escape, Colonel Scotland wrote in an official report:

> The importance of making prisoners of war en masse feel the weight of our control when they attempt to break the peace cannot be over estimated . . . the whole camp [at Devizes] was profoundly impressed by the arrest, the security measures taken and word of warning given afterwards by the camp commandant.[3]

In 1944 there were around 300,000 German POWs in England, guarded by a comparatively small number of troops (because most of the Allied forces were in Europe). The plot at Devizes was far more ambitious than anything undertaken elsewhere, and would have far-reaching consequences beyond the borders of the camp – or indeed the London Cage.

No one underestimated the seriousness of an escape plan that came close to success and which would have seen around 4,000 German POWs absconding from the camp over the quiet Christmas period, when guard duties were perhaps more lax; if it had been successful, the escapees could have wreaked havoc or carried out acts of sabotage across the country. The plan involved capturing an aircraft from a nearby military base and eventually linking up with German forces at sea. Morale in POW camps in Britain had reached a new high, with prisoners' hopes raised by the Ardennes campaign and the destruction being caused by V rockets landing on England. German prisoners began to believe that maybe Germany's fortunes could turn, in spite of the successful Allied landings at Normandy six months earlier.

Reflecting later, Scotland was impressed by the escape plan: 'If the prisoners could have surprised the guards, collected their weapons, raided the quartermaster's stores, and got themselves some transport, they could have formed a dangerous, desperate band.'[4] It would be his job to ensure this daring was properly punished.

Escape plan from Devizes

Just prior to D-Day, the camp at Devizes had come under the temporary command of the Americans until the push into Germany in 1945. British and American armies both needed more interrogators to deal with the large number of German prisoners anticipated after the Normandy landings and in preparation for the advance westwards. A special training centre for these new interrogators was run at Devizes, with instructors provided by the London Cage. The camp held 4,000 prisoners – many SS or former Hitler Youth, described as 'dangerous and violent young brutes'[5] – so there was ample interrogation material for practice. German-Jewish émigré Herbert Sulzbach, who had fled the Nazis, transferred to Devizes as an interpreter with the British army. It was here that he encountered his first Nazis since leaving Germany. 'I didn't see them as people at all. I only saw the swastika on their uniforms,' he revealed in an interview.[6] Sulzbach had been interned as an 'enemy alien' on the Isle of Man in 1940, when

Britain feared a German invasion. From the internment camp, he enlisted in the only unit available for 'enemy aliens' at that time, the Pioneer Corps. He served with 229 Company and was stationed for a time at Didcot, near Oxford. In January 1942, he was transferred to the Prisoner of War Interrogation Section, working out of Devizes. As the German escape story unfolded, he was transferred as an interpreter to Camp 21 at Comrie in Scotland, where events took a nasty turn.[7]

It was in early December that an American officer overheard a chance remark during a training course. The unnamed American officer, a former German-Jewish refugee with fluent German, had been interrogating a young German prisoner on routine subjects. After he dismissed the prisoner, the officer lit a cigarette and watched as he joined two others. The officer's curiosity was aroused – why were these prisoners casually loitering? He listened from the door. They spoke rapidly, but, catching words such as 'escape' and 'plan', he gathered that some kind of breakout plan might be afoot and reported it to his superior officer.

The alert soon reached the camp commandant, and finally there was a phone call to Colonel Scotland, who was on a short period of leave with his wife at their home, 'The Dell' in Bourne End, Buckinghamshire. He advised the commandant to call the prisoners to the parade ground on the pretence of exercise. The instructors and trainee interrogators were set the task of finding out whether a plan was actually being hatched. The entire camp was paraded. The trainee interrogators walked down the ranks, selecting prisoners at random and ordering the guards to take them to the interrogation rooms. The first few prisoners yielded little, but clearly something was amiss.

Over the next couple of days, several parades were called, and it was noticed that the same group of men invariably stood together – all tough specimens, some from the German army, others from the German navy. All had one thing in common: they were hardened Nazis.

No progress was made, and the guards were on alert for any activity at night in the camp. It was not long before two prisoners were caught returning through the single barbed wire fence. They were marched into the main interrogation room and had a barrage of questions fired at them to establish why they had been outside the camp and who had sent them. They said very little. At the same time, unbeknownst to them, their huts were being searched: stockpiles of food and crudely made bludgeons were found. The men were confronted with this, and told that they would be charged with theft and severely punished unless they proved that they had not stolen the weapons or the food. This proved to be the turning point in the case. Fearing military discipline, the men began to talk. Soon the interrogators had a rough outline of the ambitious mass escape.

One of the German prisoners, who was a doctor and trained pilot, had observed that a large number of troop-carrying aircraft used an airfield not far from Devizes. He proposed to the men in his hut that they should attempt to reach the airfield, capture a plane and fly back to Germany. His comrades supported the idea. On successive nights, two prisoners were helped through the barbed wire fence to reconnoitre the guard system at the airfield, its general layout and where an aircraft might be collected. It was a senior German NCO, Sergeant Hermann Storch, who suggested that instead of a comparatively small number of men escaping by air, a mass escape by most of the 4,000 prisoners in the camp should be attempted. The prisoners acquired accurate information that a fleet of small German craft was forming at the mouth of the River Weser in Germany. This fleet was to link with Field Marshal von Rundstedt's drive in the Ardennes, once the German army had driven a wedge between the American and British troops. The ships were to sail for the Rhine delta, to cause a diversion of Allied troops. During its investigation into the Devizes escape plot, the London Cage never discovered how the prisoners had acquired this classified information about the German naval fleet.

Storch worked out a full escape plan for over the Christmas period. The camp guards would be killed with the weapons the prisoners had made. They would then seize the dead guards' rifles, collect transport and make a dash for the east coast of England before the authorities even realised that they were missing. It was decided that en route to the coast they would attempt to free other German prisoners in camps. But, thanks to the swift action of the German-speaking American officer, it never came to pass.

As the interrogators tried to build up a comprehensive picture of who had been behind the escape plan, different sections of prisoners within the camp discussed it, clearly nervous that they could be implicated in Storch's scheme and charged with serious offences. This would be the interrogators' key tool – to play on the prisoners' fears of being severely disciplined. The interrogators tricked them into gradually letting slip details of the plan, not by questioning them directly about the escape, but by giving the impression that they were more interested in the seriousness of the offence of stealing food and making weapons. Their patience paid off, as evidence gradually built up against named individuals. The prisoners were told that they were going to be charged with a camp crime which deprived them of any defence under the Geneva Convention and that they could be severely punished. All this happened before the suspects were taken to the London Cage.

For Colonel Scotland, who was masterminding the investigation from London, it was important to understand how the escape plan had been communicated across the different segregated compounds within the camp. Interrogations established that the common meeting point had been the staff office in the camp. Here, two English-speaking German prisoners were engaged in keeping records about prisoners employed in various types of paid work near the camp. The prisoners frequently congregated in small groups, and their exchanges had gone largely unnoticed by camp guards. The prisoner overseeing the administration work was Wolfgang Rosterg, who, as the details unfolded, turned out to be a key figure. He was described as a 'good type'.[8] Although questioned closely, he denied that the office had been the central meeting point for discussing the escape. But, after hours of interrogation and sifting of the information, it was established that thirty-five prisoners had probably been involved in the escape plan. These were the men who were transferred to the London Cage in the middle of the night on 14 December 1944.

Dissenters in the cage

For five days, the London Cage was in a state of pandemonium, as the staff left the prisoners to simmer and their anger bubbled to the surface. It was a deliberate ploy to see if any of them inadvertently gave away information. Scotland described the scene:

> In the interrogation rooms our trainees watched with interest and amusement as the tough young Nazis argued with one another, denying each other's statements, shaking their fists and squaring up to fight and threatening all kinds of revenge for treachery. As they argued, so the truth gradually came out; it was about as much like a normal interrogation as a golf match is to a game of Rugby and about as physically aggressive as the latter. And, not content with arguing in the interrogation rooms, the prisoners continued to shout to one another from their rooms until lights out at 10 p.m. Remarks were bawled from room to room, and there were loud discussions about what had been disclosed and by whom. Our guards entered into the spirit of the occasion,

letting the noise continue until they flicked the switches to put the cage in darkness; and, during the day, moving the prisoners into the interrogation rooms at the trot so that they had no time to shout warnings or to make up their minds what they intended to say.[9]

In the interrogation room, an accusation – real or imaginary – would be made against the prisoner by the interrogator. If the prisoner hesitated, the interrogator would shout at him: 'Come on, out with it. Quick!' As soon as the prisoner answered, the interrogator rapidly fired another question, then another. The strategy confused the prisoner and succeeded in making him shout back his answers. As the interrogation descended into a shouting match, so the tension rose. This approach was found to be effective, revealing that, though not all the prisoners held had been involved in planning the escape, the cage did have all the men it was seeking. As the names of the guilty men became apparent, the younger interrogators turned up the temperature of their interrogations. It was easy to raise the pitch when the young German prisoners were so eager to prove their innocence. It also gave the relatively inexperienced young interrogators an excellent grounding for the tough work they would undertake from 1945 on war crimes investigations in Norway and Germany.

Most of the information pointed to Storch as the main ringleader and originator of the mass escape idea: he had sent out the reconnaissance parties through the barbed wire fence at night, and he had proposed killing the guards. Storch, who was described by Scotland as a 'congenital liar', tried to argue that the only reason for the escape plan had been to destroy incriminating evidence in Germany that showed him to be a communist. But, according to Scotland, when he was confronted with the facts of the case he became angry that his comrades had given him away. In retaliation, he began to incriminate others, principally Erich Pallme Koenig and Josef Mertens.

As Scotland pondered his next course of action, the Devizes prisoners continued to fight amongst themselves, and various men were savagely attacked. To stop the fighting, Scotland decided to act out a charade and arouse the anger of the prisoners that the main 'traitor' in their midst was Storch. Scotland now trod a thin line in pitting the anger and emotions of the prisoners against each other:

We decided that the best way was to tell them that their own leader, Storch, had given us full details of their plan; and to let them have it out with him. We had to get him away from them after ten minutes for they beat him up severely, though many of them received some useful exchanges from Storch, a powerful man who had been a butcher by trade and was normally well able to look after himself.[10]

All Devizes prisoners, with the exception of Storch, were informed that they were being transferred to a camp at Comrie in Scotland. Before they left the cage, Scotland paraded them in his office:

> They looked a tough, unruly lot, some of them with black eyes and other facial bruises from their fighting, still furious and resentful at their plan having been discovered. And I know only too well that given an inch they would willingly have torn me to pieces.[11]

He explained that he had all the information he needed, that the matter was closed and that they had had their opportunity to deal with the guilty man. The quarrelling was to stop, he said, and there was to be no more nonsense in the new camp. He issued a stark warning: 'If you misbehave, you will be brought back to London and we will treat you very differently then. You will find yourself in a court on a crime charge and you will be dealt with in civilian gaols of England.'[12]

The men were duly transferred to Comrie. Storch was left behind. In the quietness of the cage, Scotland sat down with him for an informal chat. The German told him about his family and military service, and filled in more details about the escape plan. He admitted that he should not have let matters get as far as they had, and that he had crossed a line. He did not blame his comrades for beating him up, and expressed his thanks to Scotland for not sending him to Comrie. He and Scotland were said to have parted on amicable terms, and nothing more was heard of him. The prisoners who were dispatched to Comrie were a very different matter. Their anger continued to burn, and they would take matters into their own hands – with fatal consequences.

Murder at Comrie

Camp 21 at Comrie housed the toughest and most dangerous of all German prisoners who had been captured at various stages of the war. Interpreter Herbert Sulzbach described it as 'a very fanatical and Nazi-minded camp

with four thousand privates and NCOs – Germans – fanatical ones . . .
When they marched to their football grounds, they sang horrible Hitler
marching songs . . . that was the atmosphere.'[13]

The entire camp was surrounded by a double barbed wire fence, guarded
by equally tough British and Polish guards. One misjudgement was in
allowing the prisoners to wear their uniforms and flaunt their decorations
and ranks. Consequently, morale was high, and the internees displayed
contempt for the democratic world. All attempts at interesting them in
democracy by providing carefully chosen literature, such as pro-Allied newspapers, failed. The *Lagerpost* was one such German newspaper, written by
sympathetic Germans in London; copies were regularly sent up to Comrie
in the hope that it would influence the prisoners. It proved very unpopular
with the Nazi prisoners, who declared it to be a banned publication.

The new arrivals from the London Cage were not well received by these
Nazis, who congregated in cliques in the different Nissen huts within the
various compounds of the camp. More or less ostracised by the other prisoners, it became clear that they would not be accepted into the company
of the elite Nazis unless they proved themselves worthy of the honour.
Wolfgang Rosterg, one of the men from Devizes, was singled out by his
comrades. He showed an independence of mind and was not particularly
impressed by the Comrie elite. Because Rosterg had worked in the office
at Devizes, his comrades seized on the idea that perhaps he had informed
on Storch. In Hut 4, where he was being accommodated with 120 other
prisoners, he came under the close watch of the Nazis.

On 22 December 1944, when the Ardennes campaign was in full swing,
the morning newspapers were delivered to Hut 4. Rosterg, as the most
proficient English-speaker in the group, frequently read out news of the
progress of the war. He enjoyed the popularity this brought him, but that
morning he impetuously announced that he was going to read the latest
news on the Ardennes campaign from the *Lagerpost*. He opened the bundle
of newspapers and pulled out a copy. As he began to read, the other prisoners slipped out of the hut, leaving him alone. Reading from the pro-
Allied newspaper seemed to be the proof the inmates needed that Rosterg
was not only an informer, but an anti-Nazi and traitor.

At 11 p.m. that evening, the British guards locked the Nissen huts as
usual and turned out the lights. The camp fell quiet. In Hut 4, candles were
lit as the inhabitants gave vent to dangerous emotions. Rosterg was dragged
from his bunk and hauled into the centre of the hut. A group of Nazis from

Devizes began their brutal interrogation, demanding to know if he was a British spy, and whether he had informed against them in the Devizes camp and given away information about the escape plans. When they received neither an answer nor a denial, Rosterg was brutally beaten and struck across the face with an iron bar.[14] The questioning, beatings and half-strangling carried on throughout the night, until Rosterg, racked with pain and realising the futility of denying the charges against him, answered 'Yes'.

Just before 6 a.m., when the British guard was due to unlock the huts, one of the Nazi prisoners danced around the badly beaten Rosterg and jeered: 'What shall we do with him?'

The others shouted: 'Hang him!'

The daily checks in the camp were lax. The guard unlocked the door to Hut 4, turned on the lights and left, not noticing the state of Rosterg. The gang produced a rope and dragged Rosterg out of the hut to the wash-room, where, surrounded by jubilant Nazis, he was hanged over the water pipes of the toilet. The perpetrators quietly returned to Hut 4.

Rosterg's body was found that morning in the washroom by a prisoner from another hut. The police were called, and the body was photographed and taken down. The official report concluded that it probably took him fifteen minutes to die.[15]

The following day was Christmas Eve. Colonel Scotland had not yet received news of the brutal murder at Comrie. He was on his way to Whitehall for a meeting with the chiefs of staff and various cabinet ministers to answer questions about the Devizes escape plan. The first question was put to Scotland by A.V. Alexander, first lord of the Admiralty, on how the prisoners had secured information about the small fleet at the mouth of the River Weser – a fact known only to a few in the highest circles in England. Scotland suggested that the information could only have come from a batch of newly arrived prisoners, some of whom were from the Bremerhaven area of Germany. He reassured the meeting that life had returned to normal at Devizes, the guards had been strengthened at all POW camps over the Christmas period, and that put an end to the affair.

Trial at the cage

Scotland returned to Kensington Palace Gardens to news of the murder at Comrie. The War Office informed the local police that it would now handle the case, and instructions were issued to transfer twelve men from Hut 4 at Comrie to London: Kurt Zühlsdorff, Rolf Herzig, Josef Mertens, Joachim Goltz, Herbert Wunderlich, Heinz Brüling, Erich Pallme Koenig, Hans Klein, Klaus Steffan and three others, identified only as soldiers Bienek, Recksiek and Jelinsky. Interrogators at the London Cage were to investigate who was guilty of Rosterg's murder.

There was no need for aggressive tactics in interrogation. The serious consequence of being found guilty of murder was outlined to the prisoners, and consequently they were advised to tell their story with honesty and without elaboration. It was here that psychology played a vital role. The interrogators observed the prisoners' reactions during interrogation, and that became key to cracking this murder. They noticed that the younger men seemed indifferent to Rosterg's death: they argued that it was not the business of the British, but was a German matter, to be tried in a German court. But the war had not yet been won, and Scotland knew that to send these men back to Nazi Germany for trial (which was what they were asking for) would mean that they would not face justice. He outlined to them that they were subject to British law and would be tried by a British military court.

As the men in their cells at the London Cage prepared for the trial, they were offered English lawyers to defend them, in order to ensure a fair process. Pallme Koenig refused and insisted on being represented by a German lawyer; but the other six accused agreed to English lawyers.

Insufficient evidence meant that four suspects would not be brought to trial. Eight men remained in the cells on the first floor of 8 Kensington Palace Gardens. In the former dining room on the ground floor, the military court convened on 2 July 1945, with Colonel R.H.A. Kellie presiding, alongside five officers with the rank of lieutenant colonel or major. The prosecuting officer was Major Robert A.L. Hillard of the Judge Advocate General's Office. Standing trial were four Waffen-SS men – Erich Pallme Koenig, Kurt Zühlsdorff, Joachim Goltz and Heinz Brüling – together with Hans Klein (army), Josef Mertens (navy), Rolf Herzig (army) and Herbert Wunderlich (air force). The charge laid before them was 'committing a civil offence, that is to say murder, in that they at Comrie on December 23rd, 1944 murdered prisoner of war number 788778 Feldwebel Wolfgang Rosterg'.[16] Captain Kieser was one of two interpreters loaned by the London Cage to the court that day.

The court first heard from witness Corporal Fritz Heubner. The rest of the first day was taken up with translations, to ensure that the defendants understood the proceedings. Over the next three days, there was evidence from witnesses and cross-examination of the accused. Evidence was given by an officer of the Intelligence Corps (his name was blanked out in files, but he is thought to have been Herbert Sulzbach) who had been preparing evidence for the trial at Comrie.

On 5 July 1945, medical evidence was presented to the court by the camp doctor of the Royal Army Medical Corps (unnamed in the files that have been released) and by the doctor who conducted Rosterg's post-mortem. The court heard how Rosterg's head and face had suffered extensive bruising and how his eyes and ears had been injured from blows with a heavy weapon. By now it was clear that there was insufficient evidence to convict Klein, and he was sent to a POW camp. The following day, Kurt Zühlsdorff was questioned by Major Hillard and asked whether he had been prepared to help in the killing of Rosterg. 'Yes,' he replied. 'To hang him as befits a traitor.'[17]

In the early stages of the trial, Pallme Koenig, Zühlsdorff and Brüling slouched in their chairs and made no attempt to conceal their boredom. But as the trial progressed, it became clear that the defendants were facing the possibility of a death sentence – something they had not fully appreciated. It changed their outlook and they became more attentive. Rolf Herzig denied doing anything that would have caused Rosterg's death, but believed fervently that Rosterg was a traitor. Whatever part the defendants had played in the events at Comrie, all were united in believing that Rosterg had betrayed his country and deserved to die. Pallme Koenig admitted that, after a physical struggle with Rosterg, he had found documents in Rosterg's kitbag that 'would have made any German angry'.

Josef Mertens implicated himself in the murder when he admitted to the court:

It was clear to me that he [Rosterg] was the traitor and it was also clear that the man was dead. I seized the rope and helped to pull it for the last few yards to the pipe (of the latrine). I assisted in hanging up the body . . . I was of the opinion that a traitor should be found hanging.[18]

It was now 9 July, and Goltz, too, made no attempt to hide his guilt: 'I took hold of the rope in my hand and pulled the noose tight around Rosterg's neck again. The crying stopped when I knelt on Rosterg and pulled the rope tight. I assumed at this moment he died.'[19]

On 12 July 1945, the court in the oak-panelled room of 8 Kensington Palace Gardens gave its verdict on the seven men. Wunderlich was found not guilty and Herzig was sentenced to life imprisonment with hard labour. The remaining five were found guilty of murder and sentenced to death. The condemned men were sent to Kempton Park to await their fate. From there, Pallme Koenig wrote a letter to Colonel Scotland, thanking him for the fairness of the trial:

> After the end of our trial, and most likely the end of our stay here, I should like in the name of my comrades and in my own name to express to you, sir, our gratitude. Due to your advice, we asked for British officers to be assigned to us for our defence, and we have been agreeably surprised. Without your service we would most likely have made a different choice. Due to your, and the Major's instructions, our stay here has been alleviated. We were allowed to work and time passed quickly.[20]

A second hearing was convened at the London Cage on 29 August 1945 to establish whether six of the original suspects in the Comrie murder were guilty of manslaughter. Klein, Wunderlich, Recksiek, Steffan, Bienek and Jelinsky found themselves back in Kensington Palace Gardens. There was insufficient evidence to find them guilty.

On 6 October 1945, Pallme Koenig, Zühlsdorff, Goltz, Brüling and Mertens were hanged at Pentonville prison by Albert Pierrepoint, the death warrants signed by George VI. It was the largest multiple hanging since 1883.[21] Josef Mertens appreciated the fact that he was guilty and faced his punishment. Just nineteen years old, he stepped onto the scaffold and remarked: '*So jung, doch muss ich sterben*' ('So young, yet I must die').[22] It is true, though, as Scotland himself ruminated, that 'He died more quickly and humanely than Wolfgang Rosterg.'[23]

For Scotland:

> To me personally the outcome of the Devizes case was a tragedy. I reproached myself for having allowed Rosterg to go to Comrie and for not keeping him back and sending him to a fresh camp. But I had not anticipated that all the Devizes prisoners would be lumped together in one hut at Comrie where their bitterness could be allowed to ferment.[24]

9

GERMAN-JEWISH ÉMIGRÉS

As Allied forces battled through France after D-Day and the liberation of Belgium and Holland grew nearer, uppermost in the minds of Allied intelligence chiefs were the war crimes committed by the Nazi regime. The regime had been responsible for horrendous crimes, racial hatred and the Final Solution that had led to the murder of 6 million Jews. By the time the Allies liberated Auschwitz, Bergen-Belsen and Buchenwald concentration camps, the Nazis had already wiped out two-thirds of European Jewry and devastated the continent's culture on a scale never before seen. The unimaginable crimes also extended to the murder of 5 million others: Russians, Poles, homosexuals, the infirm and the elderly. Throughout the war, British intelligence had gathered first-hand and comprehensive evidence of mass murder and atrocities via the decoded Enigma messages at Bletchley Park and the bugging operation by CSDIC under Scotland's colleague, Colonel Kendrick. Thus, the London Cage shifted its focus from intelligence gathering to hunting down those Nazi war criminals responsible for the murder in cold blood of surrendering Allied airmen and soldiers. In addition, between June and September 1944, the cage received forty-seven complaints of war crimes by German forces against civilians.

Colonel Scotland did not have sufficient time to train new officers for the enormous workload ahead, and so he sought to bolster his staff with personnel from non-commissioned ranks who were totally familiar not only with the German language, but with the German character, and who had some knowledge of German laws and customs. He turned to the British army's Pioneer Corps, where thousands of German-Jewish émigrés, affectionately known as 'the king's most loyal enemy aliens', were serving in British military uniform. Many had been interned in 1940 on the Isle of Man and in camps around Britain, before swearing allegiance to George VI and enlisting in the forces of the country that had saved them from the death camps. Among them were Martin Eversfield, Gary Leon, Felek Scharf, Wilhelm Bonwitt, Michael Ullman, Sergeant Rhodes, Sergeant Macintosh, Sergeant Herbert Kyval and Arthur Morgenthau.

Sergeants Leon, Bonwitt and Ullman all transferred to the Intelligence Corps on the same day,[1] and were later described in a report as having 'rendered outstanding service and developed considerable ability in the interrogation of prisoners, especially where the taking of statements was required'.[2] Sergeants Rhodes and McIntosh originally arrived in England on the Kindertransport, the rescue scheme that permitted 10,000 children fleeing Nazi persecution to enter the country on a special visa without the full paperwork. They became a vital part of Scotland's team, engaged in translation and interrogation work.

Lieutenant R.A. Hepton was described as being 'exceedingly keen and proving a valuable addition to the staff'.[3] Captain C.D. Macintosh had experience of handling prisoners in CSDIC (and was later loaned as an interpreter to work at the Nuremberg trials). Sergeants Kyval, Morgenthau and Scharf initially worked at Kempton Park. Scharf later teamed up with Captain Pantcheff, Sergeant Morgenthau and Warrant Officer Bonwitt and travelled overseas for a time, working on the Emsland war crimes investigation.

In the absence of any female staff (apart from two ATS sergeants who worked for just a few weeks in 1945), Sergeants Rapp and Siegel were the translator typists. They were highly efficient, but, wrote Scotland, 'cannot deal completely with the present rush of work'.[4] Major Asche, a bilingual Norwegian speaker, was detailed to keep the records of the staff in order. The work of the intelligence officers was only possible because of the support staff at the London Cage: three officers undergoing training in interrogation duties, four sergeants, and eventually two temporary ATS sergeants maintaining efficiency in language and translations.

For all the controversy surrounding Scotland and his rough approach, he did demonstrate an understanding of his refugee staff. Indeed, he may have been particularly sympathetic to their plight as he had conducted his own rescue mission in 1933, while running a company in Argentina. According to his memoirs, he had petitioned and arranged for over 250 German-Jewish families at risk in Germany to leave the regime for South America.

Not only were they resettled in Argentina, but they worked for the company. Colonel Scotland has never received recognition for his rescue efforts.

Facing evil

Now in the London Cage, the German-Jewish refugees came face to face with the SS, Gestapo and other Nazi war criminals. The irony was not lost on them. They had fled the Nazi regime, members of their family had been killed in the concentration camps and now they faced the perpetrators. For them, the war suddenly became personal. Gary Leon had witnessed the Gestapo come for his father, Bernhard; he had been thrown down the stairs and had died instantly. Gary's mother was transported to Theresienstadt, where she died. Facing Nazi war criminals in the cage was never going to be easy. It must have been tempting to exact revenge. But the staff realised that the legal proceedings of the war crimes trials had to take their course and would bring them justice.

Leon's story is quite typical of the German-Jewish refugees who came to England to escape Nazi persecution and served in the British forces. He was born Gerhard Leon in Berlin in 1911, the youngest child of Bernhard and Gertrud. Having fled Nazi Germany, he was married at Hampstead Town Hall on 2 April 1938. After the outbreak of war in September 1939, he became an 'enemy alien', subject to restrictions; but he was fortunate in not being caught up in the mass internment of German-Jewish refugees on the Isle of Man (and at other internment camps around Britain). On 1 May 1940, he enlisted in the Pioneer Corps and undertook vital labour work for the war effort in Bermondsey, clearing the heavily blitzed areas of south London with his company before they moved to Somerset.

In March 1944, Leon noticed an army advertisement for fluent German speakers and applied. A series of interviews followed, one with a panel of German-speaking officers, the other with MI5. On 5 June 1944, he received a telegram ordering him to the War Office the following day. It was D-Day, 6 June, when Leon made his way to be given his instructions. He was to report to the cage at Kempton Park racecourse – ironically the site where some of his fellow refugees had been interned in 1940, under Churchill's policy of 'Collar the Lot!' Now the racecourse was being used for assessment and interrogation of captured German prisoners of war.

Leon arrived there with nine other German émigrés and was greeted by tough guards who he described as the scum of the earth. 'Rough, dishonest, thieving and often violent,' he later wrote.[5] Within hours, he and his colleagues were dealing with a new batch of prisoners. They were paraded and their identity papers confiscated for intelligence officers to go over for vital information about their units and military service history. That first day, the new refugee staff witnessed quite chaotic scenes, but things soon settled into a pattern of daily briefings from a member of the War Office. The cage became a very efficient unit in processing German prisoners of war. Gary Leon was promoted to sergeant, then sergeant major, and was posted from Kempton Park to the London Cage. He described his job at Kensington Palace Gardens as 'interesting and responsible'.[6] Apart from the guards, the intelligence staff were billeted in accommodation elsewhere, and walked to work each day. Leon wrote very little about he did at the cage, perhaps feeling that he was still bound by the Official Secrets Act, but he did still make some reference in his memoirs to hearing about the V-1 and V-2 'secret' weapons from the prisoners' interrogations.[7]

The Wehrmacht in the aftermath of D-Day

The biggest influx of Wehrmacht prisoners came after D-Day. Captured German prisoners of war now included men from other nations who had been conscripted to fight for the Nazi regime, among them a large number of Russians who were processed through the London Cage. They included several Russian boys aged between ten and fourteen who had been captured with various German units. When the Russian Military Commission heard about them, the commanding officer arrived at the London Cage to protect their interests. Colonel Scotland showed him around the cage and interrogation rooms to reassure him about conditions there, explaining that the boys were being well treated and were receiving food and shelter. They were eventually repatriated.

After D-Day, half a million Axis prisoners passed through reception centres in Britain.[8] In all the various cages under Scotland's command, the intelligence officers classified them and selected those who merited special interrogation. It was a massive organisational and logistical task. In November 1944, 21st Army Group urgently requested interrogators from Scotland's unit to help field interrogators in Belgium. Once the Allied forces finally crossed the border into Germany, a steady stream of prisoners was transferred to England for interrogation, first of all at the cage at Kempton Park. Their numbers varied from 1,000 to 5,000 a day.

Kempton Park was now under the charge of interrogators Captain Kieser and Captain Pantcheff, assisted by Warrant Officer Bonwitt. Sergeant Scharf was responsible for taking down statements and typing them up, aided with translation work by Sergeant Kyval. Prisoners' statements could run to many pages and were frequently written in a German script that was almost indecipherable. The contents were transcribed and subjected to careful scrutiny before being sent to proceedings, because they had to be accurate. The work of copying, translating and duplicating had to be carried out at the point of interrogation, so that any alterations that the prisoners wanted to make could be incorporated into the final document. Scotland issued instructions that every prisoner must be shown all documents before they were finally passed to the Judge Advocate General's Office. To ensure the swift movement of prisoners at any time between duty stations or other cages, the London Cage had at its disposal a 15-hundredweight lorry, a four-seater car, a two-seater car, and two prisoner-of-war vans supplied by 328 Motor Transport Company, so that there was no need to rely on public transport or special escorts.

The hundreds of interrogation reports yielded some valuable intelligence. For example, interrogators learned vital information about bunkers in the Henneville region from junior officer Ernst Schmidt, who had been captured on 25 June 1944. He provided detailed structural sketches of an armoured bunker at Wimereux in France.[9] Armed with some knowledge of the bunkers at Wimereux, the interrogators were then able to question other prisoners captured in the area. Johann Bonson, who was interrogated on 5 July, supplied their measurements, and gave details of how they were constructed and reinforced. He told his interrogator, for example, that the roofs and walls were between 1.8 and 2 metres thick, and that they had iron-reinforced gun encasements. This information would be important if the RAF were planning to attack the bunkers.

Lieutenant Herbert Krupke of a Panzer division, captured on 30 June 1944 at Greville, was interrogated at the London Cage on 11 July by Captain Sinclair, who described the prisoner as 'security-conscious and unwilling to talk'.[10] Jakob Grosser was captured north of Caen on 8 July 1944. During his interrogation at the London Cage by Captain Sinclair on 18 July, Grosser spoke about SS Division Frundsberg, which had a penal platoon consisting of SS men who had complained about conditions. To prevent widespread mutiny, the SS men were sentenced to serve five months at Danzig–Matzkau, a concentration camp for regular forces and

Waffen-SS. Grosser said that there was a special unit of these men fighting in the east.

Josef Siegel was interrogated by Captain Kettler on 18 October 1944. He had surrendered in Paris on 26 August 1944. Kettler's report concluded that 'he speaks fluent English with a strong American accent and claims to be strongly anti-Nazi'.[11] Siegel was called up to the German army in 1941, and from 1944 was attached to the German Secret Service. He was subjected to very detailed interrogation by Kettler to ascertain whether his connections were as harmless as he made out. Kettler concluded: 'This prisoner cannot be considered reliable.'[12] Unreliable maybe, but Siegel did reveal the living quarters in Paris of a section of the Abwehr known as 'Adverso', a cover name for agents who were being used as stool pigeons among American prisoners of war. All spoke English with an American accent, had complete American uniforms and identification badges, and before going on a mission were given fake papers, photos, dollar bills and genuine French money printed by the Allies.

Captured soldier Bernhard Podlaszewski had been based at headquarters at Bretteville and spoke about coastal defences near Cherbourg.[13] He confirmed that his company numbered approximately 300 men with a mobile reserve of thirty cyclists, and that it defended six concrete emplacements. He provided MI19 with information that a large hotel near La Panne was being used as a German wireless station. At the top of the dunes was a series of bunkers situated 100 metres apart, and three lines of trenches from the French frontier to Nieuport. The trenches were about 70 centimetres deep, banked with sand and covered with bundled reeds, and connected by communication trenches dug under the road. Copies of information from this interrogation report were distributed to numerous branches of the intelligence services, including MI5, MI6, MI10, MI14, MI19, CSDIC, Air Intelligence ADI(K) and Naval Intelligence Division. After D-Day, a number of Panzer division prisoners were interrogated about order of battle and troop movements. They confirmed that German military vehicles were well camouflaged with tree branches.[14]

Corporal Florian Pucher handed over a photograph of a group of British prisoners in Germany taken in 1943, and told his interrogator, Captain Kettler, that they were billeted 30 kilometres south-south-east of Graz, where they worked the land under the watch of a single German guard.[15] He knew this because his father had had two rooms requisitioned by the

1 A photograph of Nos. 8 and 8a Kensington Palace Gardens, taken in 1938 by 'the German Section of the Foreign Office, Hayes' during the search for suitable premises to requisition 'for special purposes' after the outbreak of war.

2 The northern gatehouse entrance to Kensington Palace Gardens, taken by 'the German Section of the Foreign Office' in 1938. On the left can be seen Nos. 6 and 7 which later became the London Cage during the Second World War.

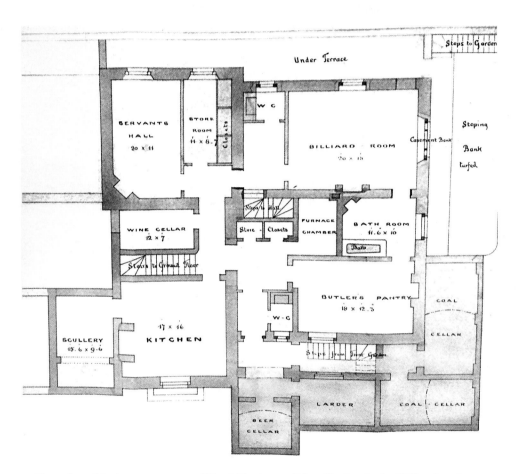

3 Floor plan of the basement rooms of No. 8 Kensington Palace Gardens in the 1930s when the building was leased by Lord Duveen. During the war these basement rooms were soundproofed and used for interrogations and various other treatments of prisoners. One of these rooms was kitted out as 'Cell 14'.

4 Colonel Alexander Paterson Scotland.

5 German prisoners of war newly arrived at the Kempton Park 'cage', being briefed by British soldiers about their status and camp discipline.

6 German prisoners being searched after the Bruneval raid, 1942.

7 Major Lovatt's forces marching for embarkation upon the raid on Bologne, accompanied by an intelligence officer from the London Cage.

8 Interrogator Randoll Coate.

9 Interrogator Kenneth Morgan, sketched by a German prisoner at the London Cage.

WHATEVER'S IN HIS POCKETS, YOU MAY **WANT** IT, INTELLIGENCE **NEED** IT! **HAND IT OVER**

10 A Second World War intelligence poster.

11 Field Marshal Albert Kesselring, who was befriended by Colonel Scotland while being interrogated at the London Cage as a possible war criminal.

12 Nazi war criminal SS General Kurt Meyer, interrogated at the London Cage.

13 An RAF aerial photograph of the paddock of Kensington Palace which became a temporary annexe camp alongside the London Cage, 'for secret purposes', in preparation for the increased numbers of prisoners captured after D-Day. It is possible to see the forty-nine bell tents and ancillary buildings used for the canteen, wash facilities and some preliminary interrogations. The camp has a triple barbed wire fence around it. This photograph was taken in 1946 just after the camp annexe was vacated by the War Office.

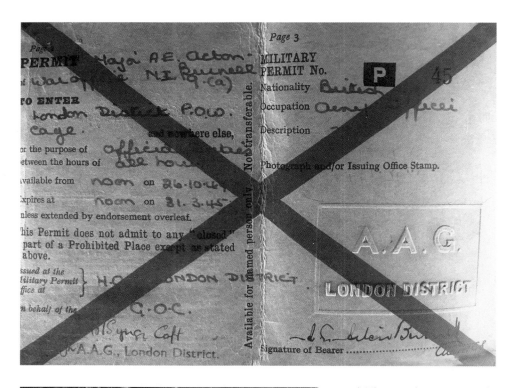

PERMIT

TO ENTER

and nowhere else,

or the purpose of

between the hours of

available from   noon on 26·10·4

Expires at   noon on 31·3·45

unless extended by endorsement overleaf.

This Permit does not admit to any "closed" part of a Prohibited Place except as stated above.

Issued at the Military Permit Office at   H.Q. LONDON DISTRICT

On behalf of the   G.O.C.

A.A.G., London District.

MILITARY PERMIT No.

Nationality   British

Occupation

Description

Photograph and/or Issuing Office Stamp.

A.A.G.

LONDON DISTRICT

Signature of Bearer ....

Non-transferable.

Available for named person only.

P   45

14 The special entry pass to the London Cage held by Major Bertie Acton Burnell of MI19.

15 Members of the battalion of SS soldiers who carried out the massacre of surrendering British soldiers at Le Paradis, France, 1940.

16 SS Lieutenant Colonel Fritz Knöchlein, the commander who gave the order to shoot the captured British soldiers at Le Paradis, which constituted a war crime.

17 The farmhouse where the Le Paradis massacre took place, the bullet holes in the wall still chillingly visible.

18 SS General Sepp Dietrich.

19 The site of the Wormhoudt massacre, 1940.

Manor
as, were
a light-
rs at the
rage in

depots are
l distribu-

me when
to about

spreading
," stated an
n Co-opera-
it is unoffi-
nd out what

n are stand-
result of a
rs at Strat-
hen they will
n the strikers.

emand

hich was de-
al garage be-
ent out to the
distributed to
got the big
risen, the men

WAR CRIMINAL
KILLS HIMSELF.

FOUND HANGED IN KENSINGTON 'CAGE'

"Evening News" Reporter

A PRISONER of war believed to be guilty of war crimes has hanged himself in the P.O.W. "cage" in Kensington Palace-gardens.

Because of his complicity in war crimes, the name and nationality of this man will be kept secret.

When the West London coroner, Dr. H. Neville Stafford, holds an inquest this week he will ask the Press, on behalf of the War Office, not to publish the name, so that justice will not be defeated.

Careful steps have been taken by military and police authorities to prevent any leakage of his identity.

LOST HIS HOME

German P.o.W.'s Suicide

Couple Retu
MAN
WITH
were

"EVE

A 27-YEAR-OLI
in a struggle
and his wife fou
from a darts clu

The injured
repairer, was ly
afternoon "in a
were fired, and
about 40 yards
Kent police this a
hunting for a man
in height, aged bet
35, hatless, and pos
a navy blue overcoa

A Scuf

20 A rare news report, one of the few to ever emerge about the London Cage during its existence, which appeared in the *Evening News*, 7 March 1946. The prisoner has not been publicly named.

21 The written statement by Major-General Hermann-Bernhard Ramcke made during his time at the London Cage, August 1946.

22 Field Marshal Gerd von Rundstedt interviewed at the London Cage in connection with war crimes.

23 The War Crimes Investigation Unit outside the London Cage. Seated in the middle of the front row is Colonel Alexander Scotland. He is flanked on his left by Miss Metzler, and on his right by Lucy Haley. On the back row, third from left is Gary Leon, and furthest left is Martin Eversfield.

24 The Russian Embassy today, Nos. 6–7 Kensington Palace Gardens.

25 At his desk, Ian Fleming, who recruited Antony Terry, senior interrogator and deputy at the London Cage, to work for the foreign section of *The Sunday Times* from 1949–80.

German government to house the prisoners. The photograph was passed to MI9's escape and evasion headquarters at Wilton Park in Buckinghamshire.

Colonel Scotland proved a match for any of the German generals, including Major-General Hermann-Bernhard Ramcke, who found himself in the London Cage in the summer of 1946. Ramcke was described as a bombastic, nasty man who sought to blame others for the crimes of the regime, 'a dark, swarthy, hairy individual, aggressive and self-assured'.[16] On arrival in the cage, Ramcke had written his memoirs and proceeded to read extracts to the guards – extracts that included alleged atrocities committed by New Zealand troops while Ramcke was serving in Crete in 1941.

Prior to questioning Ramcke, Scotland ensured that all chairs were removed from the office except his own. The 57-year-old paratroop general, who been captured near Brest after the Allied invasion of France, was then brought in by the guards. Scotland told Ramcke that he understood that the general had made trouble in the cage. Ramcke was offended by this accusation, and told Scotland that he resented it. Scotland stood up and began pacing to and fro. This was to be a battle of minds. Scotland alleged that Ramcke had breached international law by moving his fighting troops in vehicles flying the Red Cross flag. Ramcke denied the charge and became furious with Scotland.

Scotland then turned to the offending pages in Ramcke's memoirs and read aloud the section where Ramcke made allegations that New Zealand troops had cut off the ears of captured German paratroopers and mounted them on their hats as a victory prize. He reportedly bellowed at Ramcke that these allegations were unworthy of a German officer and of his rank as a general, and demanded that a letter be written immediately withdrawing the allegations. Ramcke refused. Scotland called in the guard and Ramcke was marched back to his cell to reflect on his lack of cooperation.

In his cell, Ramcke perhaps did realise that the tables might be turned on him and he could find himself accused of war crimes; the best option, then, would be to cooperate and get out of the London Cage as quickly as possible. He penned a letter immediately to Scotland:

> The derogatory remarks which I have made in my book *Cabin Boy to Paratroop General* regarding the behaviour of British troops in Crete, particularly the Maoris, resulted from ignorance and from the feeling of bitter indignation which overcame the paratroops there after the

conclusion of the fighting in Crete . . . I therefore humbly ask that this declaration be accepted and made use of to clear up existing misunderstandings. Humbly, H.B. Ramcke.[17]

His full statement withdrawing all allegations was signed on 11 August 1946.

Commando Order: No quarter

On 18 October 1942, Adolf Hitler issued the Commando Order, which stated that 'no quarter' was to be given to captured members of the special forces – in other words, there was to be no clemency. Hitler had become enraged at the Allied commando raids behind the lines and the successful sabotage missions. The Commando Order read:

> All men operating against German troops in so-called Commando raids in Europe or in Africa are to be annihilated to the last man. This is to be carried out whether they be soldiers in uniform, or saboteurs, with or without arms, and whether fighting or seeking to escape . . . I will hold all Commanders and Officers responsible under Military Law for any omission to carry out this order.[18]

The order was a direct breach of the laws of war and was intended to remain secret from the Allies; but it was discovered, and fell within the category of war crimes for investigation by Colonel Scotland.

German Luftwaffe officer Friedrich von der Heydte was brought to the London Cage for questioning about Hitler's Commando Order. He made 'a voluntary statement and without duress' in the presence of Captain Terry on 26 October 1945, in which he denied ever implementing Hitler's killing order.[19] He claimed not to remember if he had signed the order or whether he had passed it on to divisional commanders. He told Captain Terry that the only British commando unit he ever came across was in Africa in September 1942: 'I treated them in the same way in which I always treat prisoners of war, and in the way a courageous opponent is entitled to expect according to the unwritten law of chivalry.'[20]

At the same time as Heydte was held in the cage, First Lieutenant Hoff was brought in and accused of issuing Hitler's Commando Order. He denied the charges. But the cage was also holding three Polish witnesses. One, Private Edmund Zalewski, confirmed that Hoff had been given the order, and vividly remembered the day that Hoff had paraded the whole company, read it out and then destroyed the written version.[21] To verify Zalewski's story, a group of German officers was brought out of the London Cage to the parade ground in the paddock of Kensington Palace, and Zalewski was asked to identify anyone he recognised. He pointed to Hoff without hesitation. The following day, Hoff sent a note to Colonel Scotland admitting that he had been with the company at the time, but denying ever reading out the Commando Order; he did admit, however, to reading Hitler's order 'to fight to the last man, last round'.

Zalewski gave interrogators the name of a former colleague and witness, Grenadier Nagel, who was tracked down at Camp 35 at Boughton Park near Northampton and brought to the London Cage. When questioned, Nagle could not remember the order or the company briefing by Hoff. Consequently, Scotland sent two interrogators to Camp 35 to question a number of other prisoners who had served under Hoff. Only four could remember a briefing, but none recalled Hoff reading out the Commando Order. The Commando Order would surface again in the cage in the context of war crimes, and would become the focus of an important war crimes investigation.

Nazi gold

October 1945 saw the arrival at the London Cage of Major-General Otto Wagener, who had taken over command of Rhodes and the eastern Aegean on 23 September 1944, at a time when Allied forces were mounting the Ardennes offensive in Western Europe and had already captured Brussels. Wagener commanded around 6,000 German soldiers, half of them troops from 999 Division. The reputation of 999 Division was already known at the London Cage due to some of its members having arrived there after the defeat of Rommel's troops in North Africa in 1942 (see page 56). Colonel Scotland had once described them as 'rabid Nazis' who were heavily indoctrinated in Nazi ideology.[22] They were tough ex-convicts, who had spent time in concentration camps but whose sentences had been reduced when they volunteered to serve in the crack SS battalion. Wagener's testimony would be quite astonishing.

MI19 had knowledge of possible Nazi gold buried on Rhodes (the source of the information was not named). Allied intelligence was desperately trying to track and prevent the movement of Nazi gold out of

Germany, mostly – it was thought – being transported on special trains. When interrogated about the Rhodes gold, at first Wagener denied any knowledge of it. Later, however, he would tell a different story.

On 29 April 1945, just a week before Germany's final surrender and the day before Hitler committed suicide in his bunker, Wagener had been in hospital with a type of typhus. He had received a visit from his chief of staff and the quartermaster, Herr Becker. They reported that the last plane to leave Germany for Rhodes had already departed from an aerodrome near Linz, carrying the gold bound for Rhodes and Crete. A Turkish firm in Constantinople had been instructed to deliver to Crete food for the German troops there, for which it would be paid in gold. The two men at Wagener's bedside wanted to establish what should be done with the gold in the event of surrender to the Allies, which was expected imminently. Major-General Wagener recognised that it would be impossible now to dispatch the gold to Crete, and that 'the best plan would be to place the whole lot in a coffin and inter it properly in the soldiers' cemetery'.[23] Wagener expressed the opinion to Scotland that the gold belonged to the German government, and hoped that it would not fall into the hands of the British authorities.

Twelve hours after his interrogation, Wagener sent a note to Colonel Scotland to say that he realised the significance of the questioning on the gold and had some further information to add to his statement. He said that his testimony could be verified by Major-General Benthack, the commandant of Crete, with whom he had shared a room in the British prisoner-of-war camp in Cairo. Crucially, he added that he believed the weight of the gold buried in the coffin was 17 kilograms. He said that he had always intended to build a special home near the German cemetery at Kameiros in Rhodes for those soldiers who had fought in the Aegean, and maintained that the gold had been set aside for this purpose. As he told interrogators:

> The gold was buried in a proper grave where all the new graves were. I would refer to the small photo (taken of the cemetery) which I have handed over . . . The position of the grave was on the left hand side on the extreme outside; but I cannot remember whether it was the last row or the last row but one. The cross was to bear the name Stein or Steiner or something similar.[24]

Wagener added finally: 'The suspicion is unfounded that the gold was sent so that it could be hidden on Rhodes for future use.' There the paper trail goes cold. It is not known if Colonel Scotland informed the intelligence services or whether the gold was subsequently dug up and hidden in Allied territory.

War Crimes Investigation Unit

Until Germany's unconditional surrender on 7 May 1945, the London Cage's role would continue to be to gather intelligence. But that would change as it made the transition to the unique role it would play in war crimes investigations. These began at the London Cage in 1944, but on nothing like the scale seen in 1945–48. By then the concentration camps had been liberated and the full extent of Nazi brutality had been revealed. While the world expressed its shock and tried to comprehend the scale of the extermination machine, Scotland and his team quietly turned their attention to other acts of Nazi brutality. They were specifically tasked with investigating war crimes against Allied soldiers, airmen and special forces. To this end, they were formed into a new unit: the War Crimes Investigation Unit (WCIU).

The London Cage became the most important centre outside Germany to deal with high-profile Nazi war criminals. Yet its vital contribution is rarely referenced in histories of the Second World War or the war crimes trials. Between October 1945 and the end of September 1948, 3,573 prisoners of war and enemy civilians passed through its doors. Many were eyewitnesses, who provided details of war crimes for the prosecution's case against numerous Nazi war criminals; many of those Nazis were tracked down by Scotland's own teams. The strength of his staff increased to forty officers and NCOs, some stationed at Kempton Park, Lingfield Park and abroad. Their work was an administrative challenge that generated thousands of interrogation reports on atrocities committed against Allied soldiers and airmen in all theatres of the war, as well as against civilians and Allied special forces; all were for direct use in the trials that followed.

The atmosphere intensified as the cage braced itself to receive some of the highest-ranking Nazi leaders and war criminals – many of them reviled even before they crossed the threshold of Kensington Palace Gardens. Among them were the commandants of liberated concentration camps, as well as SS General Sepp Dietrich, SS General Kurt Meyer, General Nikolaus von Falkenhorst, SS Colonel General Reinhold Bruchardt (commander of a murder squad in Danzig), Colonel General Adolf Strauss and Field Marshal Albert Kesselring. Held there, too, were a number of German generals who were being interrogated as witnesses: General von Manstein, Field Marshal von Brauchitsch, Major-General Ramcke (see above) and Field Marshal von Rundstedt. A former witness to this period commented: 'Rundstedt was neatly dressed, had a moustache, high cheek bones and was very military and correct. We had him for 4–6 weeks.' Major Roger Mortimer, who occasionally visited the London Cage from Wellington Barracks, said of Rundstedt: 'I grew fond of old von Rundstedt, the best type of Prussian officer. He never complained and sometimes I used to take him for a cocktail and have a chat with him.'[25]

The purpose of holding the generals in the cage was to find out from them what they knew about war crimes, whether the orders that had led to the atrocities had been issued by commanders below them, and if so, what they knew about those orders. The generals could be held for several days if there was much to ask them.

The London Cage no longer collected intelligence from military sources, as it had done during the war. Now it was dealing with the most heinous crimes – crimes that would test the interrogators' patience to the absolute limit. The work would keep them busy for three years. In the first two of those years they would struggle to cope with the sheer number of Nazi war criminals and witnesses who crossed the threshold as part of the investigations. The rooms were crammed with men undergoing special and detailed interrogation for varying lengths of time. This placed a huge strain on the interrogators, who worked long days and evenings to get through the workload. As soon as an interrogation was completed, or a voluntary statement given by a prisoner or witness, the paperwork was dispatched to a secret location for typing up. It was an enormous logistical challenge, executed with great efficiency by the close-knit team at the London Cage. The huge volume of files surviving today in the National Archives is testament to their efforts.

In addition, time was spent trying to hunt down the whereabouts of suspected war criminals, with no assurance of success. When a wanted war criminal was finally located in hiding or in an internment camp, the paperwork had to be arranged and his formal transfer to London organised by special escort.

The London Cage witnessed plenty of drama as Scotland dealt with some of the highest-ranking leaders of the Nazi regime and commanders of the German forces. One such person was navy captain Hellmuth von

Ruckteschell, who commanded the *Neumark*, an armed merchant ship which had orders to become a raider to sink Allied ships. Ruckteschell had shown no mercy to the drowning crews struggling in the sea. He was eventually given a new raider, *R28*, and ran missions to the Far East, finally giving over his ship to the Japanese. Not relishing any further fighting on behalf of his Führer, he had no intention of going to sea again.

After the Japanese surrender in August 1945, British forces tracked Ruckteschell down in Shanghai and transported him back to England, where he appeared before Scotland in the London Cage. The slight, bronze-skinned figure standing before Colonel Scotland was described by him as a 'weedy-looking spiv dressed in a pressed Palm Beach suit, gaudy tie and white and brown shoes'.[26] Ruckteschell strutted around Scotland's office with an arrogance that would immediately be challenged.

Scotland asked him a few personal questions, then turned to technical details of raider *R28*. Ruckteschell began to shout, demanding that his interrogation be carried out by a naval commander. Scotland bawled at him: 'Stand to attention you miserable traitor! Remain at attention until I give you orders to leave this room!'[27] Scotland asked the guard to take Ruckteschell out, provide him with work clothes and set him to chores in the kitchens. Ruckteschell was told that he was not to address Scotland unless he asked permission, at which point his request would be considered. If he caused any trouble, the guards were to remind him that the only reason he was in the cage was because of his murders at sea, and that he would only leave the cage for his trial.

Just twenty-four hours later, Ruckteschell asked to see Scotland. But Scotland refused to see him, because the guards still found him arrogant and defiant. Instead he responded by increasing Ruckteschell's chores around the cage. After three days, Ruckteschell stood in front of Scotland again, this time a docile figure who had accepted his discipline. There was no more trouble from him. In May 1946, he came before a war crimes court in Hamburg and was sentenced to ten years' imprisonment. Sent to Fuhlsbüttel prison, he died there of a heart condition on 24 June 1948.

One CSDIC/MI19 interrogator, Matthew Sullivan, summed up the situation: 'The cage in its cool pursuit of justice became a hot-house of guilt, defiance and fear ... Some nasty characters were being sent for examination and the outcome now might be a jail sentence or even death. To make the bully feel small gave great pleasure to certain interrogators.'[28]

10

A MATTER OF JUSTICE

In the spring of 1945, the world was shocked by the scenes captured on film of the liberation of the concentration camps. Across Europe, towns and cities lay desolate from aerial bombing, their communities in chaos, and thousands of displaced people in civilian internment camps. The continent bore the physical and psychological scars of a bloody war that had wreaked so much suffering and death on millions of ordinary people, not least through the Nazis' horrifying systematic programme of mass extermination. The Allies began the slow process of restoring democracy to post-war Europe, a task that necessitated the denazification of every stratum of German and Austrian society, government, law and civic life. For democracy to succeed, there could be no surviving remnants of the Nazi regime to rise up and take power again. For post-war peace and stability, those Nazi war criminals who had gone into hiding had to be hunted down and brought to justice.

'The entire history of the Hitler regime is riddled with acts of grossest and most inhuman cruelty,' wrote Colonel Scotland.[1] Now, it would seem, he felt justified in showing no tolerance or mercy to Nazi war criminals in his cage. He and his staff were disgusted by what the Nazis had done to Jews, civilians and surrendering Allied personnel. Pitted now against the Nazi war criminals, Scotland was determined to bring them to justice for their crimes, if it was the last thing he did. It became a very personal mission. He vowed to track down every name on the London Cage's list of wanted war criminals.

The Allied powers had compiled a list of suspected Nazi war criminals that ran to over 60,000 names. Printed in four volumes and with two supplementary lists, it was known collectively as the Central Registry of War Criminals and Security Suspects (CROWCASS). The Allies had agreed that all security suspects and alleged war criminals were to be transferred first to one of five holding camps in Germany: Esterwegen, Fallingbostel, Sandbostel, Recklinghausen and Westertimke. Colonel Scotland's teams travelled to Germany and scoured the holding camps and civilian internment camps for war criminals who were hiding under assumed names or masquerading as refugees. When discovered, the suspects were transferred to the London Cage for extensive interrogation. The task of tracking down Nazi war criminals was slow and painstaking work. As well as CROWCASS, interrogators made use of an extensive card index of war criminals already created by the headquarters of the British Army of the Rhine (BAOR). The Allied Control Commission had numerous files with evidence of war crimes. Scotland's teams could draw on them and prisoner records across all prisoner-of-war camps.

Once suspected war criminals were in the London Cage, an effective tactic was to place a particular prisoner in solitary confinement in a room next to another carefully chosen prisoner. The men would soon discover that the flues from the fireplaces in their rooms merged further up, allowing them to have a conversation. An eyewitness recalled: 'They chatted up the chimney to each other. They thought they were so clever, but they gave away all kinds of information because we had placed bugging devices in the chimney and were able to record their conversations. It was wired back to an M Room in the basement.'[2]

Investigations into a prisoner's past paralleled police methods, and involved reconstructing events, asking the prisoner to write down his version of events and his part in the incident or war crime being investigated. The written account was useful, because it could be checked against known evidence and used to induce other prisoners to tell the truth. The interrogators always emphasised that they were not there to try a suspected war criminal. That was a matter for the courts. The purpose of their interrogation was to give the prisoner an opportunity to defend himself with his own written account, and to convince the interrogation team that he was innocent and should not be passed on to a court for trial. The interrogators presented the prisoner with the facts and evidence against him, and asked for his response. Scotland and senior interrogators made the final decision on the basis of the evidence available, and the prisoner's statement was sent over to the war crimes trials.

Scotland and his staff soon discovered that interrogating war criminals in 1945 and 1946 was very different from questioning German forces personnel for general military intelligence. The mentality of the two kinds of prisoner was very different. According to the Geneva Convention, a captured prisoner was only obliged to give his name, rank and number. The interrogation became a battle of minds between interrogator and prisoner. In contrast, a suspected war criminal usually spoke freely in order to clear his name. He tried to cover up his guilt by denying all knowledge of the war crime or by implicating others. Psychologically, if a war criminal was guilty, it was uppermost in his mind. Nazi war criminals spent a lot of time in their rooms at the London Cage fretting about how to fool the interrogator into believing that they were innocent. They adopted a number of strategies: some tried to distract the interrogator with irrelevant stories; others found fault with the manner of interrogation. The interrogator had to be astute enough to spot the weaknesses in any argument. If the interrogator lost his patience, then the interrogation had failed and another interrogator had to take over. All allegations of abuse of prisoners in the cage that arose at this time were flatly denied by Scotland and the military.

During the First World War, Scotland had not been tortured by the Germans while a prisoner in Windhoek prison, but he had been kept in solitary confinement. He knew from personal experience what it took for a prisoner to hold out and what would make him break. The official British military guidelines on captured prisoners were clear: 'Prisoners are not to be made to adopt any stress positions.'[3] The tactic used in the interrogation of suspected war criminals was to confront them with all the knowledge in the possession of the interrogators. If that did not induce them to talk, they lost their status as prisoners and became suspects, with no rights. If the prisoner was former Gestapo, then he was required to kneel during interrogation. No reason was ever given to justify that practice.[4] Scotland summed up the methods:

> It was true that all the confessions of guilt were obtained by psychology and a knowledge of the German mind. It was not difficult. No German will tell the whole truth when he is accused, but will tell a little and reserve what he can for his defence. Once he has been presented with statements made by others which implicate him, he will volunteer more information which although to his disadvantage, will also implicate others with whom he had been associated. Time after time we built

up our information by this method of getting a fact and 'putting it back' to a prisoner, invariably with the same result – eventually the writing of a full statement or confession. No force was necessary.[5]

Major Terry was back at the London Cage as the most senior interrogator below Scotland, coordinating and working on the war crimes investigations. Captain Ryder and Lieutenant Hepton continued their work as interrogators, aided by Warrant Officer Ullman, who also took down statements from the prisoners. Sergeants Rapp and Siegel carried on with the translating and typing of statements. Warrant Officer Gary Leon and Sergeant Martin Eversfield were responsible for tracing prisoners on the Allies' list of wanted war criminals. Finding the whereabouts of prisoners from records kept by the British, American and French departments was a painstaking task, and required Leon and Eversfield to be completely au fait with the details of the allegations. It was one thing for them to be native German speakers, but for their searches to be productive, they also had to have knowledge of the German army and its formations.

Sometimes an encounter with a prisoner took an unexpected turn. There was one interrogator who had been captured on a special mission during the war. When he was finally released from the German camp, he resumed his duties at the London Cage. There, he came face to face one day with a Gestapo officer who had physically abused him while he had been a prisoner of war. Although the interrogator was not named in reports or in Scotland's memoirs, he is thought to have been Major Terry, who was captured during the Saint-Nazaire Raid in 1942. No charges could be brought against the Gestapo officer, because permanent injury had not been inflicted on the interrogator; but Scotland saw no reason why they should not indulge in the same sort of treatment. The stage for the re-enactment was Scotland's office. It was a much milder version of the abuse suffered by the interrogator: a swagger cane was pushed down the back of the Gestapo officer's neck (as had been done to the British prisoner), his hair was pulled and he was gripped aggressively on the shoulder, while Scotland bawled in his ear in German. As a further punishment, the Gestapo man was given three days of cleaning toilets in the cage. It was enough to break his will to resist and he became introverted and contrite.

The London Cage investigated some of the most notorious war crimes ever committed against Allied soldiers and airmen, including the Emsland,

Wormhoudt (page 135), Le Paradis (chapter 11) and Sagan (chapter 12) cases. A significant number involved British personnel. For example, the interrogation team had to try to establish the whereabouts of Lieutenant Gerhard Preil, wanted in connection with the shooting of members of the 2nd SAS Regiment at La Fosse farm, Pexonne, north-eastern France, on 19 September 1944 (several SAS deaths were investigated at the London Cage).[6] Amidst all this, interrogators also interviewed German civilians in connection with the conditions endured by Polish workers in the Modrow and Niwka mines, where there had been numerous deaths. Heinrich Hautau was one such civilian. As the manager overseeing the treatment of Polish workers and giving out daily orders, he was brought to the London Cage for questioning. The issue of slave labour was uppermost in the mind of his interrogator, Captain Cornish, to whom he gave two signed statements on 5 and 12 March 1946.[7]

Other war crimes included the murder of five British special forces prisoners near Noailles on 9 August 1944.[8] The previous month, a party of nine SAS had been dropped near Paris, where they had been ambushed. One was shot and later died; another was wounded and taken to hospital in Paris. The remaining seven were taken to Gestapo headquarters at 84/86 Avenue Foch in Paris and interrogated, although not tortured. On 9 August, the prisoners were moved north of the capital to be executed; two made a break for it and got away. The other five were shot in a murder that was 'particularly brutal and cold blooded'.[9] All attempts by the military to find the culprits had failed, and the case was given to Colonel Scotland. He and his team tracked down the Gestapo officers and interrogators who had worked at the Avenue Foch headquarters. Their interrogation reports now survive in the National Archives.[10]

The SS and concentration camps

The vast volume of work had to be juggled with routine daily requests to the London Cage from other Allied organisations for information and evidence about certain war criminals for their own investigations. Most pertained to atrocities committed by the SS. Scotland's unit created a card index for every SS prisoner held in camps in Britain. Some 23,000 SS prisoners were catalogued – a task that took three months to complete.

Cells at the London Cage began to fill with SS prisoners, the ultra-tough die-hard men who had sworn an oath of loyalty to Hitler to fight to the bitter end. Now that they faced Scotland and his interrogators they seemed resolved to remain defiant and unrepentant for their crimes. The interrogators heard details of some of the worst crimes committed by the SS. One of the most difficult accounts to hear must have been when SS prisoners gave details of the slaughter of 42,000 Polish-Jewish men, women and children in a single fourteen-hour period near Lublin. The order had been given by SS Lieutenant-General Jakob Sporrenberg, acting on the direct orders of Heinrich Himmler, head of the SS, who had sent 2,000 SS troops and 250 expert killers from the Auschwitz concentration camp.[11] With Sporrenberg now in the London Cage, the interrogators found it difficult to restrain themselves. The SS man stood before them, accused of directing one of the most shocking slaughters of the Hitler regime.

'Sporrenberg was typical of the thugs used by the Nazis to carry out their policies,'[12] said Colonel Scotland. Sporrenberg's file describes him as a man of very little education, who had risen through the ranks of the Nazi party and into the SS, to become SS chief in the areas of Minsk (Belarus) and Lublin (Poland). It contains graphic details of Hitler's orders for the killing of the Jews in Lublin.[13] Facing Colonel Scotland across the room, Sporrenberg maintained that he and his men were innocent of the Lublin killings, but under close interrogation he appeared to know that around 16,000 Jews from Łódź had been killed, along with 14,000 from Camp Poniatowa and 12,000 from Camp Trawniki. During interrogation on 25 February 1946, Warrant Officer Ullman confronted Sporrenberg with the fact that these figures added up to a total of 42,000 people. The atrocity had involved 150 SS, who on average had each killed 250 people an hour.[14]

In the London Cage report, dated 25 February 1946, Colonel Scotland concluded of Sporrenberg that he was

one of Hitler's earliest and most fanatical supporters who, by his efficiency, zeal and success quickly rose to high rank and important position with the SS, and security police . . . His guilt in the extermination of scores of thousands of Jews, including Polish prisoners of war, is obvious, and even if the main burden of the work of killing 42,000 innocent human beings rested on his henchmen, such a task could not have been carried out by a mere handful of men in 14 hours. Sporrenberg's commanders had brought the victims to their place of execution and then provided guards to see that none would escape their fate.[15]

Sporrenberg was handed over to the Polish authorities to stand trial. He was convicted of war crimes in 1950, sentenced to death and executed in December 1952.

Prisoners arrived in the cage who had served in the Panzer divisions. One was Franz van Lent of 1st Company, 17 SS Panzergrenadier Division, who had been captured on 3 August 1944. His interrogation report shows that he was questioned at the London Cage about atrocities committed against Jews in the Warsaw Ghetto. Part of his file reads:

> 18 April 1944. 0400 hrs. Trained soldiers entered the Ghetto to round up the Jews. The Jews who were well armed put up such a defence that the SS troops had to leave the Ghetto after approximately one hour. Order was then given to the Turkestan Unit to open fire with their two Russian guns until the first houses were set aflame. The SS troops then entered the Ghetto to drive the people who had survived the shelling onto the market square where they were shot down by M.G. [machine gun] fire. This procedure was systematically carried out from block to block from the outskirts of the Ghetto towards the centre. The operation lasted one month.[16]

Franz van Lent told his interrogators that 45,000 Jews had lived in the ghetto before 18 April 1944, and that virtually no one was left after the atrocity. He was told by SS men from his company that a number of Jews had been taken to the concentration camp in Litzmannstadt (Łódź). He named SS personnel in the units whom he had witnessed murdering Jews in the streets and on the main square of the Warsaw Ghetto.

Hans Aumeier, the son of a rifle-factory worker, was interrogated on 28 January 1946 in connection with his activities as penal camp leader in Auschwitz concentration camp, between June 1942 and May 1943. Interrogators knew that between 15 January 1934 and April 1936 he had served at Dachau concentration camp, where he had first been 'trained', and then had been at Flossenbürg from 1 May 1939 until 15 February 1942.[17] He maintained that during his whole service at Dachau, he had no contact whatsoever with the prisoners, and had never committed any acts of murder or ill-treatment: he had been engaged solely in training new personnel outside the prisoners' compound.

Aumeier was not prepared to admit the full extent of his own guilt in the mass executions carried out at Auschwitz during his tenure, and blamed it on his superiors, Himmler and Rudolf Höss (the commandant at Auschwitz). It was clear, though, that he had been quite willing to pass on orders to his subordinates to undertake killings and other atrocities. His intelligence report summed him up thus:

> In appearance he does not conform to the standards set by the Third Reich leaders for the Master Race. Undersized, ugly, and unintelligent. Aumeier has resigned himself to being brought to account as a member of the Auschwitz staff for the bestialities perpetrated there and to take the punishment due to him. Prisoner has admitted to other prisoners that the information he has so far given of his activities represents only part of his story, and he is of the view that if the Allies want to know any more let them find out.[18]

The interrogators were primed to ask exceptionally detailed questions about prisoners who had worked in the concentration camps. Aumeier provided so much detailed information on the killings and camps that his interrogation report ran to several pages. Some of the information that he volunteered concerned gas chamber executions:

> Prisoner states that during his period at Auschwitz between 15,000 and 18,000 people were gassed to death in the gas chambers. He denies responsibility, alleging that gassings were carried out by a special task-force and camp guards directly responsible to the camp commandant. Prisoner says he witnessed these gassings on several occasions, some-times together with the Camp Commandant, sometimes alone.[19]

Aumeier denied selecting prisoners for the execution, maintaining that that had been the responsibility of the doctors who, on the arrival of new batches of prisoners, immediately picked out those who were unable to perform heavy work. They were then taken by lorry to the gas chambers and crematorium about 2 miles from the camp. What happened next was described in graphic detail by Aumeier:

> On arrival they were taken into a hut where they had to undress after which they were driven into the gas-chambers. They were told that they were to be disinfected, and in fact the word *Disinfection* was written on the outside of the gas-chamber. Then the doors were closed

and a member of the execution squad poured the gas into the chamber through a small opening at the top or side. The gas was Zyklon B which, prisoner states, led to death within half to one minute. On the following day the corpses were taken by lift to the actual crematorium and burnt, but not until other prisoners had been forced to remove gold teeth from the bodies. During the second half of [prisoner's] service at Auschwitz, the bodies of females had their hair cut off, but prisoner states that he does not know the reason for this. The gold of the teeth was collected by the camp dentist, and as far as prisoner knows, sent to Berlin.[20]

Steadily, the interrogators built up a picture of their prisoner, who had been in direct command of the SS camp guards. It was he who gave orders for the mistreatment of camp inmates. Aumeier had no problem in admitting that he gave orders for the flogging of prisoners, and that he and his men frequently hit prisoners in the face. As some kind of justification, he maintained that they only used their hands and fists. Aumeier admitted that he was present at most floggings. Interrogators wrote on his interrogation report:

A great many prisoners were killed at Auschwitz by members of the guard commanded by Aumeier, quite apart from the mass-executions in gas-chambers. Although Aumeier tries to shift responsibility for everything that happened on the Commandant, he admits that he interpreted the Commandant's orders and passed them on to the men under his command ... During the Commandant's occasional absences, prisoner deputised for him, and on these occasions the mass-executions, the ill-treatment and wanton killings of prisoners at Auschwitz were continued by Aumeier in sole charge.[21]

Thousands of prisoners died in Auschwitz due to the appalling conditions, in which epidemics could not be avoided. Despite their inadequate rations, prisoners were forced to carry out heavy physical work and, on many occasions, were killed during the work by the guards. Aumeier claimed that approximately 3,000 prisoners died at Auschwitz from 'natural causes'.

Evidence of Aumeier's guilt was confirmed by other prisoners who had been at Auschwitz under his command and had then served in Norway with SS personnel, before being captured and interrogated by the war crimes unit working in Norway. Major MacLeod and Captain Broderman of that unit hunted them down, interrogated them and collected their damning evidence against Aumeier to send back to Colonel Scotland. It was established that Aumeier had been attached to the SS Construction Brigade of 3 SS Panzer Corps from May 1943, building secret fortifications in the area of Oranienbaum, near Leningrad, Russia. He had been in charge of the 7,000 Jews from Russia and Lithuania who were employed by the notorious unit and who were quartered in several camps specially built in northern Russia and northern Estonia. He denied that atrocities had been committed against these Jews. As the Red Army advanced at the end of the war, he had to evacuate his prisoners several times, until they were finally transported back to Stutthof concentration camp, built in a secluded area some 20 miles from Danzig.

A number of men were now being held who had committed atrocities while under the command of Hans Aumeier, including Josef Remmele, an SS guard at Dachau and Auschwitz concentration camps.[22] Broderman wrote back to Colonel Scotland in London: 'If attempts at suicide are any indication of guilt, this man must have a very uneasy conscience.'[23] Another was Kurt Heinrich, who had served at Buchenwald, Ravensbrück and Riga, and had committed atrocities against Jews in Russia. Being held in Norway, too, were former guards at Auschwitz: Eduard Schmid, Karl Spieker and Herbert Lecker. Captain Broderman wrote to Scotland that investigations into Aumeier's men did not get far 'owing to lack of time and witnesses. It has been impossible to fix any definite guilt on these men, their war career is of such a nature that there can be little doubt that they were at least partners in crime.'[24]

The Wormhoudt massacre

News of the Wormhoudt massacre in France first emerged in early 1944, when the first British prisoners of war returned to England and told their stories. The London Cage was given the task of investigating the atrocity, which had occurred in May 1940. It had one aim: to bring those responsible to justice. Their investigations were aided by the remarkable fact that there were survivors. Under oath, on 14 March 1944, Private Albert Evans of the Royal Warwickshire Regiment swore a testimony at Birmingham and provided full details of what had happened. Two days later, Richard Tudor Parry, a gunner of the Royal Artillery, swore a statement in

Westminster. On 9 November 1944, a statement was taken under oath by Private Charles Edward Daley of the Royal Warwickshire Regiment; and on 7 August 1945, another survivor from the Royal Warwickshire Regiment, Sergeant Robert William Gill, took an oath and submitted his statement in York.[25] At that time, it took great courage for these men to recall the details of their ordeal.

The Wormhoudt massacre occurred on 28 May 1940, while the British evacuation from the beaches of Dunkirk was in full swing. Eighty surrendering men from 2nd Battalion, Royal Warwickshire Regiment, the Cheshire Regiment and the Royal Artillery, as well as French soldiers, were murdered by German soldiers after capture near the French village of Wormhoudt.[26] All evidence gathered at the London Cage pointed to the Leibstandarte SS Adolf Hitler (Life Guard Regiment of Adolf Hitler – LSSAH) as being responsible. This was an SS regiment that had been formed in 1933 as Hitler's personal bodyguard.[27] Its commander was known to be SS General Sepp Dietrich, who was commander-in-chief of the 6th SS Panzer Army.

At the end of October 1945, Colonel Scotland dispatched interrogator Bunny Pantcheff to Wormhoudt, with surviving gunner Parry, to gather evidence. They obtained statements from key eyewitnesses: farmer Monsieur Mercier, Madame Backot, Monsieur Devienne, farmer Jonchere and the grave-digger Monsieur Smagghe. Gradually, the facts began to emerge.

Just prior to 28 May 1940, General Dietrich was driving around the region looking for his 2nd Battalion, accompanied by Max Wünsche, his driver. His troops had seen fierce fighting with the British in recent days. Well camouflaged and still hidden in the hedges were men of the Royal Warwicks. They opened fire as the car approached. Dietrich and Wünsche flung themselves from the car into a nearby ditch for cover. The car caught fire, rolled down into the ditch and burst into flames. Dietrich and Wünsche remained there for several hours, with Wünsche slightly injured. Meanwhile, the LSSAH – consisting of eighteen companies, all elite hand-picked troops – was heading for Dunkirk to cut off the remaining British troops. It met with stiff opposition from the British Expeditionary Force.

LSSAH's 1st Battalion was already feeling humiliated by a recent heavy defeat at the hands of the Royal Artillery, Royal Warwicks and Royal Cheshires. What the SS regiment did not realise was that the British regiments were running out of supplies and ammunition, and hence had retreated to Wormhoudt. On 28 May, 2nd Battalion, LSSAH was given the order to clear the British soldiers from Wormhoudt. Dietrich was again driving around in his car when he strayed into no man's land and his car was hit for a second time. He was wounded and trapped in unoccupied territory. In his absence, SS Major (Sturmbannführer) Ernst Schützek took over and ordered 5th Company, 2nd Battalion, LSSAH to penetrate Wormhoudt and attempt a rescue of General Dietrich. The SS received a severe pounding from British troops and Schützek was killed in action.

Wilhelm Mohnke then took charge of 2nd Battalion. German anti-tank guns backed by German air power mounted a heavy attack on Wormhoudt. The British headquarters was overrun and prisoners were captured. Otto Baum, commander of 7th Company, 2nd Battalion, LSSAH ordered the British troops captured in Wormhoudt to be rounded up. A column of British prisoners set off under the guard of the German Corps of Signals, which had orders to take them to a location and shoot them. The prisoners were marshalled into an empty barn in La Plaine au Bois and hand grenades were lobbed in, causing panic and injuring some of the British prisoners. When the SS realised that two British soldiers, Sergeant Stanley Moore and Company Sergeant Major (CSM) Augustus Jennings, had thrown themselves on top of the grenades to shield others, the remaining prisoners were ordered out of the barn, five at a time, and shot. Those left inside witnessed the men being led out and then heard the gunfire. Some prisoners refused to leave the barn and were sprayed with bullets. The SS left the scene, believing that no one could have survived. But around a dozen of the wounded men were still alive. They lay there for two days before a unit of the German Red Cross passed by, looking for wounded SS men. The unit was shocked by the scene in the barn, where, by then, all but six of the soldiers had died. The survivors were taken to hospital, and after they had recovered were transferred to a German prisoner-of-war camp.

The French buried the dead soldiers in a shallow grave near the barn. Towards the end of the war, they moved the bodies to the Esquelbecq Military Cemetery, near the Belgian border, 24 kilometres south of Dunkirk.

Major Terry sent out a request to all POW camps for any members of the LSSAH to be transferred to the London Cage. It resulted in the arrival of two prisoners in early July 1946: Max Reimelt of 7th Company, 2nd Battalion and Otto Baum, commander of 7th Company.[28] Reimelt professed to know nothing about the shooting in the barn. However, he did provide interrogators with information on the LSSAH command structure, indicating that Mohnke had succeeded Schützek as commander of 2nd Battalion. But nothing that he said brought the investigators any closer to the truth. Otto Baum was brought before Colonel Scotland in July for rigorous questioning, but he remained equally evasive. He was interrogated again on 13 August 1946, this time by Warrant Officer Ullman; this time Baum spoke in vague terms about the German offensive on Wormhoudt.

High on the list of those wanted by the London Cage in connection with the Wormhoudt massacre was Wilhelm Mohnke. The Canadians also put out a search for him, because he had ordered the shooting of three Canadian prisoners of war on 1 June 1944. But his whereabouts were not established at the time, and it was concluded that he had died during the final battle for Berlin in April 1945. In fact, he lived on until 2001.

SS General Sepp Dietrich was also wanted by the British in connection with Wormhoudt. Having been captured by the Americans, he was handed over for interrogation and dispatched to the London Cage. In his defence, Dietrich argued that he had been stuck in the ditch and knew nothing of the shootings. His undated signed statement at the London Cage was witnessed by Warrant Officer Ullman and Captain Kieser.[29] In it, he claimed that he had given orders that no prisoners were to be shot after capture. He did not deny the killings at Wormhoudt, but stated that the incident had not come to his ears. He conceded that some SS officers may have carried out the shootings, but it was on their own initiative. Because of the SS oath of undying loyalty, Dietrich was unwilling to compromise any other SS soldiers. But Scotland remained optimistic that eventually one of the SS men might speak. Then, quite unexpectedly, during an interrogation one of the SS prisoners who had denied any knowledge of the shootings said: 'I don't know who was responsible for the shootings, but there is one man in England from the LSSAH signals and he knows. His name is Heinz Druwe.'[30]

The immediate priority became to find Druwe. A search of card indexes located him in a POW camp in Kent. There he was popular with staff and the other prisoners. Once in the London Cage, he proved no help at all and answered none of the questions in interrogation. He denied any knowledge of the shooting of British soldiers at Wormhoudt. But he was to level his own allegations of torture and brutality while at the London Cage.

The Wormhoudt case was one of the few failures of the London Cage in terms of bringing perpetrators to justice. However, Sepp Dietrich did not completely escape his past. He was eventually tried at a US military tribunal at Dachau for his part in ordering the execution of American prisoners of war and was sentenced to life imprisonment on 16 July 1946.

Scouring Europe

Some of Colonel Scotland's most experienced interrogators were dispatched to Europe to track down named Nazi war criminals and compile evidence of their crimes. This involved interviewing eyewitnesses to atrocities, photographing relevant locations in France, Germany and Norway where the mass shooting of Allied soldiers had taken place, and working closely with other Allied bodies. Bunny Pantcheff was sent to Germany to work on a number of cases, including the Emsland case, which concerned the investigation into atrocities committed in penal camps around Emsland.[31] From there he wrote to Colonel Scotland: 'Emsland is quite the most unpleasant place I've ever been to, and this must be the worst time of year for it. I know now why some sadistic swine picked it as a site for concentration camps. It would break the stiffest morale in no time at all.'[32]

On 29 December 1945, he sent another chatty six-page letter to Scotland with news of their progress. In brackets, next to the date at the top of the letter, he wrote 'My birthday!':

> Egger and Bonwitt safely made that journey to Brussels as scheduled. Morgenthau met us in Bad Oeynhausen after a record sea and rail journey. Scharf and myself spent 2½ days at Bad Oeynhausen at HQ BAOR getting everything organised in a water tight way. Bad Oeynhausen is a shocking place. In fact it stinks. If anybody's thinking of waging another war just now, I recommend them to go and have a look at Julich near Aachen, and see what we could do even before the atomic age. There are literally not two bricks on top of one another in the whole town, not one part of the wall, one room of one house standing.[33]

Pantcheff reported that his team had already located the major war criminals on their list, as well as fifty to sixty minor war criminals. They zigzagged across Europe, picking up the accused in hiding, trailing death records and collecting statements from prisoners and witnesses. Their work took them to Belgium, where they interviewed up to 250 prisoners in the camps there. Pantcheff wrote to Scotland: 'The interrogation of the accused is intended to be a preliminary measure. The final detailed interrogations will have to be carried out in more favourable surroundings with more facilities.'[34]

Bonwitt was working out of the northern area of the British zone of occupation in Germany, and Morgenthau the southern zone. Between them they had to plough through 7 tons of valuable documents and death records from concentration camps. Felek Scharf continued to interview Polish witnesses, and Pantcheff travelled to Czechoslovakia to pick up Czech witnesses. Egger also took down statements from Belgian witnesses.

In January 1946, Pantcheff wrote again to Colonel Scotland to inform him that they had found two or three mass graves 'which will have to be dug up by the accused, of course. I like a little poetic justice; the bodies medically examined and photographed and then given a funeral.'[35] On the first day of the following month, an exhumation of the grave took place at Camp Aschendorfer Moor and thirty-six bodies were subsequently given a Christian burial.[36]

The punishing schedule of gathering evidence of the most terrible war crimes took a psychological toll on Pantcheff and his team. As he wrote to Scotland, 'Whenever anyone gets to the stage of dreaming about the bastards, we take half a day off. All of us here have bad dreams at one time or another – they are such a God-awful shower.'[37] But it would not be for too much longer. On 14 February, Pantcheff wrote to Scotland again: 'This is the news I've been wanting to give you for so long. We have almost finished our job over here. We have all the major criminals and the vast majority of the minor ones safely arrested and locked behind bars.'[38]

One member of the detachment was tasked solely with recovering documents from concentration camps. In attics, cellars and buried chests throughout Emsland, tons of documents about the administration of the concentration camps were discovered.[39] Yet challenges remained as Pantcheff and his men prepared to leave Germany. Where were all the accused (half of whom needed further interrogation) to be temporarily incarcerated in England? And how would staff manage with the translation of over 250 statements and affidavits, and working through the piles of original documents?

By the end of March 1946, the team had all returned to the London Cage, where they studied the statements taken from prisoners, sifted through documents and urgently compiled reports to hand to prosecutors so that the war crimes trials could begin. Intermittent visits to the continent were made by members of the team to follow up on clues as to the whereabouts of suspected war criminals yet to be found.

In August 1946, Scotland dispatched Bonwitt, Morgenthau and Scharf to Belgium, to investigate further the shooting of British soldiers at Wormhoudt and Le Paradis (see chapter 11). From Belgium, they drove to Camp 2226 (Zedelghem) to report to Major Broderman and Company Sergeant Major Richter, both of PWIS. Between 16 and 20 August, they screened all SS personnel in the camp – around 100 men. They combed the Belgian and German countryside for eyewitnesses to the massacres. On 26 August, they arrived at the civilian internment camp at Esterwegen, where they screened 1,000 SS prisoners and interrogated 30. When they were investigating the Sagan case, they interrogated 134 Gestapo and SS prisoners of war at Esterwegen.[40] The following day, having been billeted overnight with the RAF police in Hamburg, they proceeded to the former Neuengamme concentration camp. Over the next three days, they screened all 6,000 SS personnel in order to establish where they had been in action; this led to the detailed interrogation of 300 of them.

Between 31 August and 1 September 1946, they worked in the civilian internment camp at Neumünster, screening 2,500 SS personnel (which led to the detailed interrogation of 80). From there they moved on to the camp at Sandbostel to screen 4,500 SS officers and interrogate 98 of them. At Fallingbostel they interrogated 20 SS of the 180 or so being held there. Between 2 September and 9 September, the team visited three other major camps (Recklinghausen, Iserlohn and Paderborn), screening 4,500 SS personnel.[41] The figures give an idea of the enormity of the task facing Scotland's teams – and that is just one section of the workload in one country.

From an office in 6–7 Kensington Palace Gardens, Pantcheff wrote the team's concluding report in April 1947:

> Our success was considerable. We have placed in custody 120 persons responsible for the murder and ill treatment of nationals of many countries . . . and every individual camp commandant who is still alive . . . It is fitting that the last words of praise and commendation should be for Captain Egger, RSM Bonwitt, CSM Scharf and Staff Sergeant Morgenthau. Only the high quality of their work and resource made this operation possible in anything like its present forms.[42]

11

KNÖCHLEIN
The butcher of Le Paradis

In April 1945, Colonel Scotland dispatched two officers to Le Paradis in France to investigate another massacre of British soldiers that had occurred during the retreat to Dunkirk in 1940. He instructed them to photograph anything of relevance and to find eyewitnesses. Their photographs survive in files at the National Archives and include pictures of the deserted farm-house and barn where the soldiers had been shot.[1]

It was during October 1944, as the liberating armies had been heading through Belgium towards Germany, that the British first heard details of the massacre at Le Paradis and brought it to the attention of the London Cage. The French authorities reported a mass grave of at least 100 British soldiers nearby, which appeared to be the result of a war crime. The London Cage was tasked with investigating and bringing to trial the commander who had ordered the shooting. The problem: Colonel Scotland and his team had scant details to go on. No one knew who the commander was or which German troops had been responsible; it had happened early in the war and much had occurred in the intervening years. It was far from certain that the perpetrators would still be alive and could be brought to trial. But these obstacles did not prevent the investigations from going ahead.

It turned out to be a major war crime, involving the deaths of nearly 100 surrendering British soldiers at Le Paradis on 27 May 1940. Colonel Scotland resolved that the massacre could not go unpunished. He and his teams discovered that Hitler's SS Totenkopf Division was implicated in the mass murder. With this knowledge, he instructed his staff to contact all POW camps and transfer to the London Cage every SS prisoner who had ever served in the Totenkopf Division. The cage soon had a steady stream of SS officers in its interrogation rooms – over 100 in total. Although many had joined the regiment after 1940, rumours about the horrific nature of the war crimes had continued to circulate among the newer SS officers. Work now focused on establishing which SS regiments had been in the area at the time. During the interrogations, certain names began to emerge: Emke, Schneider – and SS Lieutenant Colonel Fritz Knöchlein as the possible commander.

Information came into the London Cage that Albert Leonard Pooley and William Reginald O'Callaghan, both of the Royal Norfolk Regiment, had survived the massacre. Their testimony was to be crucial as the events of May 1940 were gradually pieced together in the rooms of the London Cage. The British Expeditionary Force had been forced to retreat and evacuate after Hitler invaded France. Small fishing vessels and boats were already involved in evacuating nearly 300,000 soldiers from the beaches of Dunkirk. It emerged that the SS units had been wholly unprepared for frontline fighting, having been told that they would be acting as Hitler's personal bodyguard, and in actuality having guarded the concentration camps where 'enemies' of Hitler were incarcerated.

Survivors of Le Paradis

By the end of May 1940, three regiments of the SS Totenkopf Division had moved into France.[2] The town of Béthune became their headquarters. Across the canal there was camped a British battalion of the Royal Norfolk Regiment and the Royal Scots. They had knocked the 1st Totenkopf Regiment out of battle, leaving the 2nd and 3rd Totenkopf Regiments to try to cross the canal. Knöchlein dispatched his friend First Lieutenant Harrer on a reconnaissance mission to check British positions across the canal. Harrer never returned, killed by a single bullet. Fighting continued long into the night before the SS regiments withdrew. At dawn, they were showered by mortar and gunfire. Many of the partially trained SS soldiers died. Even German tanks could not repel the British attack and were forced to withdraw. Eventually the SS retaliated with infantry guns. The Royal Scots lost the battle and the hamlet of Le Cornet Malo was captured.

After the fierce fighting against the British, Knöchlein found himself burying his closest friend, Lieutenant Harrer. At the graveside after the eulogy, Knöchlein suddenly declared: 'No prisoners! From now on, we take no prisoners. Every damned Britisher is to be shot!'[3]

Meanwhile, the Royal Norfolks were still engaged in a heavy battle near Le Paradis against the 3rd Totenkopf Regiment, the men battle-fatigued after eighteen days under attack. There were no imminent reinforcements and ammunition was low at their headquarters in a farmhouse just outside Le Paradis. The commander, Major Ryder MC, ordered the company to continue fighting.[4]

The 2nd Totenkopf Regiment now linked up with the 3rd Totenkopf Regiment to attack Le Paradis. By this point, the British forces had run out of ammunition and their headquarters had been hit. Major Ryder ordered all wounded soldiers to be moved from the cellar to a barn to protect them from mortar fire. He commanded his men to destroy all records and break up the wireless sets. Some of the men moved down the road towards the village of Lacon, surrendered to the 3rd Totenkopf Regiment and were taken to its headquarters.

Major Ryder ordered the rest of his men into the barn to take cover. Now they were completely cut off and surrounded by SS regiments. He gave his men the option of surrendering to save their lives or fighting to the bitter end with no ammunition. They decided on surrender and broke up their weapons. Three men slowly left the barn with a rifle draped in a white towel to surrender. The firing started and all three were shot as they walked towards the SS officers. Major Ryder ordered the rest of his men out of the barn with their hands up, to the sound of cheering SS who surrounded them. The SS instructed the British soldiers wounded in battle to sit. It was then that Sergeant Pooley squatted down as the SS shouted orders in German and began to kick the surrendering soldiers. Pooley was struck by an SS officer and fell to the ground.

At a little distance stood Fritz Knöchlein, grinning at the humiliation of the British. He walked towards his prisoners, bawling orders that he expected to be obeyed. He called three SS officers and quietly told them, 'Now we have these damned English swine. We will arrange a nice little shooting for them. I have sworn to avenge Harrer's death.'[5]

On the scene was SS Master Sergeant (Hauptscharführer) Theodor Emke, who would later be called as a key witness to the atrocity. He provided a statement to Warrant Officer Ullman on 23 October 1946.[6] With all prisoners out of the barn, they were ordered to march towards Le Paradis. SS men waited, poised by a hedge in a small field, their guns at the ready. Knöchlein ordered them to fire. The British soldiers fell into the dips in the field. Pooley felt a sharp pain in his leg as he and O'Callaghan threw themselves onto their comrades. Within seconds, the bodies of more soldiers covered them. They remained totally still as SS men walked up and down the lines, shooting any survivors. A whistle was blown and the SS moved off, their voices becoming fainter. The badly wounded Pooley passed out and O'Callaghan fell asleep from sheer exhaustion. They were the only survivors.

All this had been overheard by four French refugees who had fled the fighting and were sheltering in a nearby pigsty. As they made their way along the road they were stopped by a German soldier, who asked if they had seen any British soldiers. They said they had not. He accused them of being spies and held a revolver to the head of 60-year-old Madame Romanie Castel. She pleaded not to be shot. The German soldier showed mercy and strode off.[7]

In the field, Pooley finally stirred with a severe pain in his left leg. He pulled himself from under the dead bodies and heard O'Callaghan snoring. He woke him, and the two men climbed out of the ditch. In his statement, O'Callaghan described having walked beside the pile of bodies and seen not a single survivor.[8] As he approached the barn, he had heard German voices. He returned to Pooley, telling him that they had to get away urgently. He helped Pooley to cover behind a bush and went off to find shelter. He found a pigsty and went back to collect Pooley. This became their shelter for the next three days, hiding until the SS regiments had moved away from the area. They survived by eating raw potatoes.

On the fourth day, Madame Romanie Castel returned home to find the two British soldiers. She hated the German occupation of France and would not betray the soldiers. Instead, she dressed Pooley's wound, made a meal and agreed to shelter them. Occasionally they heard the voices of German soldiers in the distance. One day a passing German medical officer visited the farm, looking for wounded German soldiers. Observing the Geneva Convention, he arranged for Pooley and O'Callaghan to be transferred to a hospital in Béthune. Pooley was subsequently moved to a hospital in Paris, and thereafter to a POW camp in Germany. After sixteen days, O'Callaghan was discharged and taken with other British soldiers to a different POW camp. It would be more than five years before he and Pooley saw each other again.

Men in Knöchlein's regiment had been disgusted by the order to shoot surrendering British soldiers. It continued to be discussed among younger members of the SS regiments, who suggested that Knöchlein should be challenged to a duel to save the honour of the SS. A German war reporter saw the carnage at Le Paradis and counted at least fifty dead British soldiers near the barn. He assumed it was the result of fierce fighting and photographed the scene.

Heinrich Himmler summoned the divisional commander, SS General Theodor Eicke (inspection officer for the concentration camps in the 1930s) and ordered the shootings at Le Paradis to be kept a state secret. The 2nd Totenkopf Regiment was withdrawn from France to fight elsewhere, including on the Russian front. There a number of its 3rd Company lost their lives in battle, complicating Colonel Scotland's later task.

While receiving treatment in a Paris hospital, Pooley had been advised to keep quiet about Le Paradis; if he didn't, the Nazis would hunt him down and eliminate him as a witness to the atrocity. Pooley suppressed his experiences, but it took its toll on his mental health. When he finally returned to England, he told his story, but was ignored on the grounds that he was suffering from battle fatigue. He was doubtful that there were any other surviving witnesses – O'Callaghan might well be dead. He returned to Southall, London, and worked in the post office.

But O'Callaghan had survived in a different POW camp, and had also kept silent about his experiences. When he returned to England, his reports were also discredited. When Colonel Scotland heard about the two survivors, he was furious that the War Office had neither told him nor taken the men's testimonies seriously. He tracked down the two men and asked them to come to the cage. O'Callaghan agreed, but Pooley was profoundly depressed by his experiences and refused.

O'Callaghan was finally able to swear a statement before the commissioner for oaths in Westminster on 2 November 1946. Four days later, he persuaded Pooley to do the same. Their testimony, alongside the interrogation of SS soldiers from the unit and eyewitness account from Madame Castel, enabled Knöchlein to be indicted for war crimes and to stand trial.

Gathering evidence of war crimes could be harrowing. At the request of Major Terry, the French police were asked to take down a key statement from farmer Monsieur Louis Creton. Creton had evacuated his home on 20 May 1940 because of the advancing German army and had returned on 2 June 1940 to find that a communal grave with a small cross had been dug in one of his meadows. He said:

I also noticed bullet marks on the stable wall facing onto the meadow. By the wall, bits of brain and pools of congealed blood were scattered on the ground. At a distance of about 25 metres from the wall I found a pile of about 200 German cartridge cases . . . I found several buckets of blood and human brain which proves that the British soldiers had been shot from very short range.[9]

Creton's single-page testimony was typed and dispatched to London as key evidence in the Le Paradis massacre case.

Fritz Knöchlein

Finally, on 10 October 1946, the 'tall, fierce, disdainful, highly strung, excitable' SS Lieutenant Colonel Fritz Knöchlein was brought to the London Cage from American custody.[10] It was the beginning of 615 days in British detention, 64 of them in solitary confinement at the London Cage in 1946.[11] As one of the most loathed prisoners ever to cross the threshold of the cage, Knöchlein was described by Scotland as 'a Nazi of the first order, the worst order, a German who had dedicated himself to brutality; irresponsible in the possession of power, ruthless in execution'.[12]

Knöchlein was interrogated for short periods on 15, 17, 18 and 21 October and on 12 and 14 November 1946. He was required to appear for several identity parades at the cage when eyewitnesses were asked to identify him. During this time, he became extremely unstable and behaved like a half-crazed animal. He claimed that the guards came into his room every ten minutes from ten o'clock in the evening, pulled off his blankets and shook him until he woke. He frequently screamed out, calling the guards 'Bastards and British Gestapo'.[13]

Colonel Scotland was having none of this behaviour and issued immediate orders for every item to be removed from Knöchlein's room: the bed, table, chair, all toiletries, and even the fireplace to prevent him from hurting himself.[14] Knöchlein was left with two blankets and a pillow. The following day he was brought before Scotland and told that he would be in solitary confinement for at least twenty-eight days. On 15 October, he was given his second interrogation in Room 25 by Regimental Sergeant (RSM) Major Ullman, with Major Terry present.[15] Two days later, Knöchlein was seen again in Room 25 by Ullman, but refused to provide the name of his regiment. Scotland entered the interrogation room, waited and watched for a few moments. Without saying a word to Knöchlein, he turned to Ullman and barked, 'Have him sent to me.'[16]

Ullman escorted Knöchlein to Room 24, where Scotland instructed the German to sit down. Major Terry was present. Scotland explained to Knöchlein the charges being gathered against him. Knöchlein responded by citing his SS oath to Hitler as the reason for not answering any questions. He then complained bitterly about being held there. But this was Scotland's territory, and he showed no fear of the SS officer as he rounded the desk and told Knöchlein that he usually gave prisoners an opportunity to write down their version of events and account for the allegations against them.

Knöchlein interrupted him, snapping: 'I refuse to write anything down.'

Scotland replied: 'Exactly what I expected from you. You have sworn under your SS oath to your Regimental Commander that what happened at Le Paradis on the afternoon of 27 May 1940 was to remain a secret for life. Don't worry. You will not be asked any more questions here. You are denied the opportunity to write down your version of events.'[17]

Knöchlein was dismissed back to his room in solitary confinement. He was seen again on 18 October, this time by a Major Mason with RSM Ullman acting as interpreter. On 21 October, having received additional statements from other prisoners about the Le Paradis murders, Knöchlein was interrogated again in Room 25 by Major Terry and RSM Ullman. Even confronted with the evidence provided by survivors Pooley and O'Callaghan, Knöchlein remained uncooperative and denied all knowledge of the shootings.

In other rooms in the cage, under the direction of Major Terry, the interrogation of SS officers about the Le Paradis massacre continued, as interrogators gradually pieced together the circumstances surrounding the massacre. Between 10 October and 13 December 1946, a total of 136 prisoners were interrogated about the massacre, most spending an average of ten days in the cage. It was one of the busiest periods: the guards and camp staff were fully engaged in duties of feeding and guarding the prisoners, escorting them to the interrogation rooms and keeping an eye on them in the exercise grounds.

Allegations of torture

Knöchlein maintained that after his interrogation on 15 October 1946, Scotland ordered two guards to be stationed in his room at night. Then, for four days and nights he was taken to the guardroom, where the guards were playing cards and singing. He was allowed to lie down, but could not sleep. His clothes were confiscated, and he was given prison slacks to wear during the daytime and thin pyjamas at night. For three days, he had barely any food or sleep. In his formal complaint to the authorities, Knöchlein alleged that Ullman told him during an interrogation: 'There existed Gestapo methods not only in Alexanderplatz in Berlin. We can do that much better here. We will knock you [??] . . . here miserably [??] . . . you will wail!'[18] The complaint continued: 'At that he got hold of me on the front of my . . . twisted my collar until I was suffocated, and shouted into my face: "I hate you, I hate you, I have never hated anybody like you!" During this time the guards were instructed to treat me correspondingly.'[19]

Knöchlein claimed that on 17 October the guards forced him to make 100 trunk bends without pause, until he was ready to fall over. When he wanted to stop, he was told that this disobedience would be punished, and the comments were accompanied by persistent threats with a wooden cudgel. He was made to walk round a narrow, 2-by-2-metre space in a circle for four hours, always in the same direction, even though he pleaded that he was becoming giddy. For complaining, he was given a heavy kick with a boot every time he passed the guard. He claimed that between fifteen and twenty of these kicks had occurred. Finally, he had to turn around on his own axis for so long that he was unable to keep upright and collapsed to the ground. An interrogation session followed immediately.[20]

In his complaints, Knöchlein said:

Late in the evening, Captain Cornish finished these cruelties temporarily and ordered them to let me have food and sleep again. In the meantime I was made to work most heavily, mostly in an altogether useless way. For instance to scrub a flight of stairs and, when this was finished down below, to begin afresh on top, to scrub about with a brush on a tiled floor with a tiny rag. For instance, half a sock to wipe a large room, to clean the lavatory, and to carry coal (although I pointed out that my wrist had been broken and despite my reference to the international agreements involved considering officer prisoners of war).[21]

When he needed the toilet, Knöchlein claimed that the guards deliberately refused to hear his knocks. Or they came along, sneered, then left without allowing him to go to the lavatory. At one point, Knöchlein was held in a narrow room with three other prisoners, with no room to move. In answer to their repeated requests to use the toilet, the guard placed a bucket in the room and told them to use that. Through the night, the stench became overpowering in the stale air of the cell. But their complaints were met with scornful laughs from the guards. Knöchlein's fellow prisoners – Werner Schifer and Oskar Schmidt – had witnessed it all, he said.

Knöchlein always believed that because he had dared to complain, he was subjected to further mistreatment. When he returned to his room, he found it was a centimetre deep in dirty water. The guard ordered him to kneel and mop it up. Knöchlein described what happened next:

> As I had only one pair of trousers which were my own, I refused. Then I was lifted up by my legs, head downward and then dropped. About ten buckets of water were poured over my head and my clothes, and I was pushed several times down a narrow and steep flight of cellar stairs, a cudgel knocking me in the back, so that I almost broke all my limbs. Finally I had to take off my shoes and step with stockinged feet into the icy water which was several centimetres high, and that is how I had to 'clean!' Then I was forced to run about in the open where it was pouring, holding my shoes in my hand and with only my stockings on, driven on to more speed by a wooden cudgel in my back.[22]

Knöchlein was forbidden to change his clothes or underwear. Most of the meals that he was now permitted were taken standing in front of an open lavatory door, with only a few minutes to eat. Finally, he was ordered to kneel down in dirty water and scrub the guardroom. A guard sat on his back to keep him on his knees; this was witnessed by eight guards and two corporals.[23]

Knöchlein claimed that the treatment worsened: on 9 October 1946, he was put in a small corner of the kitchen with a big multi-flame gas stove. The gas flames radiated an enormous heat. He was forced to scrub a tiny piece of wood for ninety minutes without any water – an action which he described as

> quite meaningless, and with no rest. When the sweat was streaming down my face and body, I was escorted in a bathroom. Doors and windows were wide open. I had to undress and, in my heated state, I

had to step under the icy shower (a special shower which does not drop water on the body from above but also throws it from the sides!).[24]

Three guards prevented him from leaving the ice-cold shower. Standing freezing and shivering, he was then smeared with coal, so that he had to remain under the cold shower for 'reasons of cleanliness'. Finally, they poured an additional bucket of cold water over him. He claimed that this torture led to the onset of bad bronchitis, and his rheumatic disease got worse. He always maintained that he survived only because he was a fit man. But this was not the end of the matter. That evening, he was escorted into the back garden with fellow prisoner Oskar Schmidt. Knöchlein was ordered to kneel on the ground in front of a guard. When he refused, he and Schmidt had to run continuously in a circle while the guard pushed them in the back with a cudgel. Then Knöchlein was given a heavy log weighing about 50 pounds, which he had to carry while running, and Schmidt was forced to carry a wooden beam. Finally, they were both coerced into running around with a barrel partly filled with lubricating oil. It had serious consequences:

> My fellow-prisoner Oskar Schmidt, a man of 46 years who was obviously about to break down, was told that he had to suffer all this because I had refused to kneel on the floor. I was told that I was a bad comrade and responsible for Schmidt's sufferings because I would not kneel down! Schmidt then broke down with a heart attack and was unconscious. In order to put an end to his torture I said I was willing to kneel down before the guard inside the house, which I was forced to do in front of the guardroom. At these sadistic tortures, a corporal was present, apart from the guard, and many other guards looked on from the window.[25]

Oskar Schmidt survived the heart attack. He was carried to his room by Knöchlein and a guard 'after he had had his heart massaged, he soon regained consciousness'.[26] Colonel Scotland witnessed Oskar Schmidt's signed statement on 8 November 1946. The question remains open whether it was obtained through intimidation, or even brutality.

The following year, Schmidt was tried as a war criminal in Hamburg for his part in the murder of RAF airmen who had tunnelled out of Stalag Luft III (the Sagan case, discussed in the next chapter). He was sentenced to death and hanged in Hameln prison in February 1948 by British executioner Albert Pierrepoint.

Back in the cage

Knöchlein claimed to have been subjected to further humiliating treatment on 6 November 1946, treatment that, so he argued, went against military discipline: he had to stand to attention and salute an ordinary guard without rank, who kicked him on the legs. Knöchlein asked to register a complaint and found himself back in front of Colonel Scotland, complaining to him that military salutes were only to be given to an officer of the same rank or higher.[27]

Scotland had no time for such nonsense and told him: 'The German army has ceased to exist. There are no German officers any longer. You have to do everything the guard orders you to do.'[28]

On 13 December 1946, Knöchlein was transferred to Camp 17, a POW camp near Sheffield.[29] When Scotland and his staff had finished interrogating SS officers, they were transferred to the same camp as Knöchlein. It was here that Knöchlein learned that Colonel Scotland's case against him was making substantial progress, and decided to write down his own statement concerning the Le Paradis murders. He asked to see Scotland. His request was granted, and he was escorted back to the familiar rooms at the London Cage for a second time; there he stayed from 17 to 24 September 1947. It was during this particular period that he made a statement about the mistreatment of Oskar Schmidt that had occurred the previous year.

One of the interrogators was sent to his cell. Knöchlein handed over his statement on the Le Paradis massacre, in which he argued that the decision to shoot the British soldiers had been made by a Standgericht (a standing court). Such a court could be formed in the field; and at least three of its members must agree that life can be taken in the field. That could allow for the shooting of a deserter or of a man suddenly refusing to obey orders. Afterwards, for it to be legally binding in the German army and to prevent repercussions, the action had to be lodged in writing, signed and handed to a superior officer.

When Colonel Scotland read the statement, he was furious. He ordered the guards to bring Knöchlein to his office and the two men faced each other again.

Scotland challenged him: 'Just because you decided at a *Stand Gericht* [*sic*] to shoot your British prisoners does not mean that your action was legal in international law.'[30] He then went on to contest the legal validity of a Standgericht in German law, telling Knöchlein that his action was illegal because he had not lodged a written copy with his commander.[31] Scotland admitted:

> Knöchlein aroused the worst side of my nature. His evilness, his bombast, lying and brutal nature, and the thought of the brave men he had caused to be slaughtered – good British soldiers who had given the hated, vaunted, inefficient SS a bloody nose and who had only been captured because their position was hopeless and when they had used all their ammunition – all these things made me long to give him a taste of the SS medicine . . . He was, in my opinion, the worst German we ever had in the London Cage. I could hardly look at Knöchlein without wanting to hit him.[32]

On 24 September 1947, Knöchlein left the London Cage for a POW camp in Northumberland. But it would not to be the last time he would see Kensington Palace Gardens.

1948: Farewell London Cage

On 15 June 1948, Knöchlein was escorted back to the London Cage for the final time, in transit to Germany for his trial.[33] For two days, the staff were on high alert for an attempted escape or suicide, and Knöchlein was placed under constant watch. A routine search revealed money hidden in the lining of his coat, suggesting that he might have thought he could escape. Knöchlein kept the other prisoners awake all night with his shouting and demands to see Colonel Scotland. His requests were denied. Sergeant Prion was the guard on duty that night. He entered Knöchlein's room and cautioned him that if he continued shouting, someone would lose their temper and might lay a finger on him. It was believed that Knöchlein's actions were deliberately intended to provoke physical assault from the guards.

The following day, 16 June, at 5 p.m., Colonel Scotland paraded all the guards outside Knöchlein's cell.[34] He looked straight at Knöchlein and said: 'Your behaviour last night was unworthy of a German officer. We want no further nonsense from you.'

Scotland turned to Sergeant Prion and, with the other guards listening, said: 'Tonight you will leave the lights on in the prisoner's room, but you will remove his bedstead. People have been known to fall out of bed and break their necks. We'll have no accidents here. The prisoner may have his mattress and his blankets. And we hope that tonight he will behave as a German officer should.' That night, Knöchlein gave no further trouble. He spent his last hours crying in his cell.[35]

On 17 June 1948, Scotland watched in satisfaction and with some relief as Fritz Knöchlein was escorted out of the London Cage, handcuffed to the guard under standing orders from the RAF. He was moved towards the escorting van for his final journey through the capital to the airport, for a flight to Hamburg for his trial. It was not the last time he would see Colonel Scotland.

Knöchlein's trial took place between 11 and 25 October 1948. Throughout it, he maintained his innocence, arguing that he had never received or given an order to shoot prisoners, and nor did he have any knowledge that men in his division had been guilty of the crimes. Under cross-examination he told the court: 'I find the unfavourable testimonials which are held against me incomprehensible and they can only be based on confusion of persons, errors of memory or an ill-will.'[36] He maintained that he had learned about the murders at Le Paradis from rumours in the following days. The court had enough evidence to establish that he was lying. One of the key witnesses who travelled to Hamburg was Madame Castel, now almost seventy years old. In the courtroom, in her best black dress, the tall Frenchwoman pointed a finger at Knöchlein and said: 'I know this man!' Her identification of Knöchlein was a chilling moment, watched by Colonel Scotland who was present.[37]

As the trial progressed and as his fate became clear, Knöchlein became less composed. He issued a formal complaint about his treatment in the London Cage and claimed that other prisoners had been beaten up in 'Scotland's establishment', as he called it. Knöchlein recounted examples of sleep deprivation, mistreatment and torture, of beatings, trampling on fingers, kicking, use of a hippopotamus-hide whip (a sjambok) and application of an electrical device to extract confessions; he also alluded to the fact that prisoners could 'vanish without trace'.[38] He complained that he had only half a plate of food at breakfast, no midday meal, one cup of tea in the afternoon and water in the evening.

Knöchlein began to target his allegations at interrogator Captain Cornish. The unsubstantiated accusations led to Colonel Scotland taking the dock and robustly arguing in Captain Cornish's defence that he could not have been implicated in mistreatment, because he was engaged on the extensive investigation into the massacres at Wormhoudt and Le Paradis with Major Terry. It led Scotland to remark that Knöchlein was 'in the experience of the London Cage guards by far the most troublesome and difficult prisoner we ever had'.[39]

In an ironic twist, the tables were turned and Scotland found himself in the dock again to answer charges of war crimes. Under oath in court, he firmly refuted Knöchlein's accusations that he had contravened the Geneva Convention. The situation was serious enough to threaten to derail the whole prosecution case against the Nazi war criminals – and it very nearly succeeded. Scotland was required to produce his own detailed statement refuting the allegations. He called the allegations 'a rigmarole . . . the product of the inventive mind of Frau Ohlert' (Knöchlein's defence lawyer).[40] He argued that Knöchlein, like the other prisoners, had been held in a transit camp, and as such it was legitimate to ask him to carry coals to heat his room and to keep the cage generally clean and tidy. But he refuted claims that Knöchlein had been required to clean the lavatories. He pointed out that other camp staff – its administrative commandant and his officers, and Scotland's seven interrogators – would have noticed any abuse of prisoners.

In defence of Scotland and his interrogators, a witness statement was provided by Private Ballantyne of the Royal Pioneer Corps, one of three warders on duty in the London Cage on the night of 16 June 1948. He confirmed that orders were given to visit Knöchlein's room every fifteen minutes. He said that when he called on Knöchlein at half past midnight, the German was still awake and 'apart from being visited every fifteen minutes, the prisoner had nothing to complain of'.[41]

The court concluded that the allegations of mistreatment were irrelevant to the crimes for which Knöchlein was standing trial: it was 'self-evident that the allegations against Colonel Scotland, even if they have any truth in them, can have no bearing upon the findings or sentence passed by the Court'.[42] Although Scotland was cleared of any charges of brutality, the accusations and rumours would rumble on for decades. There was some satisfaction that the evidence gathered at the London Cage against Knöchlein had been sufficient to secure a conviction.[43] In August 1948, he was sentenced to death by the court for the Le Paradis massacre and was hanged at Hameln prison on 21 January 1949. Nevertheless, the whole affair left serious questions hanging over the reputation of the cage.

12

THE SAGAN CASE

One of the major war crimes being pieced together in the London Cage during 1945 and 1946 was the Sagan case – an investigation into the escape of eighty Allied airmen from Stalag Luft III, a secure German prisoner-of-war camp 60 miles south-east of Berlin, near Sagan in Silesia (now Żagań in western Poland).[1] Fifty of them had been swiftly recaptured and shot. It was on 25 March 1944 that they had made their daring night-time escape through a secret tunnel dug under the camp. The episode was immortalised in the famous Hollywood film *The Great Escape*.

Colonel Scotland first heard about the mass escape via a coded message sent to London from the British military attaché in Stockholm, just two days after it had happened. Further secret reports followed from Sweden and Switzerland, including rumours that a number of British airmen had been shot, although the precise number was unknown at that point. In discussing the situation with military colleagues, Scotland's advice was decisive: broadcast the case, because to keep it secret would give Hitler the idea that the British were afraid of causing panic among the public. Scotland said: 'Tell Hitler we shall treat German prisoners in exactly the same way as he treats ours – and we have many more German prisoners than he has British.'[2] Eventually, Scotland would travel to Germany to see for himself the cells where some of the British pilots from Stalag Luft III had been interrogated after their escape and recapture.

The role of the London Cage in bringing the Sagan war criminals to justice has been overlooked in accounts of the Great Escape, whether in books on the subject or in online articles. Yet it was considered by the Allies to be one of the most important investigations ever undertaken into atrocities committed against Allied prisoners of war. It was not known who the perpetrators were, or who had been responsible for giving the order to shoot. Two survivors and British prisoners (not escapees) who had been repatriated to Britain on health grounds provided the main evidence. The case was complicated by the fact that the escaped pilots had been recaptured in different areas at different times, then subsequently shot in secret locations. This meant that Colonel Scotland and his team had to undertake a huge amount of detective work. They often had to follow several leads before they could piece together the full story of who had committed the killings and when. The pattern was always the same: escaped airmen from Stalag Luft III were picked up in hiding, instructions were issued by the local Gestapo chief to carry out Hitler's order to shoot them, and a gang was assembled to carry out the killings.[3] All those involved were sworn to secrecy, and the bodies were swiftly cremated. At Stalag Luft III, the other prisoners learned of the fate of their comrades when the names of the victims were pinned up as a warning to the others. Horror and shock swept through the camp and a memorial service was held for the dead airmen.

The efficient head of the Gestapo in Berlin, Heinrich Müller, had amassed a large collection of reports on all the Stalag Luft III prisoners who had been shot. On 15 April 1944, Stalag Luft III was visited by a Swiss inspector and the killings were reported to the British government. Prime Minister Winston Churchill raised the matter in the House of Commons. The Germans became twitchy about the case. Himmler asked for full details from Müller, who arranged for new versions of the Gestapo reports on the Sagan case to be written, and for phrases to be inserted showing that the prisoners were shot while trying to escape or resist arrest. The files were sent to Berlin in case there should be an international inquiry. The German Foreign Office tried to cover up the unlawful killings by contacting the Swiss government in Berne to explain that a mass escape of prisoners from Stalag Luft III had necessitated 'some shootings for security reasons' and fifty airmen had been shot while trying to escape.[4] On 23 June 1944, Foreign Secretary Anthony Eden made a statement in the House of Commons telling MPs, 'It was cold-blooded butchery, and we are resolved that the foul criminals shall be tracked down.'[5] The following month, the German Foreign Office announced that no more information would be made available on the deaths of the airmen.

In autumn 1945 and during 1946, suspects in the Sagan case began to arrive at the London Cage, unrepentant and determined to cause disruption.

The Great Escape

The events surrounding the Sagan case were gradually pieced together some 1,200 miles away from the original crime scenes. Interrogators at the London Cage discovered that at 4.20 a.m. on 25 March 1944, the commandant of Stalag Luft III, Wilhelm von Lindeiner, had received a phone call to say that a group of British airmen had escaped from the camp. The exact number was initially unknown. The airmen had chosen the least expected time to execute their escape plan: the ground was still covered in thick snow and it was bitterly cold. This was not the first attempt to tunnel out of the camp; six months earlier, in October 1943, airmen had ventured an escape using a wooden gymnastic vaulting horse that they had constructed. While fellow prisoners exercised on it near the perimeter fence, others hidden inside its hollow cavity secretly dug a tunnel beneath them. It was an ingenious escape plan and almost succeeded; but the airmen were recaptured and warned then that if they ever tried to escape again, they would be shot. This is the escape attempt that was captured in the British film *The Wooden Horse* (1950).

By March 1944, the airmen had completed three tunnels under the camp, nicknamed 'Tom', 'Dick' and 'Harry'. The 2-square-foot tunnel 'Harry' was a masterpiece of engineering: an impressive 363 feet in length, 20 feet below ground and supplied with electricity, a roped trolley and primitive air conditioning. This was the tunnel that enabled eighty airmen to successfully crawl out of the camp, emerging on the other side of the perimeter fence.

The German guards discovered the tunnel's exit and raised the alarm. Commandant von Lindeiner ordered an immediate roll call and was incandescent with rage when he discovered that eighty prisoners had escaped. Four were swiftly recaptured, leaving seventy-six on the run. Two of those captured pilots were sent straight to solitary confinement; the other two were threatened with being shot. Lindeiner could see his distinguished career on the line – one that stretched back to the First World War. News of the escape travelled fast. By the end of the day, a significant line-up of prominent Nazis had arrived at Stalag Luft III: Colonel Richard Waelde (chief of staff of prisoner-of-war camps in the Breslau region), Dr Gunther

Absalon (of the security police in Breslau) and Heinrich Müller (head of the Gestapo in Berlin). Absalon fired Lindeiner from his post as a massive manhunt was ordered to recapture the remaining pilots. Fearing that they would undertake acts of sabotage, an order went out across Germany for roadblocks and searches of houses and farms.

By the end of the first night, fifty of the escapees were in jails in the Sagan area. Of the remaining twenty-six, seventeen were eventually recaptured and sent back to Stalag Luft III; four other recaptured pilots were sent to Sachsenhausen concentration camp, and two to the secure camp at Colditz. Only three of the eighty airmen managed to get back to England.

At the time of the escape, Adolf Hitler was staying at his mountain retreat in Berchtesgaden when news was passed to him from Heinrich Himmler, the supreme head of the SS. Hermann Göring, head of the Luftwaffe, was also informed. At Berchtesgaden, a heated argument over the escaped pilots erupted between Hitler, Wilhelm Keitel (supreme commander of the German armed forces) and Himmler. Hitler shouted at them that an example must be set.[6] General von Graevenitz, chief of the Prisoner of War Department, looked gravely on as Himmler and Hitler agreed that the prisoners were to be hunted down and shot as an example to others.[7] Graevenitz commented that it was against the Geneva Convention, but he was ignored. Keitel interjected and ordered that the names of those shot were to be posted up in Stalag Luft III for all to see, and the urns with their ashes returned to the camp and buried there. He issued a strict prohibition on anything being recorded in writing about the shooting.[8] On the journey back, General von Graevenitz turned to his colleague and said that there was nothing to be done, because the case had been handed to the Gestapo. They could only make sure that their own officials were not involved in the killings.

The day after the mass escape, the infamous Sagan Order was issued from Hitler's headquarters. It read, in part:

> The increase of escapes by officer prisoners of war is a menace to internal security. I am disappointed about the inefficient security measures. As a deterrent the Führer has ordered that more than half of the escaped officers are to be shot. After interrogation the officers are to be routed to their original camp and to be shot en route. The shootings will be explained by the fact that the recaptured officers were shot whilst trying to escape or because they offered resistance, so that nothing can be proved later.[9]

Himmler passed the Sagan Order to Ernst Kaltenbrunner, a leading Nazi figure and director of the Reich Main Security Office, who relayed it to Heinrich Müller, head of the Gestapo in Berlin. The order was to apply not only to the RAF pilots who had escaped from Stalag Luft III, but to all future escapers.

Piecing together the evidence

The two main regions where the majority of RAF pilots were killed were Breslau and Sagan in Upper Silesia, then part of Nazi Germany. Colonel Scotland's team discovered that no fewer than twenty-nine men had been murdered in the Sagan area, and their bodies cremated in the Breslau district. Tracking down the names of the perpetrators was to prove more straightforward now that the regions of the killings had been narrowed down to just two. The task of investigating the deaths within Germany was given to Wing Commander William Bowes of the Special Investigation Branch of the RAF, because the incident had involved British airmen. The first priority for Bowes and his team was to track down every German with any connection, or suspected connection, to the Sagan case and transfer them to the London Cage for detailed interrogation. If the suspects were being held by other European governments, they were interrogated by Bowes in Germany, and the reports sent on to Colonel Scotland in London.

The first arrest in the Sagan case was made in October 1944, seven months after the killings. Major Hans Thiede had been attached for a short time to No. 17 Inspection Centre (the centre responsible for six POW camps, including No. 3 at Sagan), where some recaptured RAF pilots had been held before being shot. In his defence, when interrogated by Captain Kettler at the London Cage on 19 October 1944, Thiede argued that he was an anti-Nazi who had not witnessed any of the Sagan events.[10] His only knowledge of the case came from reading a telegram that British airmen had been shot while resisting arrest. He explained to interrogators about security in the various camps, and said that the key individuals to interview were Lieutenant-General Walther Grosch (commanding officer of No. 17 Inspection Centre) and Colonel Richard Waelde. Thiede's testimony led to Grosch and Waelde later being brought to the cage to answer questions about whether the inspection centre had had any powers to protect prisoners.

Grosch was interrogated by Colonel Scotland on 7 December 1945 and initially refused to make a full statement.[11] Scotland found him 'haughty, an upright Prussian General who resented being interrogated'.[12] He informed Grosch that he had 'sufficient evidence to warrant a charge against you of conniving in this terrible crime. You can either prove to the court that you are innocent of a murder charge or you can demonstrate to me that you are innocent by writing a full statement of your actions following the escapes.'[13]

An hour later, having reflected on his position in his cell, Grosch asked to see Colonel Scotland again. Scotland passed him a pencil and paper on which to write down his account.[14] It was a wise decision on Grosch's part, because Scotland came to the conclusion that Grosch had actually taken no part in the Sagan crimes, and he was therefore not prosecuted.

The commandant of Stalag Luft III, Colonel Friedrich von Lindeiner, had been brought to the London Cage a few months earlier. Tall and rather distinguished-looking, Lindeiner appeared before Scotland on 14 August 1945. The Nazi regime had sentenced him to a year in a fortress for his apparent slackness as commander of Stalag Luft III in allowing the escape. Lindeiner had eventually been permitted to return to his home, where Russian forces had arrested him as they advanced across Germany. In the summer of 1945, the Russians extradited him to London for interrogation.

Scotland recalled how he had been eager to meet the man who had commanded Stalag Luft III at the time of a mass escape which had attracted so much attention.[15] He was astute in his handling of Lindeiner, who had asked to see the questions in advance of his interrogation. Scotland told him that he was being held on suspicion of having deliberately allowed the prisoners to escape so that they would be shot.[16]

Scotland said to him: 'You knew of the orders and that if further escapes occurred, shooting was likely . . . Someone wanted an opportunity to shoot a number of prisoners.'[17]

Lindeiner was visibly shocked at the suggestion, and protested that what had taken place after the escape had nothing to do with him. He said that he had warned the prisoners not to escape and was sorry for what had happened after they got away. Scotland reminded him that fifty innocent men had been murdered, and he was going to find out who was responsible. He insisted on Lindeiner's full cooperation before he would believe his version of events. It was a bluff, because Scotland knew that Lindeiner could not have been responsible for the killings, otherwise the Germans would not have placed him behind bars. But Scotland needed a statement from him, and Lindeiner was not cooperating. Scotland sent him back to his room.

It took three days for Lindeiner to review his options and decide to cooperate. Finally, on 18 August 1945, he signed a voluntary statement providing valuable information, including a timetable of security checks on the night of the escape.[18]

By spring 1946, a number of suspects in the Sagan case were incarcerated in the London Cage. These included Bodo Struck of the State Security Head Office, who signed a statement witnessed by Captain Cornish on 3 April 1946. Bodo Struck was able to provide extensive details on how the Germans had categorised their prisoners and where they had been held. The following week, Peter Mohr was being held in the cage. He was the police commissioner who had compiled the original German reports on the Sagan case, and was thought to have significant information on the killings. During his interrogation by Captain Cornish on 10 April 1946, Mohr provided the most comprehensive report thus far.[19] He explained that he was of a junior rank in the office and had to carry out the jobs that others did not want. He said that he had been shown ten or fifteen urns that were said to contain the ashes of the escaped prisoners. Only when he returned to Berlin did he hear about the Sagan Order – an order which, he said, had come straight from Himmler. Mohr had memorised the order and could quote it word for word to Captain Cornish. He said that all the killings had been carried out in the same manner: it was reported publicly by the authorities that the prisoners had been 'shot in an attempt to escape or while offering resistance on arrest after a second attempted escape'.[20] Mohr was a key material witness, because he told interrogators that this was untrue: the prisoners had not tried to escape after their recapture. This was the vital piece of evidence that Scotland and the interrogators needed to substantiate the Sagan case as a war crime.

Erich Zacharias

It was becoming apparent that the majority of the perpetrators were from the local Gestapo in the areas where the atrocities were committed. Wing Commander Bowes knew that as soon as the war was over many Gestapo and SS had disposed of their uniforms and were hiding among the civilian population under false identities, with fake papers and in civilian clothes. He and his team began to question local witnesses about the events surrounding the escape of the British pilots, and gathered statements on what they knew. It emerged that the bodies of at least three pilots had been cremated immediately at Moravská Ostrava, on the orders of the Gestapo. Two men in particular were urgently being hunted for their part in it: Hans Ziegler, who had given orders for the Stalag Luft III prisoners to be taken into the countryside and shot, and police officer Erich Zacharias, who had already admitted to his comrade Friedrich Kiowsky that he had shot two prisoners.[21] Ziegler had instructed Zacharias to take the prisoners out into the countryside at 2 a.m. He told him it was 'a nice quiet time when you won't be disturbed, order them out of the truck for a pee and then shoot them. Their bodies are to be swiftly cremated. The excuse given in the official report to be attempted escape.'[22]

Bowes tracked down Zacharias in Bremen and arrested him. In April 1946, he personally escorted Zacharias from Germany to the London Cage. But it would be nearly two years before Ziegler was found.

Although Zacharias was not the first suspect in the Sagan case to be brought to the London Cage, he was the first of the Gestapo men to be interrogated there. By the time he arrived, he already had his story worked out. He was described as a brutal man, who readily obeyed orders. Major Roger Mortimer, who carried out duties at Wellington Barracks, occasionally had to provide guards and escorts for the London Cage. He described Zacharias as 'one of the most appalling men I have ever met'.[23]

The interrogators had already heard from other witnesses how Zacharias's men had brutally beaten up two escaped pilots, Squadron Leader T.G. Kirby-Green of the RAF and Flying Officer G.A. Kidder (a Canadian), and had driven them out of town to be shot. Their bodies were cremated in Moravská Ostrava. Captain Cornish led the interrogations of Zacharias, quietly watched by Scotland. The fair-haired Zacharias, of medium height, displayed a cockiness and bared his bad teeth as he flatly refused to make any statement. It was Scotland who took the decision to re-enact the last interrogation of Kidder and Kirby-Green by Zacharias and Ziegler at Zlín. One of them had ripped the handcuffs off Kidder, broken his hand and dragged him onto his knees. Scotland described the re-enactment in his unpublished memoirs:

We knew that there had [originally] been four men in the room. We prepared a room for Zacharias; the blinds were drawn, the lights were on, and on a table we placed a microphone to record anything Zacharias might say. There were four of us in the room, two behind the table, and one on either side of the front. We had Zacharias brought in with

handcuffs. He was made to kneel in front of the table, just as we imag-
ined Kidder had done. A statement was read to Zacharias which gave
the facts about his part in the murders. Once it had been read out, I
moved over to Zacharias and put my hand on his shoulder, and said:
'What is the truth?' Whether the atmosphere and his memories of Zlin
affected Zacharias, or whether the bit of showmanship appealed to
him, he admitted shooting Kidder. The whole incident took less than
five minutes to obtain the confession.[24]

Scotland called for the guard and said: 'He has confessed. He can now
make a statement.'[25] The statement, signed 'voluntarily and without
compulsion', was witnessed by Captain Cornish on 12 April 1946.[26] The
statement gave a detailed step-by-step account of the shootings, in which
Zacharias admitted:

> I made the prisoners get out of the car and go to the kerb to pass water
> there. I took up position about one metre obliquely left behind him . . .
> I drew my service pistol, which was all ready for firing, from the side
> pocket of my coat and fired obliquely in the left side of my prisoner in
> order to hit his heart. In order to make quite sure, I fired a second shot
> at the prisoner as he was collapsing . . . I convinced myself of the death
> of the prisoner by feeling his pulse and looking at his eye.[27]

It was always maintained by staff that no physical violence was ever
used against Zacharias to obtain that confession. There is no apparent
reason to doubt the reliability of Scotland's memoirs which recounted the
re-enactment. It therefore calls into question whether such psychological
intimidation was justified, as well as the level of pressure that was acceptable to break the spirit of Zacharias – a known war criminal whose crimes
were evident – and secure a confession from him. After the full confession
was complete, Zacharias began to boast about his crimes.[28] Scotland
loathed him and arranged for his transfer to the cage at Kempton Park.
But that was not the last of Zacharias.

Once at Kempton Park, Zacharias planned his escape. He had been
allowed to keep his penknife, and every day for three weeks he used it to
saw away at the lock on the unpainted door of his cell. He filled the hole
with soft dough from his daily bread ration so that the guards would not
notice it. On the night of his escape, the guard was asleep in his own room

and the camp was quiet. With the lock broken away, Zacharias walked a few yards down the corridor before leaving through the open main entrance of the long, narrow building. He crossed the compound, climbed a tree, balanced on a branch, and jumped clear of the barbed-wire fence. There were no guards to be seen or any searchlights. At the second barbed-wire fence he struggled, and one of his shoes got stuck. He left it behind and made his escape.

It was several hours before Zacharias's cell was checked and found empty by the early-morning guards on their rounds. With the shoe discovered in the fence, the local police and Home Guard mounted a manhunt. Zacharias was soon recaptured and escorted from Kempton Park straight back to the London Cage. Scotland refused to see him immediately, and instructed the guards that his first night was to be spent handcuffed to his bed.[29]

From the cage, Zacharias was transferred to a more secure camp near Sheffield. He stood trial at the first Sagan trial the following year, in 1947, where he was found guilty. He was executed at Hameln prison on 27 February 1948. But before that, the story of Zacharias would take an unexpected turn.

Suspects and perpetrators

Towards the end of June 1946, the London Cage handled a number of other Gestapo men in connection with the Sagan case. These included Richard Hansel, a greying man in his fifties who had had a long career in the German army. He always maintained that he had been transferred to the Gestapo without any consultation. Hansel was close to tears when the guards brought him into Scotland's office, and it became clear that he lived in fear of being sent for trial. Hansel explained how he had accompanied the convoy of vehicles into the woods after a two-hour drive, and there the prisoners had been shot. He claimed to have known nothing of the shootings, and in his defence argued that Wilhelm Scharpwinkel, head of the Gestapo in Breslau, had made his men do things they did not want to do. He explained that at the time of the shootings, he had gone back to the truck to get a sandwich and was shocked to hear the gunfire in the woods.

Hansel signed a statement in the cage on 24 June 1946, witnessed by Colonel Scotland. Scotland decided that there was no need to hold him any longer, and ordered his transfer to a camp in Northumberland where he spent most of the time 'as a nervous wreck and crying'.[30]

In June 1948, Hansel was back in the London Cage en route to his trial in Germany. Scotland wrote in his unpublished memoirs, 'As the weather was fine, we put a chair in the back garden of the cage, let him sit in the sun, and gave him his meds there. We also got the doctor to look at him; to give Hansel sedatives to help him sleep.'[31] The mention of meds and sedatives harks back to questions raised in chapter 7 about the use of drugs and whether they had indeed been administered with the prisoner's consent. The court in Hamburg decided that Hansel was not guilty, and he was discharged.

Interrogators learned from another prisoner, Hans Schumacher, more about the central part played by the local Gestapo in the Sagan killings. Schumacher, a member of the Kripo (criminal police) in Breslau, pointed to Wilhelm Scharpwinkel as the man who knew all about what had happened. There was so much secrecy surrounding the killings that very little information had leaked out, he told interrogators. The case was indeed narrowed down to Scharpwinkel, the man in charge of the firing squads and head of the Gestapo in Breslau.[32] His name was already on the wanted list, but his whereabouts were still unknown. He was finally located as a prisoner of the Russians, who refused to hand him over on the grounds that he was too ill to travel. Interrogating Scharpwinkel became an urgent priority for Scotland's team. Negotiations began between the Soviet Union and the United Kingdom, involving the British Embassy in Moscow and the Foreign Office in London. These led to the Russians granting the necessary visa and permission for Captain Cornish to visit Moscow and interrogate Scharpwinkel.[33] He arrived in August 1946, interrogating the former Gestapo chief in a Moscow hospital on 31 August and 19 September. The Russians were initially suspicious of Cornish's detailed interrogation, and insisted on a full Russian translation; but they soon tired of the protracted examinations and settled for a copy in German.

During the questioning, Scharpwinkel told Cornish: 'I would have preferred that the order to shoot the prisoners had not reached my office; but if it had not been carried out there would have been a court martial.'[34] He blamed the shootings on Max Wielen, a man called Lux and others, saying that he had only received news of the shootings after they had happened. He claimed that the order to shoot had come not from him but had been received by Lux direct from Berlin. Lux could never be brought to justice by the London Cage because he had been killed in the siege of Breslau at the end of the war.

In his statement of 31 August, Scharpwinkel admitted that he had been at the headquarters in Görlitz with Lux. Displaying no emotion, he calmly explained to Captain Cornish how he had witnessed Lux telling the captured pilots that they would be shot. The pilots were driven in a convoy towards Sagan. When they reached the main highway, they were ordered out of the vehicles. He told Cornish:

The prisoners were placed in position and it was revealed to them that the sentence was about to be carried out. The prisoners showed considerable calm, which surprised me very much. The six prisoners stood next to one another in the wood. Lux gave the order to fire and the detachment fired. Lux shot with them. By the second salvo the prisoners were dead.[35]

Prosecutors always believed Scharpwinkel to be guilty because he had made no attempt to prevent the killings. Sir Robert Craigie, the UK representative on the United Nations War Crimes Commission, wrote at the time: 'It is clear that Scharpwinkel played a leading part in this war crime, and that he moved upon a higher level than any of the heads of the Gestapo in other places involved.'[36] Scharpwinkel did not face justice for the Sagan crimes, and died in a Soviet prison in 1947.

On 6 September 1945, Max Wielen, a member of the secret police in Breslau, had been interrogated at the London Cage by Major Reidel and Colonel William Edward Hinchley Cooke, one of the most senior interrogators of MI5.[37] During the war, Hinchley Cooke had interrogated some of the first German agents who had landed in Britain. He was dubbed one of Britain's greatest wartime spycatchers, and he helped turn Arthur Owens into the famous double agent Snow. Most of Hinchley Cooke's legacy still lies buried in MI5 files.

In the autumn of 1946, Wielen arrived back at the London Cage, to be interrogated this time by Colonel Scotland. A statement was finally secured from Wielen on 2 November 1946. Although by the end of that year teams at the London Cage had prepared material evidence against various criminals in the Sagan case, ready for the trial, the only men directly implicated in the deaths of the twenty-nine RAF officers whom they had in custody were Wielen and Hansel.

Another suspect brought to the cage was police officer Erwin Wieczorek, a good-looking, quiet man in his forties, a member of the Breslau Gestapo and head of one of the four sections working under Scharpwinkel. He had been with Scharpwinkel during one of the killings and had thus been sworn to secrecy. At the time of that shooting, Wieczorek said he had raised the bonnet of the truck and pretended to be mending the engine so that he did not have to witness events.[38] Standing before Colonel Scotland in June 1947, he provided the names of the killing squad and the driver, Robert Schroeder. He recollected the journey back from the shooting and told Scotland: 'Hardly anyone spoke because we were tired and depressed by what had taken place.'[39] Wieczorek said he had found various excuses not to accompany the squad on subsequent shootings. He signed a statement on 23 June 1947, and was not charged at the second Sagan trial in Hamburg in 1948.

It was not until the summer of 1948 that the driver, Robert Schroeder, was located. During interrogation by Scotland at the cage on 2 and 10 June, Schroeder confirmed the facts that had been provided by Wieczorek, and the part taken by Scharpwinkel in the killings. He provided a list of all the men in the firing squad. In his own defence, he argued that he was merely the driver and had taken no part in the shootings.[40]

Another man implicated in the Sagan case was Josef Gmeiner, head of the Gestapo in Karlsruhe. He, too, found himself in the London Cage, where he spent a week typing up his statement, only to be told by Scotland that what he had written was 'utter nonsense'.[41] During interrogation, Gmeiner quoted the Sagan Order word for word. When it came to the part stating that escapees were to be executed, Scotland barked at him: 'Stop!' He challenged Gmeiner that the prisoners had not been tried by any court in Germany, and therefore it was an order to commit murder.

'Didn't your natural sense of justice revolt against that?' he asked Gmeiner.

Gmeiner had his answer: 'No. It was an order from the Führer, therefore it was legal and binding on me.'

Scotland warned him: 'That statement will hang you, Gmeiner.'[42] Gmeiner voluntarily signed a statement in the presence of Captain Cornish on 25 September 1946.

Also in the cage was Johannes Post, the brutal Gestapo man who had been in charge of a correction camp at Kiel. Scotland admitted that 'We had a mutual hatred of each other.'[43] Of all the Sagan war criminals, Johannes Post stood out as a complete sadist. At the camp near Kiel, he had ensured that Germany's forced labourers were beaten to death for not working hard enough. When he was brought before Scotland, he was still smoking a cigarette and 'putting on an act'.[44]

'You are Johannes Post?' Scotland asked him.

'Yes,' he said, with what was seen as supercilious arrogance.

Scotland did not tolerate him and turned immediately to the guard: 'Take good care of this man. He is one of the worst bastards of the whole lot.' This was a coded message to rough him up.[45] Exactly what kind of treatment Johannes Post suffered has not been recorded. Reflecting on the matter some years later, Scotland commented that only SS officer Reinhold Bruchardt of Danzig, 'a giant of a man at over 6ft tall', was more 'physically brutal'.[46]

The precise date of Bruchardt's arrival at the London Cage is not recorded in the surviving files, but it is known that Wing Commander Bowes tracked him down in Germany and arranged for him to be transferred to the London Cage. The escorting guards were given a message for Colonel Scotland that Bruchardt was highly dangerous. By the time he arrived, the team had already reconstructed the part that he had played in the killings.

In his room at the cage, Bruchardt readily began to write down his version of events. Scotland was unimpressed and told him that he did not believe a word.[47] He told him straight: 'We know you were the man in charge of the special duty squad. You, and you only, were responsible for the murders. We already have all the evidence we want.'[48]

He called in Sergeant Prion of the guard and instructed him to see that Bruchardt was kept under constant observation until sent to a holding camp. Scotland recalled:

Prion set Bruchardt to work scrubbing floors. The German was both cocky and clever and fond of exhibiting his strength. Yet he found his match in Prion and he was so completely exhausted after a 'competition' at lifting sand buckets that he was glad to leave the cage for the prisoner of war camp in Colchester.[49]

Security at Colchester was not as strict as at the London Cage. One night, during Bruchardt's incarceration there, prisoner Lehmann passed his cell while attempting to escape. Bruchardt whispered to him to give him something to work the bars of his window. Half an hour later, the two men had made off over the boundary wall. They succeeded in living for three weeks undetected in woods near Colchester, raiding farms for food. Eventually they were both arrested by police and transferred back to the London Cage, where Colonel Scotland instructed Sergeant Prion to 'greet' them.[50] Bruchardt is said to have asked for work and chores in the cage to stop him going mad with boredom.

To prevent another escape, Bruchardt was transferred to a prison in Sheffield while the war crimes case was prepared against him. Then, in October 1948, he spent a brief time back at the London Cage before being transferred to Hamburg for the second Sagan trial which took place that same month.

The London Cage on trial

When the first Sagan trial opened in July 1947 and the second opened in October 1948, the reputation of the London Cage came under intense scrutiny for its treatment of prisoners. Colonel Scotland found himself in the dock answering serious charges about how statements were secured from Nazi war criminals. Accusations of brutality against the prisoners extended to periods of starvation, sleep deprivation and third-degree methods of interrogation and electric shock treatment. There was much at stake – not only months and years of careful detective work, interrogations and research into the whereabouts of war criminals, but, if it could be proved by the defence lawyers that Scotland and the interrogators had acquired the confessions by force, then the war crimes case might collapse and the war criminals walk free.

The first Sagan trial commenced on 1 July 1947, and soon the focus of the military court shifted from the Nazi war criminals to the London Cage itself. The defence tried to show that the statements secured for the trial were the result of coercion in the cage. This led to Scotland spending three days in the witness box under cross-examination. He realised that something was wrong when the female German defence lawyer, Dr Ohlert, addressed him as *Herr Zeuge* (Mr Witness), rather than by his full military rank.[51] The judge advocate did not correct her. It was always Scotland's belief that a remnant underground SS movement was behind the disruption in court. They knew that the SS war criminals standing trial had signed an oath of allegiance to Hitler that they would never break. Scotland believed that Dr Ohlert was under their influence, as she tried to corner him into publicly admitting that the statements had been signed under duress.

The court granted her request to cross-examine Scotland, and it became a very public affair. She put it to him that Zacharias's statement had been made under physical pressure. She asked Scotland whether prisoners had been denied food, whether their complaints were investigated and whether they had been engaged in cleaning duties as a disciplinary measure. And were they ordered to clean their rooms with a toothbrush as a punishment? She wanted to know why Zacharias had been interrogated more than ten times. She related to the court how Zacharias had been struck across the face several times, had had food withheld for several days, and on the days when he was interrogated, how the guards had refused to let him sleep.

'If that were true, Zacharias should have made a complaint and we would have done something about it,' responded Scotland, remaining outwardly unruffled by the accusations. But from comments he made later in his autobiography, he was seething at the turn of events.[52]

Dr Ohlert fired back another comment: 'Zacharias says you threatened him with electrical devices in the London Cage.'

'Quite untrue,' replied Scotland. 'We have no such weapons or devices.'

She then levelled accusations against his staff, who allegedly beat up Zacharias when he was alone with an intelligence officer. Scotland's reply was carefully worded: 'I cannot vouch for things that happened when I was not present at an interrogation, but I would have noticed marks on Zacharias if he had been beaten.'[53]

'Is it true that prisoners in the London Cage were told that they would be hanged and their wives deported to Siberia?' she asked.[54]

Scotland retorted: 'I have heard a lot of nonsense about the London Cage, but this is really the limit. It is absolutely untrue and nonsensical.'

Scotland had one key weapon at his disposal: from decades of human espionage and dealing with German prisoners of war, he understood psychology. The calmer he remained, the more agitated and frustrated Dr Ohlert became. She began shouting across the courtroom, and played her one final card that she thought would destabilise the situation. She asked him: 'Is it true that you have served in the German army?'

Courtroom observers and journalists muttered in shock at the question. Scotland did not deny it, and was forced to admit publicly that he had served in the German army during the Khoikhoi War. It led to sensationalist newspaper headlines about 'Schottland – Spy serving in the German army'.[55] The *Observer on Sunday* reported 'allegations of beatings up and third degree methods', but added the rider that these allegations 'may be baseless'.[56] The military court refused to be drawn in and ruled that these details were irrelevant to the case.

It was only when Scotland wrote up his memoirs that he provided some clue as to the treatment of prisoners; but the intelligence services censored out the following paragraph:

> Naturally we used disciplinary measures if they were required. You don't allow tough Gestapo criminals to imagine they have arrived at a Kindergarten or for a rest care. But there were ways of putting a troublesome or cocky prisoner of war in his place without beating him up. And as for work about the cage, many were happy to be given something to do to occupy their time. It is true that we tried a little showmanship with Zacharias, but this was a matter of psychology, not force.[57]

The military court sat for forty-nine days. Thirteen of the accused were sentenced on 3 September 1947 to be hanged at Hameln prison; others were given various lengths of jail sentences.

The second Sagan trial, which convened in Hamburg in October 1948, was far more efficient. It was here that Bruchardt, Zacharias, Wieczorek and Hansel were tried. Although Bruchardt was condemned to death, his sentence was later commuted to life imprisonment. Erich Zacharias, Johannes Post and Oskar Schmidt were among those sent to the gallows. Wieczorek and Hansel stood accused of the death of twenty-nine RAF officers from Stalag Luft III who been murdered near Breslau. Hansel was discharged. Wieczorek was sentenced to death, but this was later commuted to life imprisonment. He was subsequently released.

At the end of both Sagan trials, it could be said that justice had only partly been served: some of the war criminals were never caught. The case against the London Cage for torture and brutality was dismissed and Scotland was exonerated. But he always regretted that he and his team had not succeeded in bringing all the war criminals of the Sagan case to justice. As he wrote:

> Though we knew the full story of the murders in the Breslau area, it was one of the most unsatisfactory sections of the Sagan crime for, in the end, not one man went to the gallows to answer for the deaths of the twenty-nine RAF officers.[58]

13

NORWAY AND WAR CRIMES

It was May 1946 when Colonel Scotland walked into Room 22 to see General Nikolaus von Falkenhorst's name among the list of prisoners on the board. Falkenhorst had been Hitler's supreme commander-in-chief of the German army, navy and air forces in Norway, and was loathed for his part in war crimes there.[1] Norway had been invaded and occupied by the German army from 9 April 1940 until Germany's surrender in Europe in May 1945. The civilian population had suffered various kinds of brutality that extended to cruel interrogations at Gestapo headquarters in Oslo. Falkenhorst stood out as the man responsible for the atrocities. A month after Germany's unconditional surrender in May 1945, Colonel Scotland dispatched a team to Norway to investigate. The team, headed by Captain Broderman consisted of twenty-five officers and thirty-five sergeants, and took up residence in the old medieval fortress of Akershus in Oslo, once the Gestapo headquarters. They were tasked with investigating two partic-ular war crimes against British special forces during clandestine operations in Norway in 1942. The Allies were holding around 370,000 German prisoners of war in camps in Norway, and Broderman and his team had to comb the camps for any suspected war criminals.

The Americans had arrested Falkenhorst on 10 May 1945 and were holding him in Dachau concentration camp. Falkenhorst's guilt was clear; it was the job of the London Cage to gather the evidence for a court to sentence him to hang him for his crimes. Major Terry was dispatched to Dachau to interview Falkenhorst and secure a statement from him, which he did on 5 April 1946. The statement outlined Falkenhorst's military career, and in it he stated that no German soldier wanted the shootings, but he was acting on Hitler's orders. He spoke about the 'tragic conflict between honour and conscience, responsibility and a sense of duty, obedience and oath of allegiance'.[2]

The following month, Scotland had Falkenhorst in the London Cage. He asked the guards to take him to his office, where Falkenhorst waited alone for fifteen minutes before Scotland entered. Scotland wrote of the moment that he first saw him:

> I found Falkenhorst standing in the middle of my room facing a window, and I had a side view of him as I passed to my table. At 5'7", he was of slight build, a retreating forehead and beaky nose. His furrowed brow revealed an anxious man with thin grey hair.[3]

According to Scotland, he seemed a physical and moral weakling,[4] and Scotland showed him no tolerance during the hard-line interrogations in the cage. Falkenhorst refused to make eye contact as Scotland asked him to pull up a chair to the desk.

Scotland stared at him for a few minutes in silence, then said: 'I want to know why Hitler selected you as senior officer commanding the whole of the Wehrmacht forces in Norway – an appointment that no other German enjoyed throughout the whole of the war. Why?'[5]

Falkenhorst replied that he had commanded the 21st Army Corps in Poland, and that same unit had been selected to occupy Norway. Scotland interjected with his own analysis of Falkenhorst's career, saying that, in his view, Hitler had chosen Falkenhorst because he was the only member of the Prussian military aristocracy to have accepted the principles of the Nazi regime absolutely. He then explained to Falkenhorst that he would not be treated as a prisoner of war with the rights that afforded him, but rather as a war criminal, deprived of his rank as a general. He could expect to be in the cage for at least three weeks, during which time the interrogators would obtain all the information they needed for a conviction. Scotland outlined the atrocities he had committed in Norway while Falkenhorst became subdued; he tried to argue that he had had no authority over the Nazi figures who had committed those crimes.[6] Before Falkenhorst was dismissed and escorted back to his cell, Scotland told him that he had three days in which to write down his account of exactly what had happened in Norway.

The Commando Order

Between 11 and 21 September 1942, ten British commandos and two Norwegian commandos had mounted a raid on the power plant at Glomfjord. Their mission, codenamed Operation Musketoon, succeeded in blowing up the Norwegian industrial factory there and removed it from operation for the rest of the war. The explosion awoke the German troops and resulted in the capture of seven of the special forces. They were transported to the famous prison at Colditz Castle in Germany, and from there were later transferred to Sachsenhausen concentration camp and shot. They should have been treated as prisoners of war, but they were murdered under the jurisdiction of General von Falkenhorst and, as such, were the victims of a war crime.

Norway was strategically important to the Third Reich because of its key industrial sites and power plants, some vital to Hitler's developing atomic programme. The clandestine British raids on these plants, often in conjunction with Norwegian special forces, enraged the Führer. He issued the Commando Order, which amounted to the legitimisation of 'no quarter' – no clemency – to commandos captured in battle. Marked 'Top Secret' and dated 18 October 1942, the Commando Order stated:

> I have found myself forced to issue a drastic order for the extermination of enemy sabotage parties and to make non-compliance with it severely punishable . . . Should it prove advisable to spare one or two men in the first instance for interrogation reasons, they are to be shot immediately after their interrogation.[7]

The Commando Order made it compulsory for German commanders to kill captured special forces or commando raiders in any theatre of war.[8] Under no circumstances were they to be treated as prisoners of war. With no consultation, Falkenhorst took it upon himself to add a sentence to the end of Hitler's Commando Order: 'If a man is saved for interrogation, he must not survive his comrades for more than twenty-four hours.'[9] Falkenhorst dispatched the order to the commanders of the German army, navy and air force in Norway, together with his additional sentence, as if it had come direct from Hitler. Falkenhorst had personally sanctioned the killing of special forces within twenty-four hours of capture and had authorised his commanders to do so.

The following month, the Commando Order was executed against raiders of another clandestine mission called Operation Freshman, which targeted the Vemork heavy-water plant outside Rjukan. On 19 November 1942, a combined airborne operation of sappers from the Royal Engineers, SOE and 1st Airborne Division attacked the hydroelectric plant to destroy any Nazi capability to produce heavy water for its nuclear programme.[10] Operation Freshman was always known to be extremely risky and costly, with a high probability that the men would be taken prisoner. No one expected them to be executed in cold blood after capture.

The events surrounding this secret mission and the subsequent atrocity were investigated at the London Cage and gradually pieced together. A detailed picture emerged, with interrogators learning that two Horsa gliders had headed for the site at Vemork with thirty-one men on board, including two officers.[11] The weather was against them, and high winds had separated the gliders.[12] The first glider crashed on cliffs above Lysefjord, near Stavanger, when the tow rope snapped. Five survivors, all Royal Engineers, were captured by the Germans: Lance Corporal Jackson, and sappers F. Bonner, J.N. Blackburn, J. Walsh and T.W. White. All were taken to Grini concentration camp in Bærum, near Oslo.[13] On 18 January 1943, the men were taken into nearby woods and executed on the orders of Colonel Probst, chief of staff to Lieutenant-General Karl von Behrens of the 280th Infantry Division, headquartered at Stavanger.[14]

The second glider crashed near Egersund. Fourteen surviving prisoners were picked up by German patrols under the command of Colonel Probst. All were shot by members of the German 355 Infantry Regiment.[15] Both Probst and Behrens would face interrogation at the London Cage after the war. Behrens was absolved by a British military court in Hamburg of any part in the deaths of the fourteen commandos of Operation Freshman, and remained a prisoner at Camp 11 at Bridgend in South Wales until his repatriation to Germany in 1947.

Falkenhorst in the cage

Colonel Scotland wanted to understand why Falkenhorst had added the clause to the Commando Order. He waited three days for him to cooperate with a statement, which Falkenhorst duly completed. In it, the German outlined why he had been chosen by Hitler as commander in Norway and how he had had no authority over another key known war criminal, Josef Terboven, the senior political commissar for occupied Norwegian territories and head of the secret police there. Terboven had feared capture by the Norwegians for his part in atrocities and had committed suicide. Although Terboven had no command over German military forces in Norway (because they came under Falkenhorst), that did not mean he had not been ruthless: he had planned the concentration camps in Norway and had his own personal force of around 6,000 men, including 800 secret police. Terboven was known to have been responsible for the murder of at least five British prisoners of war in captivity in Norway.

Colonel Scotland sought to understand why Falkenhorst had allowed certain events to unfold in Norway without making any attempt to forestall them.[16] Why, for example, had he allowed Terboven to send British prisoners of war to their deaths in Norway or in concentration camps in Germany? As the most senior commander of forces in Norway, it was his duty to ensure that all captured prisoners were held under military law and treated according to the Geneva Convention. During a number of interrogations, Scotland made the consequences of Falkenhorst's actions very plain. He explained to Falkenhorst that he would certainly be charged with the deaths of the commandos in the Glomfjord raid.

According to Scotland, Falkenhorst had a ready supply of answers, claiming that in allowing the prisoners to be taken to Germany, he was not actually responsible for their deaths: he was only obeying Hitler's Commando Order. Scotland was one step ahead and retorted that in distributing the Commando Order throughout Norway, Falkenhorst had not kept it secret, but had made it a public document; and that by adding the clause, he was implicated in the deaths of the men of Operation Freshman. Scotland laid out the plain facts – that the men had been in uniform and only carrying weapons with which to defend themselves. He put it to Falkenhorst that these men fell within the boundaries of the Geneva Convention as prisoners of war, and as such, Falkenhorst should have arranged their transfer to a prisoner-of-war camp, not a concentration camp.[17]

Falkenhorst defended himself by saying he had no organised POW camps in Norway at that time. The only camps were under the control of Terboven, and he would not allow the men to be taken to Terboven's camps. Scotland did not accept this feeble explanation and countered that

Terboven had prisoners in the Akershus. Falkenhorst replied that he had nowhere else to put prisoners of war.

Scotland's patience wore thin as he outlined Falkenhorst's crimes:

> Crime Number one – You as the commander of all the troops in Norway were bound by the Geneva Convention to provide accommodation for any prisoners of war but you failed to do so. When Hitler's Order reached you in October, you decided to have these men removed from the Akershus to Germany. They were removed in irons – another offence against the Geneva Convention.[18]

Falkenhorst seems to have been no match for this experienced interrogator. Scotland mentions in his memoirs how the German's hands began to tremble and he became very uncomfortable. He continued his denials and became so agitated that Scotland ordered the guards to take him back to his cell.[19]

Allowing a short time for Falkenhorst to recover his composure, Scotland recalled him for another round of interrogation. Again, the central focus was on holding Falkenhorst to account for the deaths of the British men who should have been treated as prisoners of war. There was no relaxation in the intensity of the interrogation, as Scotland challenged Falkenhorst that he must have known the British men were going to a concentration camp.

He confronted him with military procedure:

> I suggest that you received a receipt from Terboven for them [the prisoners], and that they were guarded on the journey to Germany by security force men who had the right of entry into a concentration camp in Germany. You can't take prisoners from one camp to another without getting a receipt for them, and your own troops would never have entered a concentration camp.[20]

Falkenhorst flatly denied being given any receipt for the British prisoners or having knowledge of a military escort. He denied all knowledge of any injured commandos. Scotland related how he kept ahead of the game, for he knew that the prisoners had been handled by Terboven, and that Terboven and Falkenhorst were in close contact. He ventured that Terboven had gloated over the captured commandos and had spoken to Falkenhorst about their capture and death.[21] Scotland insisted on knowing the truth. At this point, Falkenhorst explained that he had contacted Wilhelm Keitel and Keitel had simply replied: 'You have the orders.'[22] (Wilhelm Keitel was the officer in command of the whole Wehrmacht, based in Berlin and found guilty of war crimes at the Nuremberg trials. He would be hanged in Nuremberg prison on 16 October 1946.)

Scotland challenged Falkenhorst that Colonel Probst had admitted to him during interrogation that Falkenhorst had given the orders to shoot the men. Concluding the interrogation, Scotland stated that the brutal deaths of the men from Operation Freshman were the responsibility of Falkenhorst, and reiterated that he would hang for the crimes. Falkenhorst was sent back to his cell.

The interrogations paid off, because finally, in a statement signed in the cage on 5 July 1946, Falkenhorst admitted distributing the Commando Order to the commanders of the army, navy and air force in Norway, and adding the sentence that prisoners were not to survive for longer than twenty-four hours. He told Scotland: 'I cannot remember the last wording of this extract but I put in the last sentence.'[23] It was one of several signed statements that Falkenhorst made at the London Cage between 21 June 1946 and 6 July 1946, all witnessed by Colonel Scotland.

The case of diver Bob Evans

Nikolaus von Falkenhorst knew about another war crime that had taken place in Norway in autumn 1942. Between Operation Musketoon and Operation Freshman, the Royal Navy Special Service Unit landed a group of men in Norway on 28 October 1942. Their aim was to sink the prized German battleship *Tirpitz*, the heaviest battleship then built in Europe, which had been deployed in Norway to disrupt Allied convoys bound for the Soviet Union. Practice for the mission had been thorough enough and involved employing special 'two-man torpedoes'. The team had learned how to cut its way through submarine nets and attach explosives to the hull of a ship. Having failed in their mission, they were within 100 metres of the border over into neutral Sweden when they were stopped by a German officer. One of the team, Bill Tebb, fired his revolver at the German, but missed. The Germans opened fire with their Luger pistols. Tebb succeeded in killing them, but his colleague, Bob Evans, was badly wounded in the stomach. Thinking him dead, the British men pressed on and escaped over the border. The gunfire had aroused other German guards who transferred the wounded Evans to hospital. Once he had recovered, he was taken to Gestapo headquarters for inter-rogation. There he suffered brutal treatment and was 'exhibited' for all to see: local Norwegians and Germans were encouraged to come in and see the frogman with his diving gear laid out on a table. After the Gestapo had had enough of 'the show', they transferred Evans to Grini, where he was murdered alongside five of the commandos captured after the failed raid on Vemork.

Colonel Scotland knew that Falkenhorst had visited Evans at Gestapo headquarters in Oslo.[24] Facing Scotland in the London Cage, Falkenhorst was interrogated over his failure to treat Evans as a prisoner of war. In his defence, Falkenhorst argued that the Commando Order forbade him from treating Evans as a prisoner. Scotland challenged him on which section of the Commando Order made that stipulation. Falkenhorst could provide no answer as he floundered and admitted that it had been useless to intervene once Terboven had a prisoner. Under the terms of Hitler's Commando Order, Terboven could do whatever he liked. Scotland pointed out that Falkenhorst could have sent some of his own men to Grini or Gestapo headquarters to release Evans, but chose not to. Scotland told him:

> You are a despicable swine. You talked to Evans for fifteen minutes at the Gestapo headquarters, knowing that he was going to be murdered shortly by your friend Terboven. You made no attempt to rescue him. You enjoyed the situation.[25]

Falkenhorst said he had felt sorry for Evans. But Scotland dismissed his attempts at remorse and told him that he was 'a regular swine of a man'.[26]

Falkenhorst was sent back to his room to write down his statement on all the charges against him. He signed a number of consecutive state-ments between 21 June 1946 and 6 July 1946 that outlined his command of Norway.[27] As he awaited trial, he was transferred to Camp 11 at Bridgend in Wales, where he was ostracised by the other German officers. He became so depressed that after a fortnight, in the middle of July 1946, he was moved back to the London Cage, and from there was transferred to Brunswick for the war crimes trials. These were also attended by Scotland, who verified that the statements had been signed by Falkenhorst.

Nikolaus von Falkenhorst was found guilty of ordering troops under his command to execute the Commando Order. The court sentenced him to death, but this was later commuted to life imprisonment. In 1953, Falkenhorst was released from Werl prison on health grounds; he died in 1968.

14

BEFRIENDING THE FIELD MARSHAL

Of all the revelations emerging from the London Cage, possibly one of the most extraordinary was the unexpected friendship that developed between Colonel Scotland and Field Marshal Albert Kesselring.

It was September 1946 when the military authorities sent news that Kesselring was due to arrive at the London Cage from Nuremberg, where he had been appearing as a witness in the trial of the top Nazi leadership. After nine months, the court proceedings were over and the world had been presented with evidence of the worst atrocities in human history. The verdict on the twenty-one defendants deemed responsible for the most heinous war crimes had yet to be pronounced (for that, the world would have to wait until 1 October). No decision had yet been made whether Kesselring himself would face charges of war crimes alongside General Eberhard von Mackensen. Kesselring and Mackensen had both commanded forces in Italy and would spend time in the London Cage answering questions about the killing of more than 300 Italians and partisans in caves outside Rome in March 1944, in an incident known as the Ardeatine caves massacre.

Kesselring had commanded the Luftwaffe forces during Operation Barbarossa, the German invasion of Russia in June 1941. Then he had served as 'commander-in-chief south' in the Mediterranean operations, including the siege of Malta, the North African campaign (1941–43) and the Italian campaign (1943–45). It was his military service in Italy – and his possible part in war crimes – that was the reason for his transfer to the London Cage in autumn 1946.

Kesselring was one of the most popular German generals, remembered today by the only surviving veteran of the London Cage as 'always smiling and cheerful'. Even before Kesselring's arrival, Scotland had decided that he would be treated differently from other prisoners. He called Sergeant Prion to his office and instructed him to prepare a room in comfortable quarters at 6 Kensington Palace Gardens. Kesselring was not going to be treated as a prisoner facing a criminal charge, but would be accorded the privilege of walking in the gardens, free from the normal supervision of the guards. He was not to be subjected to regular observation, sleep deprivation, bright lights, minimal food rations or solitary confinement – although he did have his own room.

When Kesselring was brought to the cage, Scotland was waiting at the threshold to welcome him. There would be no unmarked vans for this escort, or arriving quietly at night. Scotland looked Kesselring straight in the eye and said 'Guten Tag, Herr Feldmarschall' ('Good day, Field Marshal').[1]

Writing later about the moment he first met Kesselring, Scotland recalled 'a tall, well-built man with a strong face, a keen and direct look and an air of authority.'[2] Kesselring made a good impression on Scotland and the other staff at the cage. In the luggage that accompanied him from Nuremberg prison were several heavy coats and smart mackintosh raincoats that were now being searched by the guards. Scotland asked Sergeant Prion to take a table up to Kesselring's room, so that he could put his extra coats on it. Kesselring remarked: 'It would be better if some hooks were nailed in the door. Then I could hang them up.' It was against cage rules for prisoners to have any sharp items in their room. Scotland glanced at Prion, then back to Kesselring, and said: 'We can't allow nails and hooks in a prisoner's room.'[3]

Kesselring laughed in his own inimitable way and replied: 'I assure you, I have no other use for them!'

Scotland then accompanied Kesselring to his special quarters on the second floor of No. 6, in a room overlooking the Bayswater Road. He appeared very grateful to be on his own after the stress and hectic atmosphere of the Nuremberg prison. Having his own quarters helped him to remain relaxed and helpful to the cage's employees.

By the time Kesselring arrived at the London Cage, many of his staff from Italy had already been interrogated (see page 187). Scotland and the interrogators had formed the opinion that Kesselring was innocent of the Ardeatine caves massacre. They assumed that the Allies would not charge him as a war criminal and that he would soon be a free man. It there-fore came as a shock when Scotland received notification from the Judge Advocate General's Office that Kesselring would stand trial, and it was Scotland's job to inform him. For the first time in his long history of dealing with German prisoners of war, Scotland felt embarrassed and depressed as he sat opposite Kesselring in his quarters and delivered the news.

Kesselring stood up, his fists clenched as he raised his voice in anger:

> If the British government expects me to submit to this charge as a guilty criminal they are making a mistake. I shall not defend myself as a man on a criminal charge, but as a Field Marshal of the German army. I shall defend my honour in that rank and nothing else.[4]

Scotland rose to his feet, level with Kesselring, and told him firmly:

> I do not believe you are guilty of any crime in Italy. But if you take that attitude before a British Military Court you will be found guilty, and you will be sentenced. Sit down and write your final statement, as you will prepare it for a proper legal defence on a legal charge. You have to answer any charge made against you, but that answer is not as a Field Marshal. I am convinced that the limitation of your authority is your answer. But if you maintain that you were the Supreme Authority in Italy, then you will be condemned.[5]

Kesselring was a principled man with his own views on military respon-sibility. He refused to listen to Colonel Scotland and maintained that he would defend his honour as a field marshal and as supreme officer in Italy overseeing various German units. He stated his intention to shield Mackensen, too, of war crimes. His response not only frustrated Scotland, it strengthened his resolve to help prove him innocent. Kesselring was asked to write down his version of events and what he knew of atrocities in Italy. Scotland spent time with him most days, discussing military matters and going over his statement. He admitted in his memoirs: 'I used to spend two hours a day going over with him the ground for his statement and, as he produced his material, amending it with him to show what had been his personal duties and responsibilities in Italy at the time of the crimes.'[6]

Kesselring wrote his statement in German; the flowery language that was so typical of him was difficult for the translators to render into readable

English. Scotland was comfortable enough to advise him that, as a soldier, he should practise using short words and learn to be more precise. The two men enjoyed each other's company as military men and had an extraordinary mutual respect that did not occur between Scotland and any other prisoner.

The Ardeatine caves massacre

The war crimes investigations at the London Cage – including the massacre at Le Paradis, the Wormhoudt massacre and the Emsland case, to name but a few – already amounted to a heavy workload. Added to those now was the Ardeatine caves massacre.[7] Although Rome was spared the bombing during the war, the Italians hated the occupying forces and blamed Germany for the loss of its men and territory in North Africa in 1942. The resentment led to reprisals against German troops and attacks on the streets of Rome by groups of partisans. These acts of sabotage and murder incensed the German occupying forces. Across the different headquarters in Italy, Fascist leader Benito Mussolini, German Infantry General Rudolf Toussaint, SS General Karl Wolff and Field Marshal Kesselring were united in agreement that the partisan killing of German troops must cease. During 1944, leaflets and posters warned the population that for every German murdered on the streets of Italy, ten Italians would be killed within twenty-four hours. These reprisals would be carried out by the security police under Herbert Kappler. The authority behind the retaliation order was Luftwaffe General Kurt Mälzer, who had been appointed commander of the city of Rome in 1943. Although Kesselring had subscribed to the order, he had no authority in Rome.

One particular Italian partisan observed that the German police units kept to exactly the same schedule: at the same time every day, around 100 security police from the SS Police Regiment Bozen marched back to their barracks along the Via Rasella.[8] On 23 March 1944, he filled a street cleaner's barrow with explosives with a timer fuse set to go off when half the police regiment had marched by. The carnage that followed the explosion was horrific, and the scene on Via Rasella was utter chaos. Dead bodies of German security police and ordinary Italians were strewn across the street. Some buildings in the immediate vicinity were on fire. It was estimated that thirty-three members of SS Police Regiment Bozen were killed and sixty injured. And then there were all the dead and wounded Italians. Four men were arrested for this act of sabotage.

Luftwaffe General Kurt Mälzer called a meeting with SS Police Chief Herbert Kappler and informed him that ten Italians had to be killed for every dead SS man: 330 Italians had to die within twenty-four hours. It was Mälzer who gave the order, although the SS would carry out the killings.[9] General von Mackensen, commander of the 14th Army, conveyed to Kappler that the German army would not get involved in reprisals; but if there had to be retaliation, then it should be restricted to prisoners who had already been sentenced to death in Italy's prisons.

Kappler discovered that there were only 273 Italian prisoners being held in the prisons awaiting death. He telephoned General Wilhelm Harster in Verona, commander of the intelligence section of the SS, for advice, and they agreed that the fifty-seven Italians needed to make up the number should be Jews taken from concentration camps. The message was relayed to Kesselring that those to be executed would be Italians already sentenced to death.

The following morning, an extremely agitated Kappler contemplated the situation. He had to kill 330 Italians by the end of the day. The German army had refused to take part in the executions, and so too had General von Mackensen's men. Kappler made his final decision: he and sixty of his own officers would carry out the killings at the Ardeatine caves in the hills surrounding Rome. What happened there became known as the Ardeatine caves massacre and took place under conditions of the utmost secrecy.

On 24 March, lorries began to move the prisoners from Rome's prisons, along with fifty-seven Jews from a concentration camp, to a disused quarry by the caves. Five extra prisoners were taken in error, resulting in a total massacre of 335 people. At the entrance to the quarry, groups of six at a time were made to walk the short distance to the caves. Forced to kneel, they were then shot in the head by officers of the SS Police Regiment Bozen who had been plied with cognac to ensure that they carried out the orders. After the killings, the cave entrances were plugged with dynamite, blown up and sealed with new bricks. There the 335 bodies lay in heaps until their discovery after the liberation of Rome three months later. Rumours of the massacre did leak out, but because the caves had been sealed, the civilian population did not know the full truth until after liberation. Later, Colonel Zolling, chief intelligence officer to Kesselring, explained to the field marshal the possible reprisals after the partisan attack on Via Rasella, but said nothing about the caves massacre. That was one reason why Colonel Scotland maintained that Kesselring knew nothing of the massacre until he was confronted with the facts at the London Cage. Scotland's investigations narrowed the perpetrators down to Herbert Kappler, Erich Priebke, Karl Hass, Kurt Mälzer and the SS Police Regiment Bozen.[10]

The caves massacre was not an isolated atrocity: a number of other reprisals by German forces took place against Italian partisans between June and August 1944. As a result, by 1946 Kesselring was facing charges by the Allies on seventeen counts of giving the order for unlawful killings. Some of the killings had been carried out by the Hermann Göring Division which, although controlled by Göring himself, came within Kesselring's geographical area of command in Italy. Another reprisal took place at Bordini, a village near La Spezia, after a group of partisans ambushed a lorryload of soldiers of the 16th SS Panzer Division. Seventeen SS men were left dead. The lorry was doused with petrol, set on fire and the bodies of the dead Germans were strewn across the burning wreckage. A heavily armed SS unit later scoured the local villages for the partisans in hiding. All they found were terrified elderly men, women and children who knew nothing of the attack. The SS showed no mercy. It rounded them up and shot them.

The war crimes investigations could prove unpredictable in their conclusions: Colonel Scotland and his team came to understand that there was a difference between commanders Nikolaus von Falkenhorst and Field Marshal Kesselring. Falkenhorst had been supreme commander of all three services in Norway and was bound by the direct authority of Field Marshal Wilhelm Keitel. His crime lay in not ensuring that British prisoners of war were treated as such and placed in prisoner-of-war camps. He had allowed the German security police to determine their fate. By contrast, Kesselring had limited jurisdiction in Italy and bore no responsibility for the order to kill 330 Italians.

Commanders in Italy

The order for the mass murder in the Ardeatine caves had to be pinned on a high-ranking German officer, and it was the brief of the London Cage to find out who had been responsible. In the spring of 1946, a number of Kesselring's staff found themselves in the London Cage as witnesses or suspects, all high-ranking officers and generals from Italy. They included General von Mackensen, Wehrmacht Generals Heinrich von Vietinghoff and Joachim Lemelsen, General von Senger und Etterlin, Commander

Heer, Lieutenant-General of the Artillery Eduard Crasemann, SS General Karl Wolff, SS General Wilhelm Harster, SS Lieutenant-General Max Simon and SS Major-General Tensfeld. They were put together in a large room, given a typewriter and instructed to explain the reprisals and massacre in their own words, and to write down their own individual statements. Examining the reports from the interrogations, it became clear that, whilst a case for war crimes could be brought against these German commanders, the crimes had been committed on Italian soil and should be the subject of an Italian war crimes investigation of their own. Nevertheless, it did not prevent the British from holding war crimes trials in Italy.

As well as this imposing list of high-ranking German commanders, the London Cage was also holding SS generals and war criminals from other theatres of war, including SS Commander Fritz Knöchlein of the Le Paradis massacre, Jakob Sporrenberg, German commando Helmut Tanzmann and many others under investigation.

In February 1946, General Fridolin von Senger und Etterlin (known as General von Senger) was transferred to the London Cage. He spoke flawless English, having studied as a Rhodes scholar at Oxford University, and was well versed in world affairs. The general of a Panzer division, he had been captured at Trento and was initially held in a number of different POW camps in Italy. While in the London Cage he provided an articulate, rational argument that SS General Karl Wolff, as the highest commander in Italy, was responsible for the war crimes there, not the German army. It was an argument that resonated with Colonel Scotland, who believed that the German army was largely innocent of crimes in Italy.

When General von Mackensen arrived at the cage, interrogators found him to be from a proud military family. His father had had a distinguished career in the First World War. Mackensen was asked to write a full account of the reprisals that led to the Ardeatine caves massacre, which he completed in two days. In his own defence, he claimed that he knew there were to be reprisals by the security police, but was unaware of the massacre. Mackensen was warned by Colonel Scotland that he would probably face charges as a war criminal, at which point Mackensen became extremely agitated and muttered: 'Thank God my father is not alive.'[11]

Scotland believed that Mackensen was also innocent of the massacre, and assured him that he would offer a plea on his behalf to have the charges lifted. But the Judge Advocate General's Office was pushing for Mackensen to stand trial, and Scotland was ultimately unsuccessful.

High Commander Heer was found to be a stiff gentleman, aloof and austere, who insisted on having his own private room in the cage. In contrast to General von Senger, he argued that the German army in Italy was in fact culpable of war crimes, but that the regiment responsible had come under the command of Hermann Göring, not Kesselring.

At this time, SS Lieutenant-General Max Simon was interviewed as a witness at the London Cage, and admitted that the killing of partisans had taken place. He said that the action was reported direct to Göring's headquarters, and the original order to kill had not come from either Kesselring or Wolff. A frank and straightforward character, Simon won the respect of his interrogators.[12] Two villages had been the scene of murders of partisans by his men, but he maintained that he knew nothing of it until after the deaths. He admitted to Scotland: 'I know that the men who did it were under my command. There is nothing I can do but take the responsibility.'[13]

Max Simon did not stand trial for the Ardeatine caves massacre, but did receive the death penalty from a British military court for the Marzabotto massacre in Italy in autumn 1944; his sentence was later commuted to life imprisonment and he eventually received a pardon.

Tall, ruddy-faced SS Major-General Willy Tensfeld was a different character altogether, being described by Scotland as 'a man of no morale whatsoever'.[14] When challenged over the shooting of twelve Italians in Burgo Techino,[15] he became a nervous, stammering wreck and a doctor had to be called to give him a sedative;[16] there is no record of what was administered, but he would not have been the first prisoner in the cage to be given a barbiturate. He was promptly sent to his cell to write down his statement. Just two hours later, he handed Scotland a small piece of paper with illegible scribblings. Still very agitated, Tensfeld was helped in his statement by Max Simon. In the end, Tensfeld was not convicted.

Karl Wolff was head of the security police and all SS units in Italy. He denied any knowledge of the Ardeatine caves massacre and claimed he was away on 24 March 1944. Whenever he faced difficult questions from interrogators, he irritated them by feigning ignorance, offering a stupid grin and talking gibberish.[17] Scotland decided not to tolerate his nonsense and challenged him. Scotland reckoned that Wolff must have attended the funeral of his thirty-three policemen killed by the partisans. Wolff replied that he attended only to read the eulogy. Staff at the cage felt only revulsion for Wolff because as an SS commander he knew the intricate details of Himmler's experiments on Jews in concentration camps.[18]

Scotland discovered that General Harster had not attended the funeral of his men. Looking smug under interrogation, Harster said he had been confined to his office in Verona with a leg injury.[19] Scotland did not believe him and suggested that the real reason he could not leave Verona was because he was finishing his final report on the reprisals to send to Berlin. Harster began biting his lower lip – a nervousness that betrayed his guilt. After the interrogation of Wolff and Harster, Scotland was resolutely convinced that Kesselring was innocent.

Investigating the culprits of war crimes in Italy was challenging for Scotland and his team, because German-occupied Italy had several commanders, and untangling the chain of command for atrocities committed in the field was a complicated task. Field Marshal Kesselring reported ultimately to Wehrmacht High Commander Heer; and German lines of communication were overseen by General Plenipotentiary Toussaint, who had been appointed by Himmler. Then there were the commanders of the German navy and air force in Italy, and General Karl Wolff, head of the security police and SS. Kesselring was only in charge of German army units fighting on the front line in Italy. His authority was therefore limited.

The area where anti-partisan reprisals took place in Rome came under the command of General Mälzer. As an open city, Rome was controlled by the security police. The command structure in Italy was further complicated by the fact that Mälzer was accountable to Toussaint, and the security police were accountable to Commander Kappler, who was under General Harster. Harster was responsible to Wolff. Kappler also happened to be the German representative to the Holy See (the Vatican) and Abwehr officer in charge of counter-espionage.

In the end, not a single German commander in Italy was hanged for the Ardeatine caves massacre. Kappler and Mackensen faced trial and were sentenced to life imprisonment. Mackensen was released in 1952. Kappler had many influential friends in Rome, who did all they could to prevent him coming to trial before a British court – and they succeeded; Kappler was never brought to the London Cage for interrogation, and in October 1948, he was tried by an Italian court. In his defence, he claimed that the order for the massacre had come from Hitler; and as Hitler was dead, it was hard to prove otherwise. The Italian court found Kappler guilty of the murder of just 5 of the 335 Italians massacred in the cave. His prison sentence was short.

Kurt Mälzer was sentenced to death, but this, too, was later commuted to life imprisonment. Harster went to trial in 1949 and was imprisoned, but was released in 1953. Kesselring attended the trial of Mackensen and Mälzer as a witness and vouched for them by declaring that he had been in complete command in Italy. It made no difference to their sentences. Justice was served late on SS police officers Erich Priebke and Karl Hass, who did not face trial until 1996 and 1998, respectively. Erich Priebke was found not guilty because he was 'acting on orders', although he had allegedly fled to Argentina after the war on a Vatican passport. Karl Hass was placed under house arrest and died in 2004.

Kesselring on trial

There was nothing Colonel Scotland could do to prevent Kesselring from standing trial. The field marshal, whom Scotland had befriended, was transferred from the London Cage to the American zone in Germany and held in a camp until his trial in Venice, in spring 1947. The charge against him: that while senior commander in south-west Europe, he gave orders that led to the shooting of 335 Italians in Rome on 24 March 1944, and to the massacre of Italian civilians and partisans in caves between June and August 1944.[20] Scotland never wavered in his belief in Kesselring's innocence. Determined to defend him, Scotland travelled to Venice in February 1947 to testify on Kesselring's behalf. His personal defence of the field marshal was deeply unpopular within the intelligence services.

The controversial side of Scotland erupted in the courtroom, as Kesselring told the judge that he was not guilty of all the charges.

'Who told you that?' the judge advocate asked.

'Colonel Scotland,' he replied.[21]

Scotland found himself once again at the centre of the courtroom, as he was asked to step into the witness box to account for his comments. He articulated a simple but powerful argument that Kesselring could not possibly be guilty of war crimes, because his authority had been limited. The prosecuting member turned to the judge and asked permission to question Scotland about the organisation of the German army in Italy. This was granted. The defending counsel immediately rose to his feet and raised an objection: 'Colonel Scotland has not been a soldier in the German army and is not competent to provide this information.'[22]

The prosecuting member turned to Scotland and asked whether he had ever been a soldier in the German army. Scotland replied 'yes'.

This was not the first time that Scotland had been asked publicly about his time in the German army, but it caused a stir in a courtroom. He enjoyed the high drama and challenge of defending Kesselring; it was, after all, not dissimilar to outwitting a prisoner in an interrogation. His expertise at logical and legalistic argumentation was shown off to the court audience; but nothing he said made any difference to the outcome of Kesselring's trial: he was found guilty and sentenced to death. The sentence was later commuted to imprisonment, which was served in Werl prison, east of Dortmund in Germany.

There is a postscript to the friendship between Scotland and Kesselring. On 17 September 1949, Scotland was visiting Werl prison and asked the governor for permission to see Kesselring. The fact that Scotland made the request was quite remarkable. It was done not out of curiosity, but instead reflected the mutual trust between the two men. The governor granted the request. In the cell, Kesselring greeted him warmly. Scotland found him defiant and still with a razor-sharp mind.[23] He had retained his sense of humour and still maintained his innocence. Kesselring was released from prison in October 1952 for health reasons, and died of a heart attack on 16 July 1960 at the age of seventy-four.

Scotland embarked on writing a book defending Kesselring's innocence in 1949. But it was never published: it was banned by the intelligence services. No copy of the manuscript was ever released and it may no longer survive. All attempts to locate it have failed.

15

DEATH IN THE CAGE

The bitterly cold winter of 1945–46 meant uncomfortable conditions for staff and inmates in the cage. A shortage of fuel and firewood saw their residence become uncompromisingly sparse, as the beautiful oak panelling was torn down and burnt in the fireplaces. The harsh conditions were matched by the equally tough prisoners who crossed the threshold as part of the war crimes investigations: SS officers and some of the most loathsome Nazi officers and commanders ever to be held by the Allies. 'The reputation of the Waffen-SS stemmed from both their prowess in the field and the atrocities they had committed,' wrote MI19 interrogator Matthew Sullivan.[1] The atmosphere became extremely tense as the guards tried to keep them in order.

Among these prisoners were Infantry General Otto Roettig, interrogated by Captain Cornish on 25 January 1946; SS Lieutenant-General Jakob Sporrenberg, implicated in the killing of 42,000 Jews in Lublin in a single day; Helmut Tanzmann of the harsh Tanzmann Commando brigade; and SS man Erich Zacharias; as well as various commandants of concentration camps. Scotland enforced strict discipline, as he and the interrogators worked long days and evenings hearing the horrors of the SS's crimes, or battling with war criminals who continued to deny any part in the atrocities, despite the evidence against them. The German-Jewish émigré interrogators listened to the former commandants of the camps boasting about the number of Jews they had killed.

But how long before tempers frayed? And what would be the consequences? Scotland maintained that no physical violence was used against a prisoner to make him confess to war crimes: 'We were not so foolish as to imagine that petty violence, nor even violence of a stronger character, was likely to produce the results hoped for in dealing with some of the toughest creatures of the Hitler regime.'[2]

Up to his death in 1965, Scotland consistently denied any sadistic practices in the cage; however, his memoirs were not always consistent, because he did state that things were done 'that were mentally just as cruel'.[3] For example, one unnamed obstinate prisoner was forced to strip naked and exercise. This deflated the prisoner's ego and he began to talk freely. Other prisoners were forced to stand for hours at a time, and if one wanted to urinate 'he had to do it there and then in his clothes. It was surprisingly effective.'[4]

Was it ever legitimate during wartime hostilities to use violence or undue pressure to extract information from enemy prisoners of war, even if that information could change the course of the war and save lives? How often was decency sacrificed for expediency? These were relevant questions then, as they are now. How did the behaviour of the interrogators change once they were confronted with intransigent SS prisoners who refused to break their oath of loyalty to Hitler and who were known to have committed brutal massacres? It was a natural human reaction to loathe them. But the situation was more complicated than that.

Suicide

On Thursday, 7 March 1946, the *Evening News* carried the headline 'War Criminal Kills Himself: Found hanged in Kensington "Cage"'. It went on to report: 'Because of his complicity in war crimes, the name and nationality of this man will be kept secret.'

It was one of four suicides in the London Cage. For seventy years, the identity of the prisoner has remained a mystery, his name never publicly released. Sifting through the declassified files has revealed two key references that enable his identity to be established for the first time. The first of these comes in a report from the London Cage dated 22 March 1946 and reads: 'Following the unfortunate demise of SS Ostubaf [Obersturmbannführer – Lieutenant Colonel] Tanzmann at the London District Cage . . . (alias O'Leut. S. Koch) . . .'[5] The second reference in the same file reads: 'Since Tanzmann committed suicide, we have not tried to trace the wanted men . . .'

These references appear to solve the mystery of the suicide. Except further research found that there is no death certificate in any British death register for Helmut Tanzmann. Nor is there a death certificate for his alias 'S. Koch'.

Further enquiries established that his death was registered at the Chelsea and Kensington Registry Office under the name of Hans Erich Koch. The death certificate states that the 39-year-old Hans Koch, a lieutenant in the German navy, died at 7 Kensington Palace Gardens on 6 March 1946. The cause of death: 'asphyxia due to strangulation by Hanging at a Prisoner of War Cage. Did kill himself while the balance of his mind was disturbed.' Suicide was established from a post-mortem, and the report was written by H.N. Stafford, coroner for London. An inquest was held on 13 March 1946. A recent enquiry to the local coroner's office elicited a reply that the coroner's file for the case no longer survives.

Research into the circumstances of the death has been complicated by the fact that Tanzmann was first buried at an unknown location under the name Hans Koch, but then subsequently interred at the Cannock Chase German Military Cemetery under his real name. Today, a death certificate still only exists for Hans Erich Koch, but he was buried as Helmut Tanzmann.

What were the circumstances surrounding Tanzmann's short confinement in the London Cage? Information is patchy, and Tanzmann's own interrogation reports are not among the declassified files. In the spring of 1946, the London Cage was investigating a number of missing German army commandos of Commando Tanzmann who had fled Norway on Narvik-class vessels, masquerading as crew and carrying false identity papers.[6] They were wanted by the French authorities for atrocities committed in France during the war, and had taken the decision to flee from Norway to avoid arrest for war crimes. The first priority of the war crimes unit in Norway was the arrest of Captain Suhren, head of the German U-boat service there.

During interrogation, Suhren revealed that two U-boat commanders knew the whereabouts of the missing commandos. They were First Lieutenant Hans Falke of U-boat *U-992* and Lieutenant Otto Westphalen of *U-968*.[7] A report to the London Cage followed swiftly from Norway on New Year's Day 1946, with information that Commando Tanzmann had later been renamed Commando 21, under the command of SS Lieutenant Colonel (Obersturmbannführer) Tanzmann. The unit had originally been sent to German-occupied Norway to cover the whole of northern Norway and consisted of 120 men. As the Russians advanced through Finland in 1945, Tanzmann's men realised they were not up to the task and fled.

One vital piece of information supplied during interrogation was confirmation that Helmut Tanzmann had come to Britain aboard *U-997*, under the command of Captain Lehmann. A search for Lehmann located him at Camp 18, Featherstone Park camp, Haltwhistle in Northumberland. He was immediately transferred to the London Cage, where he confirmed during interrogation that all members of Commando Tanzmann had come to England under false names with the help of Hans Falke and Otto Westphalen. The circumstances were gradually pieced together, and a cypher telegram was received at the London Cage with the following facts: 'Lt Koch arrived UK 17 May 1945 with five of his men disguised as members of crews of U-boats surrendered.'[8] In the haste to hand over U-boat prisoners in May 1945, no proper record or check had been made of the men on board the surrendering U-boats. That was how Tanzmann and his men had evaded detection.

The hunt was on for Hans Erich Koch (aka Helmut Tanzmann) and the commandos who were hiding as U-boat prisoners under false identities in various prisoner-of-war camps in Britain. Tanzmann was located fairly swiftly, although the files do not say where. He was brought to the London Cage in early March 1946. One interrogator scribbled in pencil on a tatty scrap of paper the following description of him: 'hair: dark; eyes: brown; face: long and narrow, protruding cheeks; complexion: small wart on left cheek; speech: lisps, when talking always has wet mouth and lips'.[9] Tanzmann's identity book was made out in the name of Koch; he claimed that his original papers had been lost in an air raid and that new papers had been issued on the basis of his verbal statements. This is the extent of information about Tanzmann in declassified files. The circumstances surrounding his suicide continue to raise questions: how easy was it for a prisoner to hang himself, given that all items of possible harm were removed from the prisoner's cell, including towels, shoe laces and belts? The cell's furnishings consisted only of a bed, chamber pot and chair. There was no clue as to why Tanzmann had committed suicide – did he wish to escape justice? The use of the phrase 'the unfortunate demise of SS Ostubaf Tanzmann' seems somewhat dismissive.[10]

Investigations into the men of Commando Tanzmann continued after Tanzmann's suicide. Hans Falke and Otto Westphalen arrived at the cage, but it was almost full to capacity and so they were put in a room with six others, including three German generals. They were held at the London Cage for at least three weeks and interrogated by Major Terry, who witnessed their statements on 11 March 1946.

On Sunday, 24 March, the guard instructed Falke and Westphalen, as the most junior officers in the room, to bring up a supply of wood and coal for the fireplace from the store downstairs. Falke and Westphalen were in bed and refused to move. The corporal of the guard came in and officially ordered them to carry out the guard's instruction, at which point they moved swiftly; but their original failure to obey an order was reported to Scotland.

Falke and Westphalen were brought before Scotland. In the presence of the sergeant and corporal of the guard, Scotland reminded Falke and Westphalen of military discipline. He said that proceedings could be initiated against them for disobeying an order and suggested that they faced a considerable term of imprisonment.[11] According to Scotland, after issuing a caution, he then pronounced their punishment: to carry out all necessary chores in the cage for forty-eight hours. During this time, they would have to wear prisoner uniform, then would revert to wearing their normal clothes.[12]

That week, discipline deteriorated. By Thursday, steps had to be taken to improve the situation. Six German generals were at the centre of the unrest. On Friday, they faced Scotland and were given a frank talking-to.[13] Things settled down again. The smooth running of the cage depended on 'the strictest discipline being maintained between prisoner and interrogator'.[14]

In the end, although Falke and Westphalen had connived in the crime of smuggling named war criminals into Britain, they were not punished because 'they supplied information under interrogation which enabled us to trace these wanted men'.[15] On the list of those wanted in connection with Commando Tanzmann were Fritz Mirek (aka Fritz Kuhn), finally located in Camp 166; Georg Brandis (aka Georg Keller), located in Camp 136; and Josef Grieger (aka Josef Krüger) and Matthias Wiedemeyer (aka Matthias Krauss), both located at Kempton Park. All were held in the London Cage from April 1946. Josef Grieger signed his statement on 10 April 1946; Georg Brandis signed his on the following day. The latter claimed that he had had nothing to do with Commando Tanzmann, carrying out only telephonist and guard duties. Also on 11 April, Matthias Krauss signed a statement that before fleeing to England the men had been inclined to commit suicide rather than be captured by the Russians; but Tanzmann had offered them a way out. Finally, Fritz Mirek signed his statement on 12 April. All their statements were witnessed by interrogator Captain Arthur Ryder.

An unwanted visitor

A week after the suicide of Tanzmann, the London Cage was unexpectedly visited by an inspector from the International Red Cross. It was 13 March 1946 when Monsieur Chavan arrived unannounced at 6–7 Kensington Palace Gardens and sought entry. He was left standing on the doorstep as Colonel Scotland refused him permission to inspect the cage.[16] Chavan was apparently displeased at being turned away and deeply suspicious of the premises.[17] He followed up with a phone call, insisting on being granted entry to interview prisoners. Scotland wanted to know why the cage was suddenly the subject of an inspection by the International Red Cross. Chavan said that it had not previously appeared on any list of POW camps. Scotland explained that their work involved holding men in connection with war crimes, either as suspects or witnesses: 'Should you speak to any prisoner under interrogation on a major war crime, the effect on the prisoner might be destructive in our efforts to establish the truth and to this extent might contribute to the defeat of justice.'[18]

Two days later, Monsieur Chavan was back at Kensington Palace Gardens. Although he was not allowed to inspect any of the buildings that comprised the cage, he was permitted to interview a senior (unnamed) NCO, who provided him with information on the prisoners' food rations, bedding, accommodation, exercise facilities and camp routine. He left completely satisfied with the answers, but the visit seems to have had an unnerving effect on Scotland, who wrote to the War Office:

> Should it be decided to permit Red Cross Inspectors to have access to the London Cage, Special Investigation Branch and RAF must be advised immediately and instructed not to bring any more Stalag Luft III suspects to London. The interrogation of these criminals must proceed in Germany under conditions more closely related to police methods than to Geneva Convention principles.[19]

Far more worrying was the special equipment in the basement and the existence of Cell 14, which could not be so easily dismantled. Scotland explained to the War Office: 'The secret gear which we use to check the reliability of information obtained must be removed from the Cage before permission is given to inspect this building. This work will take a month to complete.'[20]

Also, writing to Brigadier H. Shapcott of the Judge Advocate General's Office, Scotland argued that if the London Cage and other interrogation centres were to be opened up for inspection by the Red Cross, then a solicitor would have to be appointed to be present when prisoners were interrogated on major crimes. 'Such a demand,' wrote Scotland, 'would be the logical outcome of opening the cage to welfare or protecting inspectors.'[21] The Red Cross made no further attempts to visit.

None of the prisoners ever received legal representation during interrogation; as with all military or secret service interrogations, it happened behind closed doors.

Suicides and deaths

A former eyewitness to events at the London Cage recalled one night sometime in 1946 or 1947 when cage staff noticed a German prisoner with a ghastly appearance – 'a terrible colour, collapsed and at death's doors'. Instructions were issued to call an ambulance to get the man to hospital because 'he must not die on our patch'. The prisoner was suffering from pneumonia and was rushed to the Royal Herbert Hospital in Shooter's Hill, Woolwich. The army hospital had reserved 200 beds for MI19's wounded prisoners awaiting interrogation. The prisoner died that night. It has not been possible to establish the details of his death.

The name of a second suicide at the London Cage can now be identified. (Although the identities of the third and fourth suicides remain elusive, the author is confident that their names will emerge one day, either from deep in one of the files or from an unexpected source.) In spring 1948, former inspector Hans Ziegler was finally being held at the London Cage over his involvement in the Sagan case and the shooting of RAF pilots from Stalag Luft III. Ziegler, who was a large man of 18 stone, was told by Scotland that statements about his guilt had been obtained from other prisoners – Erich Zacharias and Friedrich Kiowsky – and they had implicated him in the crimes. Ziegler denied any part in the Sagan killings and began to type up his statement. He never finished it.

On 23 February, he was found dead in his room. According to the death certificate, the 49-year-old had committed suicide at 7 Kensington Palace Gardens. Dr H. Stafford, the same London coroner who had conducted the inquest into Tanzmann's suicide, held an inquest two days later. He concluded that Ziegler had died 'from a haemorrhage wound of the neck, self-inflicted, and did kill himself while the balance of his mind was disturbed'.[22] In the unpublished version of his memoirs, Scotland recorded that Ziegler had acquired a razor blade, cut his jugular vein and bled to death.

Were the four suicides at the London Cage really suicides, or the result of brutal mistreatment when the balance of the prisoner's mind was affected by torture, both psychological and physical?

The history of another site in London has a bearing on this question. During the Second World War, a secret facility was run by the Free French Forces from 10 Duke Street, near Selfridges in central London. The address was the headquarters of an intelligence section created by General Charles de Gaulle in 1941, known as the Bureau Central de Renseignements et d'Action (BCRA). It received suspected spies and communists from Vichy France for interrogation, and worked closely with MI6 and SOE. On one occasion, after three MI6 agents came back from France, they were given an extremely harsh interrogation by BCRA, and at least one of them is known to have died in the cellar. The details contained in secret files have not yet been declassified.[23] The official verdict given on the death certificate was suicide: death by hanging. Special Branch detectives undertook an investigation and discovered various injuries that the man had suffered during interrogation: 'Intelligence men in MI6 and MI5 suspected he had been hanged (after death) to mask these wounds and to create the illusion of suicide.'[24] The men had been obeying MI6 orders not to reveal certain facts to BCRA, and this cost at least one of them his life.[25] British intelligence became extremely uncomfortable about what was going on at 10 Duke Street, so much so that MI5's head of counter-espionage, Guy Liddell, was moved to write in his diary on 14 January 1943, 'Personally, I think it is time that Duke Street was closed down.'[26] Its reputation prompted an American Naval Intelligence officer to speak about a 'secret torture chamber':

> The men at Duke Street were hard, cruel and unscrupulous. They reminded me of the Nazi Party officials and workers I knew in Berlin. Duke Street sounded very much like the notorious city concentration camp, Columbia-Haus, formerly run by the SS in Berlin.[27]

The suicide of prisoners in British custody was rare, but it did occur at other sites under Colonel Scotland's jurisdiction as head of the Prisoner of War Interrogation Section. On 24 August 1946, German prisoner Christian Assem committed suicide at Camp 186, Colchester, Essex.[28] He had most likely been contemplating suicide for several days, because he left a signed statement in German, dated 16 August 1946, in which he exonerated himself of involvement in concentration camps near Papenburg which were being investigated by Major Pantcheff as part of the Emsland case.

Even today, enquiries into deaths at the London Cage are deemed too sensitive to warrant a straightforward answer. A death certificate for one of the suicides sent to the author went missing in the post; the names of two other prisoners who committed suicide have never been released; no coroner's records survive for any of the suicide inquests; and some War Office files are reported to have been contaminated by asbestos and destroyed. All this begs the question: why such sensitivity over the suicides seventy years on? It is possible – but no longer verifiable without further evidence – that these deaths occurred as a result of brutal treatment, starvation and prolonged periods of solitary confinement, and were not suicides. The consequences of releasing such information today is discussed in the epilogue.

A criminal element: The guards

The arrival of tough new guards in 1946 did nothing for the already dubious reputation of 6–8 Kensington Palace Gardens. They were chosen 'for their height rather than their brains'.[29] It was said by an anonymous eyewitness to this period that when a request was sent to Pirbright (or some other source of guards), the commanding officer did not necessarily send his best men to London; rather, he was glad to get rid of a discipline problem. At this time, Lord Belper (Ronnie Strutt) of the Coldstream Guards took over from Lieutenant Colonel Clarence Peel as the new commander of the guards at the London Cage. He admitted that his predecessor had 'drawn men who were not of the best type',[30] and tried to restore the guards' reputation by dismissing unsuitable personnel. He described Sergeant Major Frederick White of the guard as 'a nasty character, a bit tricky and in danger of being court-martialled'.[31]

A criminal element of the guards ran what became known as the 'Ham Scam' and the 'Lead Scam'.[32] The 'Ham Scam' was discovered after prisoners complained about the lack of bacon at breakfast. The adjutant was puzzled, because rations of bacon and ham were on regular order. The catering corps confirmed that the bacon had been signed for. A team of police officers was put on the case. They followed the delivery lorry and discovered that some guards from the London Cage were intercepting the delivery and signing for the order. The bacon was then being sold on the black market.

The 'Lead Scam' was uncovered after a report that No. 2 Mess Room was flooded after heavy rainfall. This was strange, because the room was on the first floor and there was a floor above. An inspection revealed that the source of the leak was the roof: the water had seeped through the little-used second floor to the first. A member of staff went up onto the roof and found gaps where the lead had once been. It was discovered that several guards had been climbing onto the roof at night, removing small squares of lead and lowering them over the side wall into the garden at the back, and from there into the gardens of the palace near the paddock. Bit by bit, over the weeks, a substantial amount had gone missing. The discovery ended the scam, but the culprits were never caught.

In another incident, some of the guards entered the adjutant's office where there was a large, heavy safe. The back of the safe was not so secure, because it was thought that no one could move it. The guards slid it on soap across the stone floor, unscrewed the back and emptied the contents.

The behaviour of the guards left a lot to be desired. Sergeant Major Frederick White faced court martial for attending a cocktail party on 19 November 1946 in the officers' mess and getting drunk. He staggered down to the servants' quarters, wearing a trilby hat and with a bottle of whisky in his hand. The adjutant ordered him to his room, but White refused and went back upstairs. He was subsequently ordered to appear before a military court in Chelsea.[33] Lord Belper arranged for his swift removal from the cage.

Few testimonies survive from the guards, but Doug Richards of the Welsh Guards did once recall a time in early 1946, when

> a party of White Russians arrived at the London Cage. The Russian Embassy [next door] duly ordered its security men to stand in the middle of the road, armed with machine guns. We were asked to hand over the prisoners. When we asked the Russians why, they replied: 'We shoot them now.' How the Russians knew of the arrival of the prisoners we never found out.[34]

Having tough guards could sometimes be an advantage. It could prove useful for the interrogators to be able to blame the guards for a prisoner's treatment and for the conditions in the cage – and thus appear to be the prisoner's friends. It all seems to have been a charade, a kind of play, harking back to the interrogators as good 'actors'. An official report noted: 'Army guards were ordered to be somewhat inconsiderate in their treatment, thus leaving the interrogator to ingratiate himself by ostensibly improving the prisoner's lot.'[35]

Mistreatment: The allegations

To this day, the London Cage continues to be the subject of controversy about just how terrible the interrogations and conditions were for the prisoners. A rare interview at the Imperial War Museum provides further evidence of life inside the cage from former German POW Alfred Conrad Wernard.[36] A wireless operator of U-boat *U-187*, Wernard spent three weeks in Kensington Palace Gardens and spoke about threats of execution, sleep deprivation and daily interrogations at different times in the dead of the night, always after having been dragged out of bed from a deep sleep. He was taken blindfolded to a room for interrogation.[37] Interrogators were particularly interested in information Wernard had concerning a forerunner of the German radar system. 'British Intelligence was interested in it,' Wernard said. 'They even knew that I went on a course about the new equipment and the instructor's name . . . The interrogator knew more about our U-boat than we did.'[38] When Wernard refused to give information, the interrogator began to slowly rotate a revolver on the desk between them. 'When it points at you,' he said abruptly, 'I pull the trigger.'[39] 'I had no way of telling if he would,' Wernard admitted. Out in the yard, he was shown a deep trench and was threatened with being shot. 'It was all designed to make us talk . . . It looked like a prison and there were bars on the windows.'[40] Back in his room, which Wernard shared with a U-boat companion, the prisoners discovered a bugging device in the light fitting. 'We were careful what we said,' he commented.[41]

The main official complaint of physical mistreatment and torture came from SS Lieutenant Colonel Fritz Knöchlein and Heinz Druwe. Aside from Knöchlein's own claimed mistreatment (discussed in chapter 11), he maintained that other prisoners were tortured in the cage, which was 'unsuitable as a torture chamber'.[42] He said that he heard the excited voice of a German prisoner wailing all over the house: 'Do kill me, I can't stand it any longer, kill me!'[43]

Knöchlein signed a voluntary statement on 13 August 1947, witnessed by Captain Ryder, that when Oskar Schmidt returned from an interrogation 'one of his eyes was disfigured and bloodshot and he alleged that he had been beaten during the interrogation'.[44] The interrogator, whose name was not given, was described as 'particularly big and heavy physique [*sic*]'.[45] At his trial the following year, Knöchlein alleged that he and a number of his comrades were 'in a most brutal and gruesome fashion tortured at the London Cage'.[46] He raised the case of prisoner Werner Schifer, who had a medical certificate in three languages – German, English and French – from an international medical committee attesting to his 'grave injuries'.[47] Yet, during his time at the London Cage, Schifer's injured back was allegedly regularly knocked with cudgels.[48] When he showed his medical certificate, the staff were said to have sneered at him and thrown it onto the floor.[49] Schifer was subjected to sleep deprivation, being woken by a guard in the middle of the night and shown a signed order from a British officer that he, Schifer, was 'prey to any kind of treatment'.[50] After several heavy bouts of malaria, Schifer reported to a doctor and was allegedly beaten afterwards with a stick by Sergeant Major White.[51]

According to Knöchlein, there was a long list of prisoners who suffered at the hands of Colonel Scotland and some of his interrogators. Prisoners Reinhold Bruchardt and Zacharias Noa had tufts of hair pulled from their heads. Bruchardt was subjected to 'cold water cure' and other 'special', unspecified, kinds of treatment.[52] During the second Sagan trial (1948), Scotland had to answer questions in the dock about whether Bruchardt had ever been beaten by Captain Cornish or Major Terry. He answered in the negative. The court wanted to know whether Scotland had ever shown Bruchardt a hide whip, or told prisoners that they could be beaten with it. Scotland maintained that there were 'never any whips, sticks, pistols or any other weapons', referring to Bruchardt's claims as 'absolute nonsense'.[53] If these allegations were true, argued Scotland, Bruchardt should have complained while he was in the cage.

Lieutenant Colonel Neutler was apparently told by Scotland that there were sufficient possibilities for a man to disappear without trace, and that he would be the first to vanish from the London Cage. A former member of a German signal unit, prisoner Wunder, was supposedly badly beaten because he would not incriminate his battalion's adjutant in the desired way. There were allegations by another prisoner that he had received sixty punches from Scotland during an interrogation, and claims by others of beatings, strippings, forced confessions and ice-cold showers.[54]

In September 1947, another formal complaint was issued by Heinz Druwe, who was being held in connection with the Wormhoudt massacre. This time, the allegations were against two interrogators rather than Colonel Scotland. The complaint concerned violence during an interrogation on 5 May 1947, in which Druwe claimed RSM Stanton and Sergeant Conway had forced him to kneel with his hands at his sides and then beat him about the face for thirty minutes of the forty-five-minute interrogation. The beatings had ceased by the time Scotland entered the room, but Druwe said that his face was still very red and swollen. He was escorted to Scotland's office, where he was interrogated once in the morning and then again in the afternoon. Druwe said he did not complain because he feared he would never leave the cage. When he finally did leave, a week later, on 12 May 1947, he had to sign a certificate in German stating that he had no complaint about his treatment there.

A court of inquiry into Druwe's allegations was ordered by General Officer Commanding London District, Major-General J. Marriott. On 2 September 1947, the case came before Colonel M.D. Erskine, DSO, of the Scots Guards, at Wellington Barracks, Major H.G.B. Knight of 2nd Battalion Coldstream Guards, and Captain D.M.A. Wedderburn of 1st Battalion Grenadier Guards. Colonel Scotland attended as a witness, and under oath told Colonel Erskine that he permitted no violence during interrogation and nor were prisoners beaten to extract information. Colonel Scotland claimed that Druwe was standing when he entered the room; his face was not swollen or red, but he was showing signs of strain, and RSM Stanton was standing in front of him, with Sergeant Conway nearby.[55]

RSM Stanton was called to the inquiry to answer questions. In his sworn statement, he said that Druwe had been interrogated about the killings that took place in 1940:

> From the beginning of the interrogation, Druwe adopted a truculent and uncooperative attitude and gave evasive or, in some cases, untruthful replies to questions put to him. I cautioned him and his attitude, and told him it was his duty to answer the questions . . . At no time did I make the prisoner kneel, nor was he beaten or struck, either by myself or by Sgt Conway. CSM Richter was present for about 10–15 minutes. He did not strike Druwe.[56]

CSM Richter gave his sworn statement, which concurred with Stanton's evidence, and stated that he had attended twenty minutes of the interrogation. He described Druwe as 'uncooperative and sloppy', but said there was no kneeling down or violence.[57]

The final witness called to testify was Sergeant Conway, who had translated for half an hour of interrogation on 5 May. He told the court that Druwe was 'nervous and obstinate when asked questions'. Again, he confirmed that Druwe had not been abused or made to kneel.[58]

Colonel Erskine concluded that there was 'insufficient evidence to prove that physical violence was used at the Cage', but added a caveat: 'it does not, however, rule out the possibility that violence was in fact used in this case'.[59]

Scotland remained greatly troubled 'by the constant focus on our supposed shortcomings at the cage for it seemed to me that these manufactured tales of cruelty towards our German prisoners were fast becoming the chief item of news'.[60]

In a letter dated 30 March 1948, former SS Major Emil Reinhard Stürzbecher, who had spent time in the London Cage, wrote to interpreter Captain Herbert Sulzbach from a camp at Wisbech:

> As a former member of the Waffen SS, I can only expect hatred and rejection; and beyond this, since I was involved in certain events, though without my actually doing anything or knowing about it, I realise I am regarded as a specially unpleasant former enemy and as a nasty type . . . When I was confronted by all this, suddenly and fiercely, at my interrogation at the London Cage I was completely to the edge of despair.[61]

In the autumn of 1948, Colonel Scotland watched as the last two prisoners of war, manacled, left for RAF Northolt, to be flown back to Germany. The doors of the London Cage finally closed. Kensington Palace Gardens lapsed back into quiet dignity and its secrets lay dormant.

16

TORTURE
Myth or reality?

With the closure of the London Cage in 1948, the intelligence services perhaps felt that a line could be drawn under the secret wartime interrogation centre. But rumours continued to surface periodically. Using official files from the War Office, Scotland's two memoirs, and the testimony of a surviving veteran of this period, it has been possible to build up a fairly comprehensive picture of life inside the London Cage. No war diary appears to exist for the London Cage – or if does, it has not yet been declassified. And there is only fleeting mention of the cage in the MI9 and MI19 official war diaries.

The truth about Britain's secret interrogation centre was multilayered and nuanced. Was violence sanctioned there? And if so, by whom? Inevitably with a secret site, there are unanswered questions. Official guidelines stated: 'Prisoners may be *treated harshly* and in an *unfriendly manner* but they are not to be made to suffer any physical indignity nor man-handled in any way except for the purpose of guiding them.'[1]

Scotland himself was at pains to state that 'No physical force was ever used during our interrogations to obtain information, no cold water treatment, no third degrees, nor any other refinements.'[2]

What, then, was the truth? There was certainly psychological intimidation, and there is evidence that prisoners were struck during interrogation. The darker side of mistreatment and torture appears to have arisen in the post-war period, when the cage dealt with hated Nazi war criminals. Although Scotland may have claimed that there were no contraventions of the Geneva Convention, in the end it was a matter of interpretation. The

Geneva Convention clearly protected the rights of prisoners of war in the armed forces, but Scotland believed that 'Many of the war criminals at the London Cage were not members of the armed forces and were not intended to benefit from terms of the Geneva Convention. Nor was it the intention of the Convention to extend its protection to criminals within the armed forces.'[3]

When placed in the context of other Military Intelligence establishments, the London Cage was not an isolated case in its ill-treatment of prisoners. There are four known examples of disciplinary action having been taken by the War Office in cases of brutality against prisoners.[4] In 1940, Brigadier Drake-Brockman was dismissed from service for hitting two German airmen who crashed near his headquarters.[5] In 1948, Colonel Robin 'Tin-Eye' Stephens, who had headed the MI5 interrogation centre at Ham during the war, faced court martial for alleged mistreatment of internees at a post-war interrogation centre, No. 74 CSDIC Bad Nenndorf in Germany. The court convened behind closed doors and Stephens was acquitted. In 1954, Colonel Griffiths was sentenced to five years' imprisonment for mistreating Mau Mau fighters during interrogation. Four years later, Captain Lindsay and Captain O'Driscoll were charged with the ill-treatment of Cypriot EOKA prisoners during interrogation. In addition to these four examples, it is now known that internees at the Brompton Oratory School in London may have suffered torture during the Second World War: the treatment received there by the German anti-Nazi Otto Witt, for example, is specifically mentioned in his declassified MI5 file.[6]

The Directorate of Military Intelligence made a conscious decision not to investigate allegations surrounding the London Cage for the following reasons: too much time and too many staff members were needed to investigate or to trace the officers associated with them, and a search of files at the War Office and Ministry of Defence was too onerous. It meant the files could be quietly consigned to the basement.

Neither journalists nor the general public had any right of access to the interrogation cages or penal camps. If there was cause for public concern with regard to such places, the under-secretary of state for war had to be approached to hold an inquiry. In 1949, that was Michael Stewart (later foreign secretary, Baron Stewart of Fulham). In the spring of 1949, Reginald Paget MP raised a number of questions in the House of Commons about incidents at the London Cage during 1946. He asked the under-secretary of state for war whether he had considered the declarations made by Reinhold

Bruchardt and other prisoners that cruel methods had been adopted by the London Cage to secure statements and confessions. Paget wanted to know whether a full public inquiry would be held. Michael Stewart confined his written response of Tuesday, 8 February 1949, to two cases that had already been discussed in open court during the war crimes trials. He highlighted the fact that the only declarations by Bruchardt alleging cruelties at the London Cage were made at his trial, during which the counsel for the defence had cross-examined one of the witnesses and had not pressed the matter. On the second case, the Sagan trial, Stewart said:

> The allegations made at this trial were investigated with the greatest care by the court which heard the evidence of some Germans that they had been ill-treated at the London Cage. The trial (in which there were 19 accused) took fifty working days. All the accused were convicted, and it follows in the circumstances of the case that the court rejected the contention that the statements made by the accused at London Cage were induced by ill-treatment.[7]

In conclusion, Stewart refused to instigate a full inquiry. Although the matter was considered firmly closed, the rumours continued to rumble on.

Those who had once worked at the cage remained silent. Having signed the Official Secrets Act, they went to their graves without ever speaking about their work. Only Colonel Scotland tested the limits of secrecy by beginning to write his memoirs. The intelligence services seemed to want to suppress any damaging revelations, especially those that could lead surviving Nazi war criminals behind bars to have their cases reopened and their sentences repealed; or that could induce the relatives of those who had died in custody to try and claim compensation from the British government. The truth of life in the London Cage over its ten-year history remained obscured for decades.

Fate of intelligence personnel

Many of those who had worked at the London Cage went on to have distinguished careers after the war. On 1 October 1948, Scotland transferred to the depot of the Intelligence Corps at Maresfield, near Uckfield in West Sussex.[8] The following December he retired; but that retirement was short-lived: he was recalled for special security duties under an agreement with the American government for the trial of Nazi war criminal Field Marshal Erich von Manstein.[9] Manstein had already spent time in Nuremberg prison as a key witness at the Nuremberg trials. Now he faced the court for crimes committed, although he always maintained that the German army had never been involved in war crimes. Scotland was responsible for 'top security' documents produced during the trial. Afterwards, Scotland returned to his home in Bourne End and spent the next year going through documents that he had removed from the London Cage 'for security reasons'.[10] He then burned the papers which he believed were of no further official value. All that was left were those papers impounded by the security forces in 1957. After taking early retirement, Scotland and his wife moved into a flat at 19 Clarence Gate Gardens in north London.

Of the other intelligence personnel from the London Cage, the subsequent careers of only a few are known. Scotland's deputy, Antony Terry, became one of the most highly respected British journalists of the Cold War, and never really retired. In 1949, he was invited by Ian Fleming, the Naval Intelligence officer of James Bond fame, to work on the foreign section of *The Sunday Times*. From 1949 to 1980, he worked on major assignments, and from 1972 until 1980 he was the paper's European editor. He became the longest-serving foreign correspondent at *The Sunday Times*, covering Middle Eastern affairs and the Cold War (working out of Budapest), and in the process gaining an intimate knowledge of secret arms deals and corruption in the Eastern bloc. Later, in 1970, he went to Biafra and covered the war there. Given his background and subsequent employment, including covering conflicts in Africa, it is likely that he worked for MI6. Terry died at home in New Zealand on 1 October 1992, at the age of seventy-nine.[11]

Interrogator Bunny Pantcheff worked for SIS/MI6 after the war, being stationed for a time with the British Army of the Rhine, first with the Intelligence Division of Control Commission Germany and later with the Joint Operations Research Group at Rheindahlen.[12] He was appointed Companion of the Most Distinguished Order of St Michael and St George (CMG) in 1977 after tours of duty in Lagos and Leopoldville in the Belgian Congo, as well as in Germany, and was listed as a 'Counsellor, Foreign & Commonwealth Office' in the *London Gazette* entry. He retired in 1979 and wrote about the wartime occupation of the Channel Islands in *Alderney: Fortress island*. His collection of papers was donated to the Military Intelligence Museum Archives at Chicksands. He died in Alderney on 28 November 1989, at the age of sixty-eight.

After the war, interrogator Kenneth Morgan left MI19 with the rank of captain and joined the German section of the Foreign Office as a lecturer at Wilton Park, Beaconsfield. It was here that the Foreign Office ran a re-education programme for German prisoners of war to promote values of democracy, in preparation for their repatriation to Germany. In 1951, when these courses were moved to Steyning, West Sussex, he joined the BBC World Service at Bush House as a news sub-editor, retiring in 1972 as a chief sub-editor. He died in October 2000 in the village of Jordans, Buckinghamshire.

Interrogator Randoll Coate joined the diplomatic service of the Foreign Office and served in Salonika, Oslo, Leopoldville, Rome, The Hague, Buenos Aires, Stockholm and Brussels, where he was the head of press and information. During a state visit to Belgium by Her Majesty the Queen, he was appointed a Member of the Royal Victorian Order. For his services to Belgium, he was made a Chevalier of the Order of King Leopold II. Coate was an internationally recognised expert on the design of mazes and labyrinths, planning and building more than twenty in the United Kingdom and abroad. These included the maze at Blenheim Palace near Oxford, Longleat in Wiltshire, the Château de Beloeil in Belgium and the 'Beatles Maze' at the 1984 International Garden Festival in Liverpool. He retired in 1969 and lived in London. In 2005, he died at the family's second home in Le Rouret, France, at the age of ninety-six.

The German-Jewish émigrés at the London Cage were demobbed from the Intelligence Corps and the British army, applied for British nationality and settled down to rebuild their lives in the country that had saved them from Nazism.

The exclusive street of Kensington Palace Gardens has always retained an air of mystery. It was suggested that No. 8a could be used as a special research facility on a temporary basis. A letter dated 6 October 1945 from Fort Belvedere, Surrey, where the Office of the Crown Commissioners had been evacuated during the war, stated that the Crown Estate was prepared to lease No. 8 and No. 8a to 'erect, equip and maintain a new building to be used as an Establishment for Fundamental Scientific Research'.[13] It is not known whether it was in fact used for this purpose; if so, it would have functioned for a time alongside the War Crimes Investigation Unit, located at Nos. 6–7 and No. 8.

After the war, a member of the family of the late Lord Duveen inspected the premises at Nos. 8 and 8a to assess the war damage, estimating the repair bill at £1 million. On 23 February 1948, accounts were submitted for work carried out on the houses: 'The apportionment of the part of the works attributable to war damage is made more difficult because of thefts of lead and other vandalism which occurred at these premises.'[14] On 20 May 1949, Nos. 6, 7 and 8 Kensington Palace Gardens were formally relinquished by the War Office to the Commissioners of Crown Lands.[15]

During the Cold War, there were rumours of spies watching spies in the shadows there, and of rooms in some of its buildings being lined with cork to prevent any remote eavesdropping. But this was probably all the product of an overactive imagination on the part of spy enthusiasts and James Bond devotees. Kensington Palace Gardens retained (and does to this day) a Russian presence in the street, as it had throughout the Second World War, with the Russian consular section at Nos. 6–7. Snippets about this have emerged in official files and other sources. An entry in the 1950s in the post-war diaries of Guy Liddell, then MI5 director of counter-espionage, recorded: 'The Soviet Embassy have had ten new telephone lines installed, in addition to the five that were already there at 18 Kensington Palace Gardens where the Soviet Press Section is to be housed.'[16] Another file discusses the Russian use of premises in the street in June 1965, of which some pieces have been retained under Section 3(4) and are not available under a freedom of information request.[17]

During the 1960s, Nos. 1, 2 and 3 Kensington Palace Gardens were handed back to the Crown Estate Commissioners; No. 5 was on lease to the Russians; and another house was occupied by the International Rubber Group. Nos. 8 and 8a were demolished and rebuilt as a modern glass block of luxury apartments. A retired diplomatic protection officer, Peter Lawrence, recalls the time he went into the vacant premises of 6–7 Kensington Palace Gardens in the 1980s to view it for possible use in training:

> I was shown into a room with a full-height metal stationery cabinet in one corner, invited to open it and found the back of the cabinet opened into a small windowless room lined with cork.[18]

The precise use of that room is a matter of speculation – but cork is a good material for sound-proofing. Whether the room was there in Colonel Scotland's day is unknown. It could have been a remnant of Cold War espionage that was rumoured to have taken place in certain buildings in Kensington Palace Gardens in the 1960s.

Daily Mail headlines

It was at the height of the Cold War, in 1960, that rumours about the London Cage interrogation centre broke very publicly in the *Daily Mail*, with sensationalist headlines that it had been the scene of brutality, torture and psychological abuse. Overlooked was the fact that the London Cage had gathered material and evidence that was used at fifteen different war crimes trials – including the Sagan case, the Kesselring case, Wormhoudt, Emsland and Le Paradis – which resulted in a considerable number of Germans being sentenced for their crimes.[19] Some twenty years after its closure, the London Cage had once again become the centre of controversy. Liberal MP Jeremy Thorpe began an investigation into possible malpractice at the wartime cage – and even into whether it had been the scene of war crimes. A *Daily Mail* journalist tracked down Sergeant Major White, the guardsman who had been removed by Lord Belper in 1946, and interviewed him.

Even then, a nervous intelligence service sought not to publicly disclose the evidence. Behind the scenes, another branch of Military Intelligence, MI11, liaised with Lord Belper over how to handle the affair. There seems to have been a reckoning in dialogue and conversation. Previously unpublished files that have been released into the National Archives now show that officials agreed privately that White might have acted discreditably during his time at the London Cage.[20] Lord Belper was questioned by Arthur Christopher Soames, a Conservative MP and secretary of state for war under Prime Minister Harold Macmillan. Lord Belper admitted that the alleged activities might have occurred during his predecessor's time, and partly during his own. No satisfactory conclusions were drawn. Publicly the intelligence services maintained their silence. But the War Office wrote to the *Daily Mail*:

> Brutal treatment of prisoners is, and always has been, contrary to War Office policy. Whenever instances have come to light, severe disciplinary action has been taken. An officer was court-martialled in 1948 for brutality to prisoners under interrogation and more recently in 1954 and 1958 officers were court-martialled and sentenced for maltreating members of the Mau Mau and EOKA terrorist organisations. The fact is that no such disciplinary action was taken over activities at the London Cage.[21]

During 1960, there was an exchange of letters between Thorpe and Soames about the allegations. The questioning went deeper than the London Cage and began to probe the training of personnel in the Intelligence Corps, after a former trainee by the name of Strickland claimed to have received training in torture at the Intelligence Corps depot at Maresfield. Strickland cited numerous examples of training in how to torture a prisoner and leave no physical trace, including beating a prisoner who had been wrapped in a wet blanket and holding him against a hot stove.[22]

In a letter of 16 June 1960, Jeremy Thorpe queried two suicides at the London Cage between 1942 and 1945. He wrote:

> There is a fair amount of evidence which I have on this matter which appears to be somewhat disquieting, and I am wondering whether your categorical assurance that no brainwashing techniques were ever used during the Second World War can be held to apply to the questioning, and other methods used, at this particular centre?[23]

Soames replied categorically: 'There was no question of the employment of techniques commonly described as brainwashing at the London Cage.'[24] Thorpe delved further and asked about the other suicides there: Hans Ziegler, implicated in the Stalag Luft III murders, who allegedly killed himself after he realised that the evidence of guilt against him was too overwhelming. Soames replied:

> After this period of time it would be extremely difficult to identify the other suicides which German prisoners-of-war may have committed, but I have no reason to think that they were caused either by ill-treatment or by employment of brainwashing techniques. It is, and always has been, contrary to the policy of the British Army to use any form of torture, physical or mental, on prisoners-of-war, and whenever such treatment has come to light, the offender has been severely dealt with ... As to the London Cage, we can find no records of any complaints of brutality, nor of disciplinary action having been necessary.[25]

Soames took the opportunity to comment on Colonel Scotland's contentious unpublished manuscript. He told Thorpe:

The book mentioned certain instances of severity towards arrogant Germans which, although in our opinion very far from being breaches of the Geneva Convention, might be represented as such by ill-disposed persons . . . I expect you realise that the so-called brainwashing techniques are quite a different thing from physical brutality. In any case, I can assure you that the army does not condone, and never has condoned, either.[26]

The issue of the mistreatment of prisoners refused to go away. Prime Minister Macmillan received a letter in July 1963 from the MP Francis Noel-Baker in connection with a general review of the security services at the height of the Profumo affair, in which Noel-Baker proposed:

that during the [Second World] war a technique of brainwashing was certainly used by Major Kennedy and other interrogators at Combined Services Detailed Interrogation Centre outside Cairo and elsewhere. Unfortunately similar techniques were also employed during the emergency in Cyprus. I understand that Kennedy's methods included such devices as the suggestion of thirst in interrogations under drug-induced hypnotism and the deprivation of sleep.[27]

He concluded the letter: 'I should appreciate your assurance that formal instructions have been given forbidding these practices. Could you also give assurance that they are not taught to British interrogators when they are being trained?'

At the end of that year, on 10 December 1963, a hand grenade was thrown at a party of senior officials at Aden airport, including the high commissioner, as they were about to board a plane for the United Kingdom. In response to a request from the Colonial Office for an investigation into the incident, a team of interrogators from the Intelligence Corps was sent out and the detained suspects interrogated by a team from Special Branch (Aden). Relatives of the detainees complained that the detainees were

being held in small, narrow cells, two in each cell, unable to move their limbs freely. They looked extremely tired and weak, although their morale was quite high. They told us that they were not allowed to leave their cells except to go to the lavatory or to be interrogated by Scotland Yard officers. Interrogation, we were told, continues non-stop, four hours at a time. A detainee is ordered to stand upright for the full length of the interrogation.[28]

It all sounded very familiar. The intelligence services would have had everything to lose from such revelations. Their authority, the legitimacy of their methods and the very credibility of their reports and evidence were at stake – something they couldn't afford at such a sensitive time in the Cold War, when tensions were already heightened between East and West. The British government depended on the information it was given to make judgements on whether to act. Strategically the revelations were extremely damaging, because they forewarned the enemy of the methods used to obtain information during interrogation, thus forearming them. Attempts were made to discredit the rumours as not being part of official military guidelines, but the truth had emerged. In times of war and extreme tension, moral boundaries can often become blurred.

The death of Colonel Scotland

In January 1958, the year after the publication of his censored memoirs, Colonel Scotland wrote to the Home Office asking for the return of all impounded copies of the original manuscript. His request was denied. He died on 3 July 1965 in a nursing home. He was quite a wealthy man – his estate was valued at £13,254. His wife Roma had predeceased him in October 1962.

After Scotland's death, as the estate was being tidied up after probate, publisher John Farquharson Ltd requested copies of the manuscript to be returned. The intelligence services now faced a legal challenge that they believed they would lose. Perhaps they knew that anyone who worked through the files and Scotland's manuscript would be hard pressed to prove conclusively that mistreatment and torture had occurred. And there were secrets which even Scotland was apparently not prepared to reveal about the use of truth drugs, hypnosis and experimentation in interrogation. Such matters would go on to constitute the murky side of espionage in the early Cold War. And so it was that the War Office was instructed to quietly release the manuscript into the National Archives, where it lay undiscovered for decades.

Today, Nos. 6–7 Kensington Palace Gardens are part of the Russian Embassy. No trace is left of its clandestine wartime role. Occasionally the street makes headline news – as after the British verdict on the murder of Russian dissident and spy Alexander Litvinenko, when a Russian official appeared outside the embassy to issue a statement to the media. Kensington Palace Gardens continues as an enclave of foreign embassies and high-class residences for billionaires, under heavy armed guard and still owned by the Crown Estate. The two gatehouse entrances are guarded by the armed police who patrol this exclusive and enigmatic street.

EPILOGUE
The legacy

Sensitivity over the London Cage can be felt even after seventy years. There is a nervousness in official circles that has nothing to do with the fact that it was an interrogation centre or that it held German prisoners of war and Nazi war criminals. The sensitivity lies in what went on behind closed doors – particularly the rumours of mistreatment of prisoners in the basement of No. 8 and the four suicides within its walls. Is there still an attempt going on to protect the truth?

No files for the London Cage have been declassified into the National Archives for the years prior to 1943. A request several years ago by British journalist Ian Cobain to gain the release of all files was denied, and they remain locked deep in the archives of the War Office. Other key files have been 'contaminated by asbestos and destroyed by flood water',[1] and were therefore too damaged to be scanned before their destruction, in order to establish their date and contents.

A death certificate ordered by the author from the local registrar went missing in the post. Enquiries to the coroner's office about the inquests for the four suicides drew the response that the files have not been retained and only files of important cases are kept in the coroner's library. So are files pertaining to the suicide of four German prisoners in custody at a clandestine interrogation centre run by an intelligence agency during the war not deemed important? This begs the question whether the files have in fact been destroyed or are being withheld from public release.

It also came to light during the writing of this book that coroners are among those government bodies exempt from the freedom of information act. Neither was there any clarification from the Commonwealth War Graves Commission, which did not reply to questions about why Helmut Tanzmann was interred at Cannock Chase Cemetery without a death certificate in his real name.

Even though certain files for the London Cage appear to have been retained by the government, it has still been possible to reconstruct for the first time a vivid picture of life in the cage, and to shed light on the shadier side of intelligence. Colonel Scotland's unpublished memoirs appear remarkably accurate when compared against the official files that have since been released.

What could be the consequences of declassifying any remaining information today, if it does still exist? In this age of increased legal challenges and compensation, it could open the way for relatives of prisoners to make claims against the British government for their family members' ill-treatment, manslaughter or even murder. If a legal challenge were successful, it could mean compensating the descendants of some of the worst Nazi war criminals ever held in England. Whilst the state did not authorise the mistreatment and torture of prisoners, it looks as if certain departments of state have subsequently been responsible for covering up the truth. What is more, if it were proved that statements were obtained from Nazi war criminals under duress, that would undermine the guilty verdicts that sent many of them to their deaths. It would also call into question the verdicts of all Nazi war criminals who faced justice after the war. Of course, it could be argued that the Allies had sufficient independent evidence to convict them. Nevertheless, a democratic society prides itself on upholding the judicial system, and to undermine that system would call into question the ability of bodies like the International Criminal Court in The Hague in the Netherlands to continue to bring war criminals to justice. In an age of global terrorism, these questions are profoundly relevant. When democracies are faced with terrorist threats, is it acceptable to take a rough approach during interrogation? Where are the boundaries? There could be protracted consequences of a very public debate about the interrogation methods being used in Britain and America today, particularly when it is still an extremely sensitive and contentious issue in relation to countries like Iraq and Afghanistan.

Was what was done in the cage justifiable? Between 1939 and 1945, as Britain was waging an existential war of possible obliteration, and democracy itself was placed at risk, what happened at the London Cage and other similar intelligence sites raise important moral questions. They also pose a tough problem for critics of torture. From the perspective of espionage, when dealing with die-hard fanatics, whether religious or political, history has shown that no results can usefully be achieved by being soft on them. A tough approach is necessary. But that approach must be within the boundaries of the Geneva Convention, to which all civilised countries adhere. Otherwise, how can such civilised societies uphold justice and deal with future war crimes? The only rationale is the realisation that brutality in interrogation produces unreliable results at best – and at worst, wrong and unjust outcomes.

So, what is the lasting legacy of the London Cage? The cage is scarcely dealt with in books on the Second World War. Yet, through its interrogation of thousands of German prisoners of war, it made a contribution to intelligence gathering that had an impact on the war, military campaigns and operations across five years. As part of the famous commando raids of 1941 and 1942, it dispatched brave intelligence officers to bring back German prisoners from behind enemy lines for MI19's interrogation sites. But perhaps most importantly, it successfully brought to justice a number of major Nazi war criminals – sending them either to prison or to the gallows. Ironically, there is a degree of uncertainty over whether the London Cage was guilty of its own war crimes.

And what view are we to take of Colonel Scotland? He ran the cage in his own way. A competent military figure of the old school, he was uncompromising on discipline and expected his prisoners to cooperate. The intractable SS and Nazi officers who refused to do so were shown a darker side of British intelligence. Colonel Scotland did not believe in taking a soft approach towards truculent prisoners. And nor – with the exception of Field Marshal Kesselring – did he befriend them: that kind of approach was reserved for other MI19 sites at Trent Park, Latimer House and Wilton Park. The London Cage was reserved for prisoners who held information that could not be acquired through bugged conversations – prisoners who needed tough interrogation. Here it is important to keep the backdrop of the London Cage in focus: Colonel Scotland and his staff had to deal with some of the toughest prisoners of war ever held by the British; and not just prisoners of war, but war criminals. The detailed catalogue of atrocities which he and his staff listened to is beyond comprehension – the vilest acts of inhumanity, genocide and cruelty on an unprecedented scale. Coupled with this extreme cruelty, those German officers had sworn an oath of undying loyalty to Hitler. The only way in which Colonel Scotland could have had any chance of breaking their will to resist was through rough treatment. But few can deny that he went too far. Today, the military still does not condone mistreatment or torture. Branches of Military Intelligence have often learned the hard way that torture and brutality do not produce a cooperative prisoner; they only serve to make the prisoner tell you what you want to hear.

What is certain is that the reputation of the London Cage will endure – and not for the justice that it secured against the evil Nazi perpetrators of mass murder. The rumours surrounding it will forever cast a shadow over British intelligence.

APPENDIX
Staff at the London Cage

This appendix provides a list of known staff who worked at the London Cage or one of the other cages in Prisoner of War Interrogation Section (Home Command) during the period 1940 to 1948. The information is taken from WO 208/4294 and WO 208/4970.

Colonel Alexander Scotland OBE (commander of the unit).

Capt. R.A. Allen, WOII P.S Ashe, Capt. M.B. Baron, Capt. W. Bennett, WOI W. Bonwitt, Lieut. F.O. Brann, Capt. A.C. Broderman, Capt. E.G. Burdett, Capt. P.H. Burges, Capt. Burrows, Capt. Victor Caroe, Capt. Randoll Coate, Capt. R.B. Colvin, Capt. Maurice F. Cornish, Capt. K.A. Cottam, Capt. E.A. Davies-Cook, Capt. J.M. Denison, Capt. W. Dewhirst, Capt. J. Dill-Smith, Capt. R.P. Edwards DSO, Capt. E. Egger, Sgt M.E. Eversfield, Lieut. J.S. Fawell, Capt. F.C. Fenton, Lieut. D.B. Gregor, Capt. C. Hay, Lieut. R.A. Hepton, Capt. H.M. Hoffman, Capt. R.D. Jeune, Capt. A.H. Keane, Capt. C.C. Keith, Capt. H. Kettler, Lieut. V. Khoroche, Capt. W.E. Kieser, Sgt H. Kyval, Capt. R. Le May MBE, WOII Gary Leon, Capt. T.J. Leonard, Capt. C.D. Macintosh, Major Cyril MacLeod, Major A.V. Magnus, Capt. A.J. Marsden, Lieut. M.W. Meyer, Capt. J. Moorhouse, Capt. Kenneth Morgan, Sgt A. Morgenthau, Capt. Ian Munro, Lieut. G.J. New, Capt. D.E. Oglander, Capt. L. Okell, Capt. R.A. O'Rorke, Lieut. Theodore X.H. Pantcheff, Capt. G.W. Paton, Sgt J. Rapp, Capt. C.J. Raven, Capt. Eric Rhodes, CSM Richter, Capt. A. Ryder, Sgt Felek Scharf, Capt. H. Sheldon MBE, Sgt H. Siegel, Capt. George Sinclair, Capt. A. Soldatenkov, Capt. H.E. Spearman, Capt. P. Stampe, RSM Stanton, Capt. C.H. Stokes, Capt. M.F. Strachan, Capt. G. Sugden, Capt. A.E. Teare, Major Antony Terry, Capt. B. Tucker, WOI M. Ullman, Lieut. J.A. Viccars, Capt. H.A. Vischer, Capt. A.E. Wernly, Lieut. G.D. West.

Lucy Haley and Miss Metzler (ATS sergeants).

Major Ted Lessing (Grenadier Guards, liaison officer).

Robin Forbes (308 Field Security Section, responsible for security at the London Cage).

Other cages: Command

Scotco – Major Cyril MacLeod; Northco – unknown (Catterick); Eastco – Capt. J. Leonard (Newmarket); Seco – Capt. A.V. Magnus (Lingfield); Southco – Capt. Sugden (Swindon); Westco – Capt. Jeune; Adjutant at Wilton Park, Beaconsfield – Capt. J. Dill-Smith, succeeded by Capt. Kenneth Morgan; Adjutant at Kempton Park and Devizes – Capt. Raven, then Capt. Allen.

NOTES

Introduction: Impounding the evidence

1. WO 208/5381.
2. Ibid.
3. Ibid.
4. Letter to the War Office, 16 March 1955, in WO 208/5381.
5. Ibid.
6. Contained in WO 208/5381, dated 26 January 1955.
7. WO 208/5381, pp. 77–8.
8. Scotland, unpublished memoirs (WO 208/5381), p. 73–4.
9. Ibid., pp. 74 and 77.
10. Ibid., pp. 95–6.
11. Ibid., pp. 199–200, 233, 293–4 and 347.
12. Ibid., pp. 126, 130–4 and 135–40.
13. Ibid., pp. 297–8.

1 Genesis of the cage

1. Forthcoming book on Kensington Palace, edited by Tracy Borman, to be published by Yale University Press in 2018.
2. Helen Fry, *The M Room: Secret listeners who bugged the Nazis in WW2*, 2nd edn, Thistle Publishing, 2015.
3. Sir Joseph Duveen (d. 1908) lived at Hawthornes, Golders Green, a smart detached house on the corner of Finchley Road and Golders Green Road, long since demolished and now a parade of shops.
4. Helen Fry, *Spymaster: The secret life of Kendrick*, 2nd edn, Thistle Publishing, 2015.
5. 'H' in PWIS(H) stood for 'home'.
6. Under the command of 905 Squadron of the RAF.
7. WO 208/5615.
8. Ibid.
9. Ibid.
10. The section of Air Intelligence that carried out the interrogation of German prisoners of war was ADI(K); this had previously been dealt with by Air Intelligence Section AI1(K). It was not dissimilar to army Military Intelligence MI9, which later in the war split to form

MI19 for the interrogation of prisoners of war. Examples of ADI(K) files at the National Archives include AIR 40/2636, AIR 40/2868–77 and AIR 40/2833.
11. WO 208/4970.
12. Courtesy of Mark Scoble, from an unpublished wartime intelligence diary.
13. Ian Cobain, *Cruel Britannia: A secret history of torture*, Portobello Books, 2013.
14. The full story of this can be read in Fry, *The M Room*; and also in Sönke Neitzel (ed.), *Tapping Hitler's Generals: Transcripts of secret conversations, 1942–45*, Frontline, 2007.
15. See, for example, WO 208/5016, WO 208/5017 and WO 208/5018. See also Fry, *The M Room*.
16. Barry Sullivan, *Thresholds of Peace: German prisoners and the people of Britain*, Hamish Hamilton, 1979.
17. WORK 16/1564.
18. Military photographic interpretation of the 1946 aerial photograph of the tented POW compound.

2 A very 'German' Englishman

1. The other was MI5's Edward Hinchley-Cooke.
2. It is my belief that Scotland went to South Africa to do intelligence work for the British, perhaps as a contact person providing the eyes and ears on the ground in and around the empire; but he could not admit as much during his lifetime, because any official British intelligence organisation or network was always denied.
3. Alexander P. Scotland, *The London Cage*, Evans Brothers Ltd, 1957, p. 15.
4. His official British military record gives his occupation from 1902 to 1914 as land and mining.
5. This period of Scotland's life can be read in more detail in his unpublished memoirs, pp. 17–23.
6. Fry, *Spymaster*. Alexander Scotland had contact with SIS circles for decades, many of his closest friends being members of SIS. He wrote one of the references required for Thomas Kendrick to join the Intelligence Corps in France in the First World War. Kendrick had a long career with SIS.
7. Scotland, unpublished memoirs, p. 27.
8. Ibid., p. 27–8.
9. Marshall-Cornwall joined the Intelligence Corps in Le Havre in 1915, later serving in General Headquarters of the British Expeditionary Force under Sir Douglas Haig. Towards the end of the First World War, Marshall-Cornwall became the head of MI3, the military section that dealt with geographical information. During the Second World War, he served with Special Operations Executive and SIS.
10. Scotland, *London Cage*, pp. 38–48.
11. Letter in Scotland's personal military file, Army Historical Disclosures, Glasgow.
12. Scotland's personal military file.
13. It is the author's belief that Alexander Scotland was undertaking work for British intelligence while in South America as an SIS contact man, although Scotland was never able to mention it in his memoirs because officially SIS did not exist. He does, however, provide scant references to his intelligence work for the British.
14. Personal military file from the army's Historical Disclosures section, Glasgow.
15. Scotland, *London Cage*, p. 52.
16. Ibid., p. 53.
17. Ibid.
18. Scotland, *London Cage*, p. 57.
19. Scotland, unpublished memoirs, pp. 29–30.
20. WO 208/5381.
21. Scotland, unpublished memoirs, p. 352.
22. Ibid.
23. Ibid.
24. Ibid., p. 355.
25. WO 373/148.

3　Cage characters: The interrogators

1. Scotland, unpublished memoirs, p. 99.
2. The one exception was Matthew Sullivan, who wrote about his work as an interrogator at another MI19 site, Latimer House in Buckinghamshire, in his book *Thresholds of Peace*. In it, he wrote a short section about the London Cage, but he was not intimately acquainted with its day-to-day work.
3. From 1942, Naval Intelligence Division used female interrogators at Latimer House in Buckinghamshire, headquarters of Combined Services Detailed Interrogation Centre. Confirmed in 2015 in the author's interview with Evelyn Barron, former member of the Naval Intelligence team at Trent Park, then Latimer House.
4. Scotland, unpublished memoirs, p. 40.
5. Much of the information on the interrogators here has been provided by the Military Intelligence Museum, Chicksands.
6. WO 311/61.
7. Letter dated 23 March 1942 to No. 1 Commando from MI9, copy provided to the author by the family.
8. Unpublished papers of Randoll Coate, with kind permission of Pamela Coate.
9. Coate was mentioned in dispatches for his service there. Obituaries in the *Independent* (14 January 2006) and the *Daily Telegraph*. He is thought to have served in MI5, SIS, SOE and MI19.
10. WO 311/61.
11. Announced in the *London Gazette* in February 1946. See also *The Honours and Awards of the Intelligence Corps*, Military Intelligence Museum, Chicksands.
12. Sullivan, *Thresholds of Peace*, p. 49.
13. Interrogator Kenneth Morgan, quoted in Ibid., p. 49.
14. Cobain, *Cruel Britannia*, p. 64.
15. His collection of papers ('The Pantcheff Papers') was donated to the Intelligence Corps archives.
16. WO 311/61.
17. According to the Military Intelligence Museum, no official entries have been found confirming his membership of the Intelligence Corps, although he is described as 'Intelligence Corps' in the Pantcheff Papers, where he is included in the staff list of the Prisoner of War Interrogation Section (the 'London Cage') in 1942.
18. Military Intelligence Museum archives (Pantcheff Papers); *Honours and Awards of the Intelligence Corps*.
19. WO 373/100.
20. Sullivan, *Thresholds of Peace*, p. 244.
21. Ibid., p. 49.
22. Information on Campbell Dundas Macintosh kindly supplied by the Military Intelligence Museum.
23. Macintosh is referenced in TNA files KV 2/11, KV 2/18, KV 2/13.
24. Guy Liddell, *The Guy Liddell Diaries*, Vol. 1, *1939–1942*, ed. Nigel West, Routledge, 2009, diary entry for 17 December 1940.
25. B8L was a counter-intelligence branch of 'B' Branch of MI5, responsible for security of the camps in the war.
26. Information provided by the Military Intelligence Museum.
27. Medal Card Reference WO 373/111/2, Bundle 1. Information supplied by the Military Intelligence Museum.
28. WO 311/61.
29. WO 165/41.
30. Scotland, unpublished memoirs, pp. 61–2.
31. Ibid., p. 39
32. ADM 223/475.
33. WO 208/5381.

4 Cage characters: The 'guests'

1. Reports in WO 208 and AIR 40.
2. FO 1093/1–16.
3. Scotland, unpublished memoirs, p. 53.
4. DEFE 2/83.
5. Initially part of Air Intelligence, AI1(K), later the Air Documents Research Centre, see AIR 40/2636.
6. Scotland, unpublished memoirs, p. 80.
7. WO 208/5494.
8. Ibid.
9. Ibid.
10. Ibid.
11. Ibid.
12. AIR 40/2636.
13. Commodore E.G.N. Rushbrooke, head of Naval Intelligence Division, an experienced interrogator from the First World War, drafted a comprehensive report on interrogation techniques for 'C' (the head of MI6). See ADM 223/475.
14. AIR 40/2636.
15. Scotland, unpublished memoirs, p. 60.

5 Downstairs: Interrogation methods

1. Scotland, unpublished memoirs.
2. Scotland, unpublished memoirs, p. 348.
3. WO 33/2335: manual entitled *Interrogation in War*, p. 18. Although published in 1955, it was written during the Second World War and updated for the Cold War.
4. These included pp. 57–8, 67–8, 69–70, 73–4, 78–9.
5. Sullivan, *Thresholds of Peace*, pp. 53–4.
6. Gary Leon, *The Way It Was*, Book Guild Ltd, 1997, p. 59.
7. Scotland, unpublished memoirs, p. 77.
8. Sullivan, *Thresholds of Peace*, p. 50.
9. Scotland, unpublished memoirs, p. 68.
10. Ibid.
11. Ibid.
12. Ibid., p. 71.
13. Ibid., p. 84.
14. Memo dated 19 October 1942 in KV 6/33.
15. Koenig's personal SOE file in HS 9/855.
16. KV 6/33.
17. Ibid.
18. Ibid.
19. HS 9/855–7.
20. Extensive MI5 personal files exist on Otto Witt. See KV 2/471–479, and also FO 371/48038.
21. KV 2/471.
22. Guy Liddell, *Guy Liddell Diaries*, Vol. 2, *1942–1945*, ed. Nigel West, Routledge, 2009, pp. 52–3.
23. KV 2/479.
24. Ibid. The school had been evacuated and from 1940 was used for vetting and interrogating refugees to Britain, before the move to the Royal Victoria Patriotic School, Wandsworth.
25. Liddell, *Guy Liddell Diaries*, Vol. 2, *1942–1945*, diary entry for 8 March 1943.
26. Ibid., diary entry for 11 March 1943.
27. Ibid.
28. KV 2/477.
29. Liddell, *Guy Liddell Diaries*, Vol. 2, *1942–1945*, diary entry for 15 March 1943.

30. KV 2/479.
31. KV 2/477.
32. KV 2/476.
33. KV 2/279.
34. KV 2/476.
35. KV 2/477.
36. Liddell, *Guy Liddell Diaries*, Vol. 2, *1942–1945*, diary entry for 18 March 1943.
37. KV 2/479.
38. KV 2/477.
39. Ibid.
40. Ibid.
41. KV 2/479.

6 Prison quarters

1. CRES 35/3074.
2. Author's interview with the son of a London Cage veteran.
3. Roderick De Normann, *For Führer and Fatherland: SS murder and mayhem in wartime Britain*, Sutton, 1996, p. 28.
4. Ibid., p. 29. SHAEF is the abbreviation for Supreme Headquarters Allied Expeditionary Force.
5. Ibid., p. 29.
6. Scotland, unpublished memoirs, p. 43.
7. Ibid., p. 73.
8. WO 208/4461.
9. Ibid.
10. Ibid.
11. Personal interview with the author.
12. Personal interview with the author.
13. Cobain, *Cruel Britannia*, pp. 60–1.
14. Ibid., p. 74.
15. Ibid., p. 75.
16. Liddell, *Guy Liddell Diaries*, Vol. 2, *1942–1945*, diary entry for 14 January 1943.
17. Tommy Jonason and Simon Olsson, *Agent TATE: The wartime story of Harry Williamson*, Amberley, 2011.
18. KV 2/61.
19. Liddell, *Guy Liddell Diaries*, Vol. 1, *1939–1942*, diary entry for 22 September 1940.
20. Sullivan, *Thresholds of Peace*, p. 291.

7 Caged lies: The truth drugs

1. Liddell, *Guy Liddell Diaries*, Vol. 1, *1939–1942*, diary entry for 22 September 1940.
2. The experimentation with truth drugs by NID is reported in ADM 223/475.
3. Ibid.
4. Ibid.
5. Ibid.
6. Ibid.
7. Ibid.
8. Ibid.
9. KV 2/471, Operation Neapolitan.
10. WO 208/4661.
11. Dominic Streatfeild, *Brainwash: The secret history of mind control*, Hodder and Stoughton, 2007.
12. WO 193/791.
13. Research into the effects of the drug on RAF pilots was being carried out by Professor Bartlett at the Psychological Laboratory, Cambridge.

14. WO 193/791.
15. Ibid.
16. Ibid.
17. Ibid.
18. WO 208/4661.
19. HS 1/189.
20. Ibid. Memo dated 18 April 1942, as part of Operation Neapolitan.
21. Ibid.
22. HW 14/44.
23. Streatfeild, *Brainwash*, p. 21
24. Ibid.
25. Ibid., p. 23.
26. Ibid., p. 47.
27. WO 208/5561.
28. See, for example, WO 241/1.
29. Streatfeild, *Brainwash*, p. 35.
30. Rees went on to become the first president of the World Federation for Mental Health.
31. Liddell, *Guy Liddell Diaries*, Vol. 1, *1939–1942*, diary entry for 22 September 1940.
32. George Bimmerle, '"Truth" drugs in interrogation', CIA website, https://www.cia.gov/library/center-for-the-study-of-intelligence/kent-csi/vol5no2/html/v05i2a09p_0001.htm
33. Use of truth drugs in the 1950s, HO 45/25333.
34. FO 1093/1–16 series of files shows that the head of MI6 was orchestrating Hess's movements and placed three MI6 officers in charge of him: Thomas Kendrick, Frank Foley and 'Captain Barnes'. The real identity of the latter has not been revealed. Bizarrely, MI6, it was revealed decades later, held Hess's trousers behind a safe at headquarters in Broadway, discovered when MI6 tried to relocate the safe to the new premises at Vauxhall: see John Le Carré, *The Pigeon Tunnel: Stories from my life*, Viking, 2016. The Foreign Office still refuses to release some of the Hess files.
35. H. Freeman, 'In conversation with William Sargant', *Bulletin of Royal College of Psychiatrists*, 1 (1987).
36. FO 1093/1–12.
37. Charles Fraser-Smith, *The Secret War of Charles Fraser-Smith*, Michael Joseph, 1981.
38. FO 1093/11.
39. FO 1093/1–16.

8 The German 'Great Escape'

1. WO 208/3651.
2. Sullivan, *Thresholds of Peace*, pp. 97–8.
3. WO 208/3651.
4. Ibid.
5. Ibid.
6. Sullivan, *Thresholds of Peace*, p. 63.
7. At the end of the war, Sulzbach carried out vital denazification work for the British army, involving thousands of German prisoners before they were repatriated to Germany.
8. Scotland, unpublished memoirs, p. 107.
9. WO 208/5381, p. 108.
10. Ibid., p. 109.
11. Ibid., pp. 109–10.
12. Ibid., p. 110.
13. Herbert Sulzbach interview, The Sound Archive, Imperial War Museum, ref: 4338/3.
14. WO 208/4633.
15. Ibid.
16. Ibid.
17. Ibid.

18. Ibid.
19. Ibid.
20. Ibid.
21. De Normann, *For Führer and Fatherland*, p. 159.
22. WO 208/5381, p. 117.
23. Ibid.
24. Ibid.

9 German-Jewish émigrés

1. They transferred to the Intelligence Corps on 17 November 1944.
2. WO 311/61.
3. Ibid.
4. Ibid.
5. Leon, *The Way It Was*, p. 57.
6. Ibid., p. 58.
7. Gary Leon left the army in May 1946.
8. WO 208/4970.
9. WO 208/3646.
10. Ibid.
11. Ibid.
12. WO 208/5494.
13. WO 208/3621.
14. WO 208/3647, Interrogation of Grenadier Dadaczynski, 18 June 1944.
15. Report dated 28 August 1944.
16. Scotland, unpublished memoirs, p. 89.
17. Ibid., p. 93.
18. WO 208/4677.
19. WO 208/3661.
20. Ibid.
21. Ibid.
22. Scotland, unpublished memoirs, p. 83.
23. Interrogation report in WO 208/3661.
24. Ibid.
25. Postcard in the author's archives.
26. Scotland, unpublished memoirs, p. 95.
27. Ibid.
28. Sullivan, *Thresholds of Peace*, p. 50.

10 A matter of justice

1. Scotland, unpublished memoirs, p. 355.
2. Interview with war veteran who wishes to remain anonymous.
3. WO 208/5572.
4. WO 208/4685.
5. Scotland, unpublished memoirs, p. 342.
6. WO 208/4670.
7. WO 208/4668.
8. WO 208/4669.
9. Ibid.
10. Ibid.
11. Scotland, unpublished memoirs, p. 356.
12. Ibid.
13. Interrogation report dated 25 February 1946, in WO 208/4300
14. WO 208/4300.

15. Scotland, unpublished memoirs, p. 356.
16. WO 208/3647.
17. WO 208/4661.
18. Ibid.
19. Ibid.
20. Ibid.
21. Ibid.
22. Yad Vashem Archives, ref: 5318/64.
23. WO 208/4661.
24. Ibid.
25. Sworn affidavits of the survivors are in WO 208/4300.
26. WO 208/4300 contains photographs of the German battalion and the farmhouse where the atrocity took place.
27. In his unpublished memoirs (pp. 207ff.), Scotland talked about the investigation into the massacre.
28. The signed statements of Max Reimelt and Otto Baum are in WO 208/4300.
29. Ibid.
30. Scotland, unpublished memoirs, p. 229.
31. London Cage summary reports of the Emsland case: WO 208/4297 and WO 208/4299.
32. WO 208/4299.
33. Ibid.
34. Ibid.
35. Ibid.
36. Ibid.
37. Ibid.
38. Ibid.
39. Ibid.
40. AIR 40/2265.
41. Detailed diary contained in WO 208/4647.
42. WO 208/4299.

11 Knöchlein: The butcher of Le Paradis

1. WO 208/4300.
2. Source for this material is WO 208/4300, WO 208/4685 and Scotland's unpublished memoirs.
3. Scotland, unpublished memoirs, p. 172.
4. WO 208/4300.
5. Scotland, unpublished memoirs, p. 184.
6. WO 208/4300.
7. Testimony of Madame Romanie Castel in WO 208/4300.
8. Pooley and O'Callaghan's signed statements in WO 208/4300.
9. WO 208/4300.
10. Scotland, unpublished memoirs, p. 196.
11. WO 208/4685.
12. Scotland, The London Cage, p. 73.
13. Ibid.
14. Statement given by Private J. Johnstone, WO 208/4685.
15. WO 208/4685.
16. Scotland, unpublished memoirs, p. 196.
17. Ibid.
18. WO 208/4685. The original typed statement is now very fragile and damaged.
19. Ibid.
20. Ibid.
21. Ibid.
22. Ibid.

23. Ibid.
24. Ibid.
25. Ibid.
26. Ibid.
27. Ibid.
28. Scotland, unpublished memoirs, p. 199.
29. Camp 17 was known as Lodge Moor Camp, on Redmires Road, Sheffield.
30. Scotland, unpublished memoirs, pp. 198–9.
31. Scotland, *The London Cage*, pp. 85–6.
32. Scotland, unpublished memoirs, p. 200.
33. WO 208/4685.
34. Ibid.
35. Ibid.
36. Ibid.
37. Scotland, unpublished memoirs, p. 205.
38. WO 208/4685.
39. Ibid.
40. Ibid. This file contained some of the court proceedings, in addition to statements by the accused and witnesses.
41. Ibid.
42. Ibid.
43. WO 311/566.

12 The Sagan case

1. Material in this chapter is taken from the thick, official bound volume on the Sagan case (WO 208/4301), which contains all the interrogations, summary reports, witness reports and final conclusions of the case. This chapter also draws on Scotland's unpublished memoirs.
2. Scotland, unpublished memoirs, p. 287.
3. Ibid., pp. 274ff.
4. WO 208/ 4301.
5. Ibid.
6. Ibid.
7. Scotland, unpublished memoirs, pp. 239ff.
8. WO 208/4301.
9. An original copy of the Sagan Order is in WO 208/4301.
10. WO 208/4301.
11. AIR 40/2266 and WO 208/4301.
12. Scotland, unpublished memoirs, p. 290.
13. Ibid.
14. WO 208/4301.
15. Scotland, unpublished memoirs, p. 290.
16. Ibid.
17. Ibid.
18. WO 208/4301.
19. All contained in WO 208/4301.
20. Ibid.
21. Kiowsky was interrogated in the London Cage and signed a statement on 22 February 1946, in WO 208/4301.
22. Scotland, unpublished memoirs, p. 286.
23. Ibid.
24. Ibid., p. 298.
25. Ibid.
26. WO 208/4301.

27. Ibid.
28. Scotland, unpublished memoirs, p. 299.
29. Ibid.
30. Ibid., p. 310.
31. Ibid., p. 311.
32. FO 371/57595.
33. Ibid.
34. Ibid.
35. Ibid.
36. Ibid.
37. WO 208/3660.
38. Interrogation reports in WO 208/4301.
39. Ibid.
40. Ibid.
41. Scotland, unpublished memoirs, p. 325.
42. Ibid.
43. Ibid., p. 330.
44. Ibid.
45. Details given in an interview with the son of a veteran who wishes to remain anonymous.
46. Scotland, unpublished memoirs, p. 330.
47. Ibid.
48. Ibid., p. 332.
49. Ibid., p. 333.
50. Ibid.
51. WO 208/4301.
52. Scotland, unpublished memoirs, p. 340.
53. Cobain's book *Cruel Britannia* provides details that MI5 was working to develop methods of torture that left no physical traces on the body, particularly with psychiatrist Harold Dearden, who was attached to Camp 020 near Richmond.
54. WO 208/4301.
55. Ibid.
56. Ibid.
57. Scotland, unpublished memoirs, p. 342.
58. Ibid., p. 322.

13 Norway and war crimes

1. Falkenhorst was assisted by Admiral Boehm, Lieutenant-General Milch and Air Flying General Stumpf.
2. WO 208/4677.
3. Scotland, unpublished memoirs, p. 124.
4. Ibid., p. 124.
5. Ibid., p. 125.
6. WO 208/4677; Scotland, unpublished memoirs, p. 126.
7. WO 208/4677.
8. Copy of the original order in WO 208/4677.
9. Falkenhorst's signed statement of 5 July 1946 in WO 208/4677.
10. DEFE 2/222–224, DEFE 2/1408, and AIR 20/11930.
11. Scotland, *The London Cage*, p. 167.
12. AIR 39/45, AIR 20/3648.
13. The camp operated from 1941 until 1945.
14. WO 331/16–17, WO 311/383–387.
15. WO 309/720.
16. Scotland, unpublished memoirs, p. 131.
17. Ibid., pp. 133–4.

18. Ibid., p. 131.
19. Ibid., p. 132.
20. Ibid., pp. 133–4.
21. Ibid. See also Falkenhorst's signed statements in WO 208/4677.
22. Falkenhorst's signed statement of 6 July 1946 in WO 208/4677.
23. WO 208/4677.
24. Scotland, unpublished memoirs, pp.139–40.
25. Ibid., p. 140 (edited out of the published version).
26. Ibid.
27. WO 208/4677.

14 Befriending the field marshal

1. Scotland, unpublished memoirs, p. 162.
2. Ibid., p. 163.
3. Ibid., p. 164.
4. Ibid, p.166.
5. Ibid.
6. Ibid., p.165.
7. Interrogation reports in WO 208/4663 and WO 208/4671.
8. Scotland, unpublished memoirs, pp. 153–5.
9. WO 208/4663.
10. In 1968, American composer William Schuman dedicated his Ninth Symphony, *Le fosse Ardeatine*, to the victims. The massacre became a feature film *Massacre in Rome* (1973) starring Richard Burton.
11. Scotland, unpublished memoirs, p. 157.
12. SS Lieutenant-General Simon signed a statement in the London Cage on 31 January 1947, witnessed by Colonel Scotland.
13. WO 208/4671.
14. Scotland, unpublished memoirs, p. 159.
15. Ibid., p. 154.
16. Ibid., p.159.
17. Ibid.
18. WO 208/4663.
19. Ibid.
20. Files of Kesselring's trial: WO 235/367–375; LCO 53/91.
21. Recounted in Scotland, unpublished memoirs, p. 169.
22. Ibid.
23. Ibid., p. 170.

15 Death in the cage

1. Sullivan, *Thresholds of Peace*, p. 284.
2. Scotland, unpublished memoirs, p. 100 and *The London Cage*, p. 154.
3. Ibid., p. 70.
4. Streatfeild, *Brainwash*.
5. WO 208/4670.
6. WO 311/61.
7. WO 208/4670.
8. Ibid.
9. Ibid.
10. Ibid.
11. Ibid.
12. Ibid.
13. Ibid.

14. WO 311/61.
15. Report dated 29 April 1946 in WO 311/61.
16. Ibid.
17. Ibid.
18. Ibid.
19. Ibid.
20. Ibid.
21. Letter dated 29 April 1946 in WO 311/61).
22. Death certificate signed on 25 February 1948.
23. Information about the secret unit in Mark Birdsall and Deborah Plisko, *The Insider's Guide to 500 Spy Sites in London*, Eye Spy Publishing Ltd, 2015, p. 253.
24. Ibid., p. 253.
25. Ibid.
26. Ibid.
27. KV 4/191, diary entry for 14 January 1943.
28. WO 208/4298.
29. Scotland, *The London Cage*.
30. WO 32/17501.
31. Ibid.
32. Based on a personal interview with a veteran who wishes to remain anonymous. The 'Lead Scam' is briefly mentioned in L 25/10/1945.
33. *Evening Standard*, 17 December 1946.
34. De Normann, *For Führer and Fatherland*, p. 29.
35. AIR 40/2636.
36. Reference 18573, Reel 5, Sound Archive, Imperial War Museum, London.
37. Ibid.
38. Ibid.
39. Ibid.
40. Ibid.
41. Ibid.
42. WO 208/4685.
43. Ibid.
44. Ibid.
45. Ibid.
46. Ibid.
47. Ibid.
48. Ibid.
49. Ibid.
50. Ibid.
51. Ibid.
52. Ibid.
53. Ibid.
54. WO 32/17501.
55. Ibid.
56. WO 208/4685.
57. WO 32/17501.
58. Ibid.
59. Ibid.
60. Scotland, *The London Cage*, p. 153.
61. Sullivan, *Thresholds of Peace*, p. 283.

16 Torture: Myth or reality?

1. WO 208/5572 (author's italics).
2. Scotland, unpublished memoirs, p. 32.

3. Ibid., pp. 98–9.
4. WO 32/17501.
5. Ibid.
6. KV 2/477 and KV 2/479.
7. WO 311/566.
8. A copy of Scotland's personal army record is in WO 208/5381.
9. FO 1060/215, FO 1024/103, WO 311/676 and PRO 57/3032.
10. WO 208/5381.
11. *Independent*, 2 October 1992.
12. Information on Pantcheff's post-war career courtesy of the Military Intelligence Museum, Chicksands.
13. L 25/10/1945.
14. Ibid.
15. CRES 35/3074.
16. KV 4/468, p. 59.
17. FO 366/3440.
18. Extract from a book which Peter Lawrence is writing with a colleague about the history of diplomatic protection work in London.
19. WO 208/4294.
20. WO 32/17501.
21. Letter dated 22 March 1960 in WO 32/17501.
22. Ibid.
23. Ibid.
24. Reply sent on 19 July 1960, in WO 32/17501.
25. WO 208/5572.
26. Ibid.
27. Ibid.
28. Ibid.

Epilogue: The legacy

1. WO 208/3548.

BIBLIOGRAPHY

National Archives

ADM 223/84; ADM 223/475; AIR 20/3648; AIR 20/11930; AIR 39/45; AIR 40/2265; AIR 40/2266; AIR 40/2636; CRES 35/3074; CRES 35/3104; CRES 43/78; CRES 43/81; CRES 57/26; CRES 65/49; CRES 65/108; DEFE 2/83; DEFE 2/222–224; DEFE 2/1408; FO 366/3440; FO 371/48038; FO 371/57595; FO 939/458; FO 1024/103; FO 1060/215; FO 1093/1–16; HO 45/25333; HS 1/189; HS 9/855–857 (personal SOE file of Kurt Koenig); HW 14/44; KV 2/11; KV 2/13; KV 2/18; KV 2/61; KV 2/470–479: KV 4/191; KV 4/302; KV 4/468; KV 6/33 (files relating to Kurt Koenig's interrogation at London District Cage); L 25/10/1945; LCO 53/91; LRRO 1/4459; LRRO 1/5038; PRO 57/3032; TS 50/3; WO 32/14552; WO 32/17501 (correspondence with Jeremy Thorpe MP, and references to suicides); WO 33/2335; WO 165/41 (MI19 official war diary); WO 188/2800; WO 193/791 (military use of drugs); WO 199/3303; WO 204/362; WO 204/11469; WO 204/12798; WO 208/3458; WO 208/3513; WO 208/3525; WO 208/3530 (reports from Camp Comrie); WO 208/3548; WO 208/3621; WO 208/3646; WO 208/3647; WO 208/3651 (the Devizes plot); WO 208/3660; WO 208/3661; WO 208/4200; WO 208/4294; WO 208/4295 (interrogations on the massacre at Wormhoudt); WO 208/4297; WO 208/4298; WO 208/4299; WO 208/4300; WO 208/4300/1 (closed extracts, two pages recovered from Colonel Scotland's miscellaneous papers); WO 208/4461; WO 208/4633 (murder of Rosterg); WO 208/4643; WO 208/4647; WO 208/4655; WO 208/4661; WO 208/4663; WO 208/4667; WO 208/4668; WO 208/4669; WO 208/4670; WO 208/4671; WO 208/4685; WO 208/4970 (history of MI19 and list of officers); WO 208/5013; WO 208/5381 (impounding of Scotland's memoirs, and copy of his uncensored memoirs); WO 208/5494; WO 208/5561; WO 208/5572; WO 208/5615; WO 235/367–375 (Kesselring's trial in Venice); WO 241 (files of the Directorate of Army Psychiatry); WO 241/1 (includes article 'The Physiological Foundations of the Wehrmacht' by Lieutenant Colonel H.V. Dicks); WO 309/720; WO 309/2197; WO 311/16–17; WO 311/61 (list of prisoners of war, complaints against WCIU); WO 311/356 (Ardeatine caves massacre); WO 311/566 (Knöchlein and Bruchardt allegations of mistreatment); WO 311/632; WO 311/383–387; WO 311/676; WO 373/100; WO 373/111/2; WORK 16/1564.

Other archives

Papers of interrogator Captain A.E. Haswell-Miller of PWIS, held at the Military Intelligence Museum archives, Chicksands; interview with Alfred Conrad Wernard, Reference 18573, Reel

5 at the Sound Archive at the Imperial War Museum (London); and unpublished memoirs and papers of Randoll Coate, kindly loaned by Pamela Coate (copies also exist in the Military Intelligence Museum).

Unpublished papers

From Military Intelligence Museum archives at Chicksands: The Pantcheff Papers; Gil Hayward, *Dollis Hill in the Desert: 1940–44 (CSDIC Cairo)*; Fred Judge, *Special Duties and the Intelligence Corps 1940 to 1946*.

Published works

Atkin, Nicholas. *The Forgotten French in the British Isles, 1940–44*, Manchester University Press, 2013.

Birdsall, Mark and Deborah Plisko. *The Insider's Guide to 500 Spy Sites in London*, Eye Spy Publishing Ltd, 2015.

Cobain, Ian. *Cruel Britannia: A secret history of torture*, Portobello Books, 2013.

—— *The History Thieves: Secrets, lies and the shaping of a modern nation*, Portobello Books, 2016.

De Normann, Roderick. *For Führer and Fatherland: SS murder and mayhem in wartime Britain*, Sutton, 1996.

Foot, M.R.D. *MI9: Escape and evasion 1939–1945*, BCA, 1979.

Fraser-Smith, Charles. *The Secret War of Charles Fraser-Smith*, Michael Joseph, 1981.

Freeman, H. 'In conversation with William Sargant', *Bulletin of Royal College of Psychiatrists*, 1 (1987).

Fry, Helen. *The M Room: Secret listeners who bugged the Nazis in WW2*, 2nd edn, Thistle Publishing, 2015.

—— *Spymaster: The secret life of Kendrick*, 2nd edn, Thistle Publishing, 2015.

Hoare, Oliver (ed.). *Camp 020: MI5 and Nazi spies – The official history of MI5's wartime interrogation centre*, Public Record Office, 2000.

Jackson, Sophie. *British Interrogation Techniques in the Second World War*, The History Press, 2012.

Jeffery, Keith. *MI6: The history of the SIS, 1909–1949*, Bloomsbury, 2010.

Jonason, Tommy and Simon Olsson. *Agent TATE: The wartime story of Harry Williamson*, Amberley, 2011.

Jones, R.V. *Most Secret War*, Penguin, 2009.

Lee, Martin. *Acid Dreams*, Grove Press, 2000.

Leon, Gary. *The Way It Was*, Book Guild Ltd, 1997.

Lewis, Damien. *Hunting Hitler's Nukes*, Quercus, 2016.

Liddell, Guy. *The Guy Liddell Diaries*, Vol. 1, *1939–1942*, ed. Nigel West, Routledge, 2009.

—— *The Guy Liddell Diaries*, Vol. 2, *1942–1945*, ed. Nigel West, Routledge, 2009.

McLachlan, Donald. *Room 39: Naval Intelligence in action 1939–45*, Weidenfeld, 1968.

Neitzel, Sönke (ed.). *Tapping Hitler's Generals: Transcripts of secret conversations, 1942–45*, Frontline, 2007.

Neitzel, Sönke and Harald Welzer. *Soldaten: On fighting, killing and dying*, Simon and Schuster, 2012.

Sargant, William. *Battle for the Mind: A physiology of conversion and brainwashing*, Doubleday, 1957.

—— *The Unquiet Mind*, William Heinemann, 1967.

Scotland, Alexander P. *The London Cage*, Evans Brothers Ltd, 1957.

Streatfeild, Dominic. *Brainwash: The secret history of mind control*, Hodder and Stoughton, 2007.

Sullivan, Matthew Barry. *Thresholds of Peace: German prisoners and the people of Britain*, Hamish Hamilton, 1979.

ILLUSTRATION CREDITS

INDEX